"Married couples: Become married lovers! This book offers some of the most practical help and biblical insight I've read in a long time."

— PAULA RINEHART

author of *Strong Women, Soft Hearts* and *Sex and the Soul of a Woman*

Intimacy Ignited is a biblical, insightful, chockful-of-ideas kind of book. It's for couples who together — hand in hand — want to step carefully into the water and walk with love into the deep of sexual intimacy."

— JACK AND CAROLE MAYHALL

authors of *Marriage Takes More Than Love*

"Wow! After reading this book just once, we can hardly wait to read it again. Filled with honesty, helpful ideas, and incredible insight into God's perspective on sex and passion, *Intimacy Ignited* is a book we'll recommend again and again."

— TOBEN AND JOANNE HEIM

authors of *Happily Ever After*

"We highly recommend *Intimacy Ignited* for couples who desire to be inspired, encouraged, and strengthened in their intimate lives. This book should answer any question you've ever had about your sex life."

— PAUL AND PHYLLIS STANLEY

international vice president, The Navigators; author of *Celebrate the Seasons*

Fire Up Your Sex Life with the Song of Solomon

Intimacy Ignited

CONVERSATIONS COUPLE TO COUPLE

DR. JOSEPH & LINDA
DILLOW

DR. PETER & LORRAINE
PINTUS

NAVPRESS®

BRINGING TRUTH TO LIFE

OUR GUARANTEE TO YOU

We believe so strongly in the message of our books that we are making this quality guarantee to you. If for any reason you are disappointed with the content of this book, return the title page to us with your name and address and we will refund to you the list price of the book. To help us serve you better, please briefly describe why you were disappointed. Mail your refund request to: NavPress, P.O. Box 35002, Colorado Springs, CO 80935.

The Navigators is an international Christian organization. Our mission is to reach, disciple, and equip people to know Christ and to make Him known through successive generations. We envision multitudes of diverse people in the United States and every other nation who have a passionate love for Christ, live a lifestyle of sharing Christ's love, and multiply spiritual laborers among those without Christ.

NavPress is the publishing ministry of The Navigators. NavPress publications help believers learn biblical truth and apply what they learn to their lives and ministries. Our mission is to stimulate spiritual formation among our readers.

ISBN 1-57683-640-1

Cover design and photo/illustration by Arvid Wallen
Creative Team: Dan Rich, Liz Heaney, Cara Iverson, Glynese Northam

Some of the anecdotal illustrations in this book are true to life and are included with the permission of the persons involved. All other illustrations are composites of real situations, and any resemblance to people living or dead is coincidental.

Unless otherwise identified, all Scripture quotations in this publication are taken from the *New American Standard Bible* (NASB), © The Lockman Foundation 1960, 1962, 1963, 1968, 1971, 1972, 1973, 1975, 1977, 1995. Other versions used include: the HOLY BIBLE: NEW INTERNATIONAL VERSION® (NIV®), Copyright © 1973, 1978, 1984 by International Bible Society, used by permission of Zondervan Publishing House, all rights reserved; the *New Revised Standard Version* (NRSV), copyright © 1989, by the Division of Christian Education of the National Council of the Churches of Christ in the USA, used by permission, all rights reserved; the *Amplified New Testament* (AMP), © The Lockman Foundation 1954, 1958; *THE MESSAGE* (MSG). Copyright © 1993, 1994, 1995, 1996, 2000, 2001, 2002. Used by permission of NavPress Publishing Group; the *New King James Version* (NKJV). Copyright © 1982 by Thomas Nelson, Inc. Used by permission. All rights reserved; and the *Holy Bible, New Living Translation* (NLT), copyright © 1996. Used by permission of Tyndale House Publishers, Inc., Wheaton, Illinois 60189. All rights reserved.

Intimacy ignited : conversations couple to couple : fire up your sex life with the Song of Solomon / Joseph Dillow ... [et al.].
    p. cm.
  Includes bibliographical references and index.
  ISBN 1-57683-640-1
  1. Marriage--Religious aspects--Christianity. 2. Intimacy (Psychology)--Religious aspects--Christianity. 3. Sex--Biblical teaching. 4. Bible. O.T. Song of Solomon--Criticism, interpretation, etc. I. Dillow, Joseph C.
  BV835.I58 2004
  241.6'6--dc22

                                    2004013566

Printed in the United States of America

1 2 3 4 5 6 7 8 9 10 / 08 07 06 05 04

FOR A FREE CATALOG OF
NAVPRESS BOOKS & BIBLE STUDIES,
CALL 1-800-366-7788 (USA)
OR 1-416-499-4615 (CANADA)

Contents

SECTION TWO: KEEP THE FLAME BURNING

Acknowledgments

A book is always the work of a team. In this case, God handpicked the best, and we'd like to express our gratitude.

A heartfelt hurrah to our super editor and friend Liz Heaney, who waded through this book concept by concept, line by line. Your exceptional talents made this a better book. Thank you to Dan Rich, Terry Behimer, and the creative group at NavPress. All of you have supported the vision of this book with your talents. May God be glorified through the final work.

Thank you to the lively group that sacrificed many Wednesday evenings to field-test the Bible study: Brian and Pam Clifford, Mic and Sharon Davis, John and Valorie Havercamp, Phil and Karla Kroeker, David and Julie Kuss, Ron and D.J. McCormack, Terry and Sherry Middleton, and Doug and Tina Van Schooneveld. We laughed much together, didn't we?

Thank you to Kim Troyer for her insights and suggestions. We want to especially thank Don and Sally Meredith and the ministry of Christian Family Life for their impact on our lives and marriage ministry focus. Some of the insights from the Song of Solomon in this book were originally in Christian Family Life messages.

Thank you to the thousands of women at the Intimate Issues conferences who openly and honestly shared their stories with us, and to the men at Tri-Lakes Chapel who provided input on sensitive subjects.

Thank you to Barry and Tamra Farah for a quiet place to write.

And finally, we give thanks to God for the privilege of commenting on His Word. Truly, God's Word is living and active and profitable for every aspect of life!

Sex At Its Best

Married couples are talking:

- ◊ "Best romance story ever written."
- ◊ "Inspiring, erotic, *very* steamy."
- ◊ "This guy is hot!"
- ◊ "I was shocked and thrilled that it was so explicit and erotic in talking about sex."
- ◊ "This book gave me permission to be wild and crazy with my husband in bed."

Would you believe these couples are talking about the Song of Solomon?

Wait a minute! you're thinking. *Isn't that in the Bible? And Solomon? Wasn't he the guy who had hundreds of wives? Why should I listen to anything he has to say about sex or marriage?*

Good question. After all, Solomon accumulated seven hundred wives and three hundred concubines during his lifetime. He's not exactly a role model when it comes to marriage! What godly insights could he offer married couples today?

WHY SHOULD I LISTEN TO SOLOMON?

First of all, we want to point out that Solomon inherited many of his wives and concubines from his father; others he acquired for political alliances. Also, 1 Kings indicates that it wasn't until later in his life that Solomon accumulated all his wives, which were his downfall: "When Solomon was old, his wives turned his heart away after other gods; and his heart was not wholly devoted to the LORD his God" (11:4).

Even so, Solomon seems to lack the proper credentials for giving anyone — let alone Christians — marital advice. Like you, the four of us aren't sure we trust Solomon. But we do trust God.

Solomon's résumé has one positive credential that overshadows all his weaknesses as a writer for a book about married love. God chose Solomon to write the Song. What other credential does he need?

The one whom God chose, he also equipped. In his youth, the likely time in which the Song was written, Solomon was completely devoted to the Lord (see 1 Kings 3:4-15; 8:14-66). As a young leader he cried out to God, "Give your servant a discerning heart to govern your people and to distinguish between right and wrong" (1 Kings 3:22-23, NIV). God, moved by Solomon's heart, answered his prayer and gave him "wisdom and very great insight, and a breadth of understanding as measureless as the sand on the seashore" (4:29, NIV). God said there never would again be anyone as wise and discerning as Solomon — past, present, and future (see 3:12).

The wisest man of all time wrote the Song of Solomon. Granted, he was not perfect. But our imperfection has never stopped the Almighty from delivering a perfect message, and although the human vessel was flawed, God's message was not. Just as we do not discount the wisdom of Proverbs because Solomon became foolish later in life, so we do not discount the rich, inspired teaching that permeates the Song.

Now that we've discussed Solomon's credentials, we'll tell you about ours.

WHY SHOULD I LISTEN TO *YOU*?

Jody and Linda have been married for forty years, and the Song of Solomon has been their "sex manual." They have benefited from the wisdom in this book and have spent hundreds of hours studying it. Jody holds a doctorate in theology and has dissected the Song in Hebrew. In the 1970s, he wrote a popular commentary on the Song of Solomon called *Solomon on Sex*. Linda first wrote about the Song in 1977 in *Creative Counterpart,* a book that encourages wives in their biblical role as helpers to their husbands.

Peter and Lorraine also have been married a long time — twenty-four years. Peter has a doctorate in educational leadership and wrote his dissertation on spirituality and servant leadership. Lorraine wrote her first book, *Diapers, Pacifiers, and Other Holy Things,* on parenting, but when she met Linda two years later, she graduated from kids to sex!

Linda and Lorraine have written two books together: *Intimate Issues*, which answers twenty-one questions Christian women ask about sex, and *Gift-Wrapped by God,* which gives single women a biblical perspective on sex. They also teach Intimate Issues conferences around the country. (Log on to www.intimateissues.com for more information.) All of their writing and teaching is based on the Song of Solomon.

Like Solomon, we are not perfect. Nor are our marriages perfect. Nevertheless, we believe God has asked us to write this book. Just as Solomon cried out to God, we also asked something of Him: We prayed that He would use us to encourage others by making His Word come alive so that they might receive instruction, hope, wisdom, and healing. We believe that the book you hold in your hands is God's answer to our prayers.

WHAT KIND OF BOOK IS THIS?

While many Christian marriage books provide great insight, most primarily reflect the author's thoughts and then use God's Word to supplement their ideas. *Intimacy Ignited* is different. We wanted God's Word to drive this book. Nothing written in ages past, nor anything written in the ages to come, can compete with the "flawless" Word of God (Psalm 18:30, NIV). Only Scripture can claim to be "living and active, able to judge the thoughts and attitudes of the heart" (Hebrews 4:12). Only Scripture can boast that it is the very breath of the Almighty (see 2 Timothy 3:16). This is why we begin each chapter with God's Word and then follow it up with application for married couples. As we wrote we prayed that our thoughts would reflect His thoughts and that God might graciously infuse the text with the power of His Spirit to instruct, teach, and build you up.

This book is not only unique in its starting point but also in its purpose. *Intimacy Ignited* is three books in one:

A popular commentary. The beginning of each chapter examines a portion of the Song and offers verse-by-verse commentary that will help you picture the cultural and historical context as well as understand the symbolism and meaning of the original Hebrew text.

A marriage manual. Each chapter also contains a section called "Applying the Song." This section provides you with tried-and-true ways to put into practice the biblical principles discussed in the chapter. Some of these practical ideas come out of our own marriages, others come from people who have told us their stories. All of the quotes and stories in this book come from real people, although we often changed the identifying details in order to respect personal privacy. While we directed most of the application toward couples, on occasion Linda and Lorraine wrote specifically to women ("Applying the Song for Wives") and other times Peter and Jody wrote application points that apply to men in particular ("Applying the Song for Husbands").

A Bible study. At the end of the book is an eight-week Bible study designed to take you deeper into God's Word. Couples may wish to do this privately or as part of a small group.

In order to help you better understand what you are about to read, we wanted to provide you with some background information that will enhance your appreciation of the Song.

WHO SHOULD READ THIS BOOK?

This book is for married couples and mature engaged couples who are close to their wedding day. If you are disappointed with your marriage, this book can help you. If your marriage is good, this book can help make it better. If your marriage is already "better," this book can take it up another level.

But if abuse or addictive behavior characterizes your marriage, we encourage you to seek help beyond what is offered in these pages. Your marriage doesn't have to be such a painful place. We urge you to get professional help from a counselor or pastor and pursue resources that will serve your specific need.

HELPFUL THINGS TO KNOW ABOUT THE SONG

WHO ARE THE MAIN CHARACTERS?

The two main characters are King Solomon and his bride, the Shulammite. *Shulammite* is the Hebrew feminine noun for Solomon and can be translated as "Mrs. Solomon." But because it felt too cumbersome to refer continually to the bride as Mrs. Solomon, we took the liberty to name her Tirzah. Tirzah was a city in Israel that was renown for its beauty. In the Song, Solomon tells his bride, "You are as beautiful as Tirzah, my darling" (6:4).

An imaginary chorus of virgins called "the daughters of Jerusalem" acts as the third character in this drama. This chorus periodically interrupts the story to convey warnings or other messages of importance. Solomon used this chorus as a literary device to transition between scenes or emphasize certain points.

WHAT IS THE SONG ABOUT?

The first part of the Song addresses the passions and insecurities faced by most newlyweds. We witness the king and his lovely virgin bride as they run to the bedroom to consummate their marriage. Heat rises from the pages as we view the steamy, yet appropriate, exchange of endearments and caresses. Then, toward the middle of the Song, problems surface. Selfishness rears its ugly head as Tirzah dreams about a recurring problem in their sexual relationship. In the dream, Solomon comes to Tirzah late at night, demanding sex. She rejects him because she wants to sleep, and then she feels badly and runs after him. They work through their problems and learn to become servant lovers to one another. The book ends with one of the most powerful statements in the Bible about married love, one lifted as a light of eternal hope for every couple: True love is stronger than death; it is eternal and everlasting, the very "flame of the LORD" (Song of Solomon 8:6).

WHAT ARE THE PREVAILING VIEWS OF THE SONG?

The two most common viewpoints are:

It's allegorical. Jews down through the ages see the Song as a "magnificent metaphor for the relationship between God and the Jewish people."[1] They believe that Solomon represents God and the wife represents Israel. Christians who hold this view believe the Song is an allegory of Christ (Solomon) and the church (the bride).

It's literal. This view says that the Song is the actual love story between a husband and his wife and that the story teaches God's view of love, marriage, and sex.

In our desire to understand any book of the Bible, we must ask ourselves, *What is the most obvious message the author is trying to communicate?* While it is possible that the Song tells a story of spiritual love between God and His people, we have embraced the literal view of the Song throughout *Intimacy Ignited*.

WHY IS THE SONG DIFFICULT TO UNDERSTAND?

People often scratch their heads in bewilderment after an initial reading of the Song, asking, "What is going on here?" This reaction has to do, in part, with the manner in which the Song is written. For instance:

We don't understand how to read Hebrew poetry. Solomon wrote this book as poetry, not prose. Hebrew poetry is didactic and rhythmic, stressing and unstressing certain syllables and sounds. The Song also contains word parallelism, a technique in which similar (or opposite) ideas are offset between the lines of poetry. While these rhythmic phrases create an alluring tempo for the unfolding of a drama in Hebrew, all of the intended nuances make it difficult to accurately translate into the English language.

The scenes in the drama are not in chronological order. The poetic style used in the Song is called lyric idyl. One of the characteristics of this style is that the scenes are a series of flashbacks; they are not in order.[2] Be prepared to witness erotic sex scenes and *then* reminisce about the wedding!

Sexual references are explained through illusive imagery and symbolism. God inspired Solomon to use poetic imagery to portray explicit sexual acts. For example, when the husband entered his wife's "garden," the image refers to . . . well, let's save that for a detailed discussion in chapter 10. *Mandrakes* and *pomegranates*, which spill forth their seed when opened, symbolize fertility and virility; "honey" and "wine" convey intense, erotic desire. Because all the sexual references are cloaked in symbolism, a child could pick up the Bible, read the verses, and find no offense. But a husband and wife could understand the terminology and find specific sexual instruction.

What Is the Theme of the Song?

"Put me like a seal over your heart, like a seal on your arm. For love is as strong as death, jealousy is as severe as Sheol; its flashes are flashes of fire, *the very flame of the LORD*" (8:6, emphasis added).

This, the key verse of the Song, speaks of a love between a husband and wife that is white-hot, passionate, burning, and unable to be extinguished because it comes from God. The promise of the Song to married couples is that your love will last forever — if you become servant lovers. This book is dedicated to helping you do just that.

A SONG AMONG SONGS

God ordained Solomon to write this timeless little instruction book on sex. The task before him must have seemed impossible. How would you feel if God told you: "Write a real-life drama that captures the passion, adventure, and mystery of marriage, but do not ignore the problems of daily life. Be frank and precise when speaking of sexual intimacy, but write in such a way that if a child reads the words, his or her innocence remains intact. Regarding sexual activity, be specific enough to be helpful, but sensitive enough not to offend. Be spiritual, yet practical; wholesome, yet sensuous. And do it all in one hundred twenty verses or less"?

Quite a tall order, wouldn't you say? Yet, Solomon did not balk.

The result is a book on sex that is specific, yet poetic; frank, yet innocent; simple, yet profound; confusing, yet straightforward. Truly, the Song is the best among all songs!

We are excited and expectant as we lead you into the riches of the Song of Solomon. We promise you that Solomon's best song will act as a match to ignite intimacy in your marriage.

Ignite the Flame

chapter one

Where Did All the Passion Go?

"I woke up one morning and discovered a stranger
in my bed — my husband."

"My dog is more affectionate and loving toward
me than my wife is."

In speaking with thousands of couples across the country, we've heard many comments like the two you just read. Intimacy in America is in trouble. More specifically, intimacy in Christian marriages needs revival. Read on:

Eric slipped under the covers, filling the bedroom with the musky scent of Pleasure. The message was not lost on his wife. Inwardly, Katie groaned, Oh, no, not again — not tonight!

Eric slowly stroked Katie's arm, hoping she'd respond to his unspoken plea: I wish you'd roll over and attack me as if I'm the most desirable man in the world.

Katie lay there, silent and unmoving, but her heart rebelled: How can you be so insensitive? Can't you see how exhausted I am, what kind of day I've had, that my brain and body are dead?

Jennifer and Jeff sat on the couch, munching popcorn and watching The Family Man. *During a playful scene in which Jack Campbell (Nicolas Cage) chases his wife around the bedroom in an attempt to seduce her, Jennifer sighed.* Why doesn't Jeff desire me sexually? Is it because I don't look like the sexy blonde in this movie? What's wrong with me?

Jeff crunched down hard on his popcorn, angry. Why do movies always portray men as sex-crazed maniacs? I don't get it.

Candace pulled the covers over herself and turned onto her right side, a signal to Jared that she was going to sleep. She lay only six inches from him, but emotionally they were miles apart. For the thousandth time, he cursed his stupidity. The affair—if you could call it that—was over. One night of foolish indiscretion with a coworker had cost Jared fifteen years of trust with his wife.

They had been to counseling. He'd begged her to forgive him, and she said she had, but they hadn't made love in a month. Jared lay awake, staring into the night, trying to figure out how they had come to this. In the early years of marriage their love had been a blazing bonfire, but even before the affair, it had cooled to a few dying embers. Now all that remained was a flickering spark. God help us! Will we ever feel close again, or are we destined to live forever like strangers?

Wait a minute! God never intended sex to be the cause of such heartache between a husband and wife. The Creator of the universe gave the gift of sex so that the two could become "one flesh" (Ephesians 5:31-32). How is it that the very thing God intended to unite married couples often tears them apart? How is it that something God created to bring pleasure causes so much pain? Why does sex in marriage often move from passion to boredom? Why are the sexual relationships of so many Christian couples in such a mess? How did we get here?

We'll answer the last question first, as we address the other questions throughout the book. It's a fair question, one that deserves an answer. How did we get in the mess we're in?

FROM PURITANISM TO PERVERSION

We doubt that the church fathers ever called a meeting and declared, "Let us make it our goal to distort biblical teaching on sex and thereby weaken the mortar of this cornerstone in marriage." Yet, certain events formed a collective mindset on the part of the church, a mindset that viewed sex as an indulgence of fleshly pleasure that must be restrained.

Let's go back in time, way back to the year AD 200, and see how the church viewed sex:

> Church authorities issued edicts forbidding sex on Thursdays, the day of Christ's arrest; on Fridays, the day of his death; on Saturdays, in honor of the Blessed Virgin; and on Sundays in honor of the departed saints. Wednesdays sometimes made the list too, as did the 40-day fast periods before Easter, Christmas, and Pentecost, and also feast days and days of the Apostles, as well as the days of female impurity. The list escalated until only 44 days a year remained available for marital sex![1]

Now leap forward a thousand years and look at the prevailing mindset. We see a gentle shift from piety to propriety as England's influence resulted in Victorian attitudes characterized by extreme modesty and utter silence on issues related to sexuality. A woman wasn't even supposed to expose a naked ankle. Such behavior was considered brazen and shameful. This attitude so permeated Victorian society that people began covering the legs of furniture lest they arouse impure thoughts![2]

We laugh at such absurdity — being "turned on" by table legs! — but truly it is not a laughing matter. The seeds of Victorianism were planted deeply into the minds of our church fathers and took root in the subsequent generations, as seen in this letter from the late 1800s, written by a pastor's wife to a young woman about her upcoming wedding night:

> To the sensitive young woman who has had the benefits of proper upbringing, the wedding day is, ironically, both the happiest and most terrifying day of her life. On the positive side, there is the wedding itself; on the negative side, there is the wedding night, during which the bride must "pay the piper," so to speak, by facing for the first time the terrible experience of sex.
>
> At this point, let me concede one shocking truth. Some young women actually anticipate the wedding night ordeal with curiosity and pleasure! Beware such an attitude! One cardinal rule of marriage should never be forgotten: GIVE LITTLE, GIVE SELDOM, AND

ABOVE ALL, GIVE GRUDGINGLY. Otherwise what could have been a proper marriage could become an orgy of sexual lust.[3]

This soon-to-be-bride was not the only one to be given such unbiblical advice. In 1907, a popular book expressed these words of instruction to a groom about how to love his bride sexually:

Thousands of married men and women are suffering from the effects of excessive sexual indulgence. They drain their physical powers, weaken the intellect, and fail to attain the happiness and grand results which would otherwise be possible to them. It might be said that no man of average health, physical power and intellectual acumen can exceed the bounds of once a week without at least being in danger of having entered upon a life of excess both for himself and for his wife.

Marital moderation is most easily secured and maintained where married persons occupy separate beds. Sleeping in the same bed is the most ingenious of all possible devices to stimulate and inflame the carnal passion. Often the best arrangement is to occupy separate rooms because then you can escape the sexual excitement which comes daily by the twice-repeated exposure of undressing and dressing in each other's presence.[4]

For centuries, church leaders and laypeople have wrongly believed that sex is not to be enjoyed but rather it is a duty that husbands and wives must perform with restraint and propriety. We can see this attitude in the following quote from Lady Hillingdon, a British aristocrat:

I am happy now that Charles calls on my bedchamber less frequently than of old. As it is, I now endure but two calls a week, and when I hear his steps outside my door, I lie down on my bed, close my eyes, open my legs, and think of England.[5]

Even if we have never read about how the church and society viewed sex or have yet to meet a woman who "thinks about England" so that she can make it through the ordeal of sex with her husband, these distorted views have affected us. Attitudes and beliefs such as these have filtered down through the years, leaving a residue of negative thinking about sex in our generation. In the twentieth century they spawned a revolt: the sexual revolution.

In the 1960s, America thrust off the constraining bustier of Puritanism and bared her chest in defiance. Sexual freedom became the cry of the country. Freedom meant no rules, no restraints, and society gradually slipped into a pervasive attitude that proclaimed, "Do it — anywhere, anytime, with anyone." This sexual "freedom" created its own kind of bondage; it resulted in unrestrained lust that sought sexual fulfillment but could not find it.

Today the sexual pendulum has swung from Puritanism to perversion. Flip on the computer and you can shop a wide assortment of pornography. Click on the television and see two *men* in bed together. Scan a current magazine and read about Washington's latest sex scandal or about some movie star's shock gimmick designed to promote personal fame. Sadly, our culture is so perverted that the shock factor is all but gone.

NOW WHAT?

While a look at the past can offer us insight into how we got to where we are today, it doesn't help us solve sexual problems or transform distorted and harmful attitudes. What we really need to know is this: How do we get out of this mess? Simple. Look to the wisdom found in the Song of Solomon:

The Song has answers. "I can't believe it! All this time, the answers to my marriage's sexual frustrations have been right in front of me — in God's Word. The Song of Solomon is beautiful and probably the most romantic thing ever written — a wonderful hidden secret!"

The Song is practical. "I learned new lovemaking techniques *in the Bible* — words to speak, ways to touch — that have put the sizzle back into our sex life."

The Song is holy. "After reading the Song, I understood for the first time how deeply God cares about our intimate relationship, that He wants to bless it and be a part of it."

The Song is life-changing. "I will never be the same again. Never. What I learned in the Song of Solomon literally saved our marriage."

The wisdom found in the Song can transform your marriage. We know this to be true because it has changed *our* marriages. As we've traveled around the country and taught these truths to thousands of men and women, we've seen transformation in their marriages as well. This book is about sex. Is sex the most important thing in marriage? No, but when the beauty, holiness, fun, and passion that God desires to be present in your intimate relationship are absent, it affects every other aspect of marriage.

Do you need to ignite intimacy in your marriage? The Song will show you how to make sex sing. It will show you sexual communication and creativity at its best. As you study the Song, you'll find:

Wisdom
    Passion
        Explicit sexual instruction
            Romance
                Honesty
                    Inspiration to ignite intimacy in your marriage

And you will learn how becoming a servant lover will enable you to nurture a love between you that is so hot, so passionate, and so intense that nothing will be able to extinguish it. So get ready for passion at its best. Before you turn the page, we ask you to open your heart and pray,

> *God, I don't want my marriage to be mediocre. I want passion and intimacy, not boredom and predictability. Speak to me as I read. May the power of your Spirit and your Word transform my heart and mind and help me to become the lover you desire me to be.*

SERVANT LOVERS: Are teachable and desire to ignite intimacy.

SELFISH LOVERS: Have stubborn and unteachable hearts.

TIRZAH TO SOLOMON:
"*May he kiss me with the kisses of his mouth!*
For your love is better than wine.
Your oils have a pleasing fragrance,
Your name is like purified oil;
Therefore the maidens love you.
Draw me after you and let us run together!
The king has brought me into his chambers."

THE CHORUS:
"*We will rejoice in you and be glad;*
We will extol your love more than wine.
Rightly do they love you."

SONG OF SOLOMON 1:2-4

〥

Give Permission for Passion

"Our sex life has no passion. He gives me a quick
kiss on the lips, one minute of foreplay, and then straight in
for the touchdown. We've been married eight years.
Is this all I have to look forward to?"

We are about to walk into a holy place, a place of passion where kisses are "better than wine." God beckons us to enter into His Word and into the privacy of a couple who will help us light the flame of passion in our own marriages by showing us how to become servant lovers. We are about to discover romance at its best.

UNDERSTANDING THE SONG

The opening verse of the Song of Solomon skips preliminary introductions and catapults us straight into a steamy bedroom scene.

Tirzah: "May he kiss me with the kisses of his mouth! For your love is better than wine." (1:2)

Tirzah hungers for her lover's kisses. No formal peck on the cheek will do. Longing to feel his deep kiss inside her own, she reaches out to him with abandon. In Hebrew, the words for "kiss" and "kissing" are onomatopoetic. Like our English word *buzz*, they sound like what they mean. This verse could literally be translated "O, that he'd give me some of his smacking kisses that take my breath away."[1] It's been said that a kiss can be a comma, question mark, or exclamation point.[2] Obviously, Tirzah thought Solomon's kiss felt like an exclamation point.

She says that Solomon's love is like wine, a rich and sensuous liquid. The Song uses three different Hebrew words for love: *rayah*, which refers to companionship; *ahabah*, which refers to sacrificial, loyal commitment; and *dod*, which usually refers to sexual love or lovemaking.[3] The reference to love in this verse is *dod*. While Tirzah's lips drink deeply of Solomon's kiss, her body cries out for further intimacies. In the Hebrew culture, joyful banquets of celebration were often referred to as wine. In mentioning wine, Tirzah is saying that Solomon's extravagant love gives her more joy and pleasure than the most lavish celebration.

Tirzah: "Your oils have a pleasing fragrance, your name is like purified oil; therefore the maidens love you." (verse 3)

In Solomon's time people prepared for a festive occasion by bathing and then rubbing their bodies with oil. The Hebrews had adopted the Egyptian practice of applying fragrance not only on themselves during a feast but also on their guests (see Psalm 133:2). Hosts placed small cones of perfumed ointment on the foreheads of their guests, whose body heat gradually melted the ointment, which then trickled down their faces onto their clothing, producing a pleasant aroma.[4]

In the previous verse, Tirzah reflects on Solomon's kisses. Here she meditates on the erotic scent of the perfumed oils he had smoothed over his body. She also tells him that his name is like purified oil. In other words, he is a man of character and his honorable reputation goes before him like a fragrance. Tirzah values her beloved so highly that the very sound or thought of his name creates a longing in her heart for him. Solomon captivates her heart, her thoughts, and her lips. Everyone sees her beloved's worth, yet he chose her. How blessed she is!

Tirzah: "Draw me after you and let us run together! The king has brought me into his chambers." (verse 4)

Dwelling on Solomon's kisses, his caresses, and the coming fulfillment of her sexual longing, Tirzah becomes even more aggressive in her invitation. She begs her beloved to seize her and race with her to the seclusion of their private bedchamber. Believe us, this is no sedate stroll to the bedroom. In contemporary English, she is saying something like, "Hurry up, honey! I can't wait any longer. I need you. I want you. Now!"

The Chorus: "We will rejoice in you and be glad; we will extol your love more than wine. Rightly do they love you." (verse 4)

As the couple put on their Nikes and sprint to the bedroom, the imaginary chorus bursts into open song, rejoicing with Tirzah. In essence, the chorus provides a blessing on the relationship.[5] They agree with the young bride that the love she and Solomon share is truly as intoxicating as the best wine.

APPLYING THE SONG FOR COUPLES

Tirzah and Solomon were drunk with love. They had sipped from each other's lips and were inebriated with the wine of passion. Perhaps Solomon was thinking of this moment when he wrote, "Let your love and your sexual embrace with your wife intoxicate you continually with delight. Always enjoy the ecstasy of her love" (Proverbs 5:19, our paraphrase).

As we see here and in many passages throughout this Song, God gives permission for passion. His Word says, "Relax. Let go. Give in to your erotic feelings. Allow yourself to become *intoxicated* by your mate's sexual touches." Stop for a moment and consider what happens when people become intoxicated. Alcohol impacts the way they think, see, hear, walk, and talk; it overtakes them. What does it mean when the Bible says that we are to intoxicate our mate with the "wine of lovemaking"? It means that our beloved is to be *overtaken* by the pleasure of our sexual love.

It is as if God reaches down through the pages of Scripture and says to a wife, "Enjoy your husband, give pleasure to him, receive pleasure from him. Delight yourself in the erotic feelings of your sexual love." And to the husband, God urges, "Enjoy your wife, give pleasure to her, receive pleasure from her. Delight yourself in the erotic feelings of your sexual love."

How is passion ignited? For Solomon and Tirzah, it began with a kiss.

Build Anticipation Through Kissing

Many couples tell us that after being married several years, they relegate kissing to the bottom of their list of intimate touch. They simply bypass the lips. These couples are forgetting how a slow, probing kiss can make your heart pound and your knees weak.

A medical doctor explains: "There is a physical reason our lips cry out to be kissed. The lips have a proportionately larger number of nerve endings than other parts of the body."[6]

Consider these additional observations about the importance of kissing:

Marriage counselor: "Kissing is an indicator of the quality of a sexual relationship. When kissing is passionate, it is likely the couple has a satisfying sexual relationship."

Author: "Kissing is the most intimate and personal sharing of ourselves because we are touching another with a part of our body that we use to communicate and nurture ourselves."

And this zinger from a woman in "the oldest profession in the world": "I tell my clients I'll have sex with them but I won't kiss them. Kissing is too intimate."[7]

The ancient Chinese felt that kissing belonged only in the intimate, erotic world of the Jade Chamber (a reference to sexual relations) and that kissing in public was tantamount to having sex in public.[8] While this is an extreme view, it suggests that kissing is a key to igniting intimacy. We agree!

Kissing May Be Good for Your Health

An article in *Health* magazine titled "Kiss Me, Please" cited the following kissing facts:[9]

- Kissing relieves stress by releasing mood-elevating endorphins in the brain.

- It burns two calories per minute — and could lead to more exercise.
- It firms the muscles in your face (and it's cheaper than a face-lift!).
- Swapping saliva with someone boosts your immune system by helping the body bolster its defenses.
- It's fun.

When was the last time the two of you shared a long, lingering kiss? If it has been a while, plan to rediscover tonight the joys of kissing. Start with the lips, but don't stop there. Consider other parts of your beloved's body that beg for the brush of a kiss. Press your lips against firm muscles and into soft curves. Touch, taste, and linger in hidden areas available to only you. Allow anticipation to build. As you do, you will discover how easy it is to turn everyday, ordinary kisses into "better than wine" kisses.

MAKE IT YOUR GOAL TO BECOME A SERVANT LOVER

You've witnessed Solomon and Tirzah's burning kisses. Let us warn you that this is only the beginning. Future scenes are even more steamy. When the four of us first understood all the nuances of the Song of Solomon, we were stunned that God's Word would be so specific about sex. But we are grateful that our Creator cared so much about sexual oneness in marriage that He included an instruction manual to help us. God wants married couples to have a love so hot, so passionate, so intense that nothing will be able to extinguish it, and He knows the key for such love is becoming servant lovers to each other. But rather than ordering us — "be a servant lover!" — He shows us how through the lives of Solomon and Tirzah.

Growing up we heard the Golden Rule: "Do unto others as you would have them do unto you." It seems natural to serve in the kitchen, at the workplace, at church, and in our neighborhood. But we don't often make the effort to be a servant in the bedroom. However, that is the heart of a servant lover!

SERVANT LOVERS

WHAT *DO* THEY DO?

Serve:

- They place the intimate needs of their spouse above their own.
- They help their spouse appreciate and enjoy intimacy.
- They are patient.
- They are willing to try new ways of expressing their intimacy that are pleasurable for their spouse.
- They look for ways to help their spouse grow in intimacy.
- They are creative in their expression of intimacy.
- They seek to give more than to receive.

Love:

- They love their spouse unconditionally.
- They are willing to put aside the meeting of their own intimate needs if their spouse is unable to meet those needs due to sickness, disabilities, emotional issues, and so on.
- They are willing to be intimate when their spouse wants intimacy, even if they may not be in the mood.

Protect:

- They protect their spouse from any harmful forms of intimate expression.
- They protect their own purity from negative and sinful influences, such as pornography.

Forgive:

- They freely forgive (see "Offer a Cup of Forgiveness," page 209).
- They do not keep a record of past sexual sin, either for themselves or their spouse.
- They do not hold grudges if their spouse is unable to express intimacy in the way they want.

What *Don't* They Do?

- They don't push intimacy just for their own satisfaction.
- They don't demand their own way of expressing or receiving intimate pleasure.
- They don't act or behave in ways that cause physical, emotional, or spiritual harm to their spouse.
- They don't withhold sex when their mate has wounded them.

Philippians 2:3-4 says, "Do nothing out of selfish ambition or vain conceit, but in humility consider others better than yourselves. Each of you should look not only to your own interests, but also to the interests of others" (NIV). This passage describes the heart of the servant lover:

- Servant lovers sacrifice *sexually* for their mates.
- Servant lovers place their mate's *sexual* needs above their own.
- Servant lovers give *sexually* with selfless abandon.

As you continue to read, you will see how a servant lover demonstrates these actions. While being a servant lover involves certain actions, it is first an attitude of the heart. Are you willing to grow as a lover to your mate? Are you willing to allow the Spirit of God to transform you so you can be the lover God wants you to be? If so, will you pray?

God, I want to give myself permission for passion. Please teach me as I read. Where I am ignorant, give me wisdom. Where I am reluctant, make me willing. With each page I turn, help me to become the servant lover you desire for me to be.

SERVANT LOVERS: Give themselves permission to extend and receive passion.

SELFISH LOVERS: Remain stuck in their old ways of thinking and acting.

TIRZAH SPEAKS:
"I am black but lovely,
O daughters of Jerusalem,
Like the tents of Kedar,
Like the curtains of Solomon.
Do not stare at me because I am swarthy
For the sun has burned me.
My mother's sons were angry with me;
They made me caretaker of the vineyards,
But I have not taken care of my own vineyard.
Tell me, O you whom my soul loves,
Where do you pasture your flock
Where do you make it lie down at noon?
For why should I be like one who veils herself
Beside the flocks of your companions?"

SOLOMON REPLIES:
"If you yourself do not know,
Most beautiful among women,
Go forth on the trail of the flock,
And pasture your young goats
By the tents of the shepherds."

SONG OF SOLOMON 1:5-8

chapter three

◊

Soothe Insecurities

"Everywhere I look, I see beautiful women flaunting their
flawless faces and trim bodies — on television, on billboards,
in the newspaper. I feel fat and ugly by comparison. I wish I could get
excited about making love with Sam, but I don't want him touching
my body, because I don't feel good about myself."

Nothing halts lovemaking faster than shifting your focus from your spouse's intimate advances to your own insecurities. How can a husband help his wife forget her insecurities and recapture sexual passion? We find insight in God's Word as we study Solomon's response to Tirzah's abrupt mood shift from driven lover to insecure wife.

UNDERSTANDING THE SONG

Tirzah: "I am black but lovely, O daughters of Jerusalem, like the tents of Kedar, like the curtains of Solomon." (1:5)

Tirzah's dark coloring, acquired from living in the open, apparently makes her feel out of place beside the fair-skinned palace maidens. Her black hair is lustrous and fine, like the valuable black goat hair used by the nomadic people of Kedar to make their tents.[1] When bathed in the flood of early evening's golden light, these tents were strikingly beautiful. As they swayed gently in the wind, they spoke of mystery and enchantment. Precious tapestries also made from beautiful black goat hair adorned the walls in Solomon's palace. Tirzah stresses the "lovely" part of herself by comparing herself to these tapestries.

Tirzah: "*Do not stare at me because I am swarthy, for the sun has burned me. My mother's sons were angry with me; they made me caretaker of the vineyards, but I have not taken care of my own vineyard.*" *(verse 6)*

The *New Living Translation* makes Tirzah's feelings clear: "Don't look down on me, you fair city girls, just because my complexion is so dark." As she compares herself to the pretty yet pampered women of the court, Tirzah gives in to her feelings of insecurity and says something like, "You were raised in bonnets and bows and kept from the burning sun. But I had to work under its fierce rays, taking care of my family's vineyard while my personal vineyard received no pampered care."

Tirzah to Solomon: "*Tell me, O you whom my soul loves, where do you pasture your flock, where do you make it lie down at noon? For why should I be like one who veils herself beside the flocks of your companions?*" *(verse 7)*

Commentators have various interpretations for verses 7 and 8. It seems to us, however, that in verse 7, Tirzah is playfully inviting her lover to a rendezvous during his lunch hour. She addresses him with deep emotion, as the one her soul loves.[2]

Solomon is a shepherd of Israel, for just as a shepherd guards and guides his flock of sheep, so Solomon leads his people with protective love. Tirzah uses the imagery of a shepherd as a way of asking Solomon where they can be alone together. In the Song, pasturing speaks of male sexual activity, and here Tirzah evokes a pastoral scene for their lovemaking.[3] She asks Solomon for directions to the place where they will meet so that she does not have to sneak out of the palace as a veiled woman in order to find him. If she must search for him, she will appear like a prostitute.

Solomon answers: "*If you do not know, most beautiful among women, go forth on the trail of the flock and pasture your young goats by the tents of the shepherds.*" *(verse 8)*

Solomon speaks to Tirzah's insecurities and declares that in his eyes she is stunningly beautiful. He then picks up the shepherd imagery as he tells her to "go forth on the trail of the flock" — that is, meet him somewhere outside the palace for a secret encounter.

According to some commentators, Solomon and Tirzah are involved in a playful, sensuous game of hide-and-seek. The invitation for an intimate encounter is there, but it's under the surface. The pastoral imagery is a cover, a veiled reference to the reality that Tirzah is stealing out of the palace to be alone with her lover. The reference to sheep, goats, and shepherds is all part of the romance, evoking a pleasant scene away from the public eye of the city.[4]

Tirzah wants to be alone with Solomon. His presence soothes her insecurities. Many wives feel insecure about how they look and seek reassurance from their husbands that they are beautiful and desirable.

APPLYING THE SONG FOR WIVES

Insecurity about appearance has reached epidemic proportions among women living in the United States. We asked the women at a recent Intimate Issues conference, "How many of you are 100 percent satisfied with your body?" Eyes searched the room to see if *any* woman was pleased with everything about her body — the shape of her legs, the look of her face, her shoe size, and her cup size. Among nine hundred women, only one brave soul raised her hand.

We are convinced that women receive a "body critic gene" at birth that makes us critical of ourselves and of others. We come out of the womb saying, "Hi, Mom. Piled on the baby pounds while I was in there, didn't you?"

> *Linda:* My mom, who is a petite size six, defined my image of beauty. Consequently, I've been dieting since I was twelve. When my daughter was little, she looked at me one day and said, "I don't want to grow up to be a mommy because that means I'll always be on a diet." The lie I've battled all my life is that beauty is defined by a certain dress size.

> *Lorraine:* In elementary school I was "pleasantly plump." When I was a sophomore in high school, I lost fifteen pounds. All of a sudden,

everyone began to tell me how beautiful I was. The lie I've had to battle
all my life is that beauty is defined by a certain number on the scale.

We don't know any woman who has not battled lies about her appearance.
Other common lies include:

- ◊ "My legs have so much cellulite that I look hideous!"
- ◊ "I'd be beautiful if I had bigger breasts."
- ◊ "Botox will make me look twenty-five and pretty again."
- ◊ "I found my first gray hair. I'm ancient!"

Too often we focus on the negative, obsessing over flaws our husbands
would never notice if we didn't continually point them out. Our friend
Mallory was in a department store trying on clothes when she looked over her
shoulder into the mirror behind her and shrieked with horror, "How did my
mother's rear end get on me?" This initiated a series of constant comments to
her husband about her expanding derriere. One day he gave her a card that
had a picture of a large woman looking over her shoulder into a mirror that
highlighted her backside. The message inside read, "Objects in mirror are not
as large as they appear." He wrote on the card, "I got you this card *only* because
you talk about this all the time."

Often we whine about extra pounds or being an A cup instead of a B.
Meanwhile, women with serious body issues look at us and think, *I'd exchange
my problem for hers in a heartbeat.*

Not long ago we were teaching on body image at an Intimate Issues conference. We were talking (read "whining") about the agony of trying to keep off
unwanted pounds once your body hits menopause and your metabolism slows to
a snail's pace. We also commented (read "complained") about the painful rigors
of diet and exercise we'd both endured in our valiant attempts to subdue cellulite.
But then we noticed a lovely young woman without arms or legs sitting in a
wheelchair in the center aisle. We both wondered what we must have sounded
like to her. But instead of judging us as two vain women obsessing over trivialities,
Brandi nodded empathetically. We knew we had much to learn from this woman!

During a break, we approached Brandi and discovered that she was at the conference to learn how to better love her husband sexually. We asked her if her physical limitations ever made her feel insecure about making love. Her wise answer convicted us both:

> I think most husbands pick up on the insecurities of their wives. We are always saying something negative about how we look, and this causes our husbands to focus on the negative. So I focus on what I like about my body, and this causes my husband to see the positive too.

Brandi is right! We need to focus on the positive, to praise God that we are fearfully and wonderfully made (see Psalm 139:14).

We want to share with you an important principle in Scripture that will help you view your body as God sees it rather than as the world judges it. Let's ask the Lord to make our hearts right so we can receive His Truth:

> *Lord, we live in a society obsessed with unattainable beauty standards, and it has warped our thinking. We moan and complain when we can no longer fit into our favorite pair of pants or when we notice a few new wrinkles around our eyes. Oh God, forgive us. Help us to quit complaining about what we can't change (the natural process of aging, our body type, our skin type, and so on) and to do something about the things we can change (our weight, fitness, and nutrition). God, teach us to view our bodies as You view them. Please open our hearts to what You want to speak to us through Your Word.*

Are you ready? If so, let's lay down the mirror of the world, which reflects unrealistic beauty standards, and pick up the mirror of God's Word, which offers a reflection of true beauty.

VIEW YOUR BODY AS GOD'S TEMPLE

What does God say about beauty and about your body?

> Do you not know that your body is a temple of the Holy Spirit who is in you, whom you have from God, and that you are not your own? For

you have been bought with a price; therefore glorify God in your body.
(1 Corinthians 6:19-20)

These verses teach that:

◊ Your body is a temple.
◊ God designed your temple.
◊ The Holy Spirit lives in your temple.
◊ Your temple does not belong to you but to Christ.
◊ You are to glorify God through your temple.

Being a temple for the living God is both an awesome privilege and an awesome responsibility. God wants you to maintain His dwelling place and to keep it holy for Him, for yourself, and for your husband.

TAKE CARE OF YOUR TEMPLE FOR GOD

In order to gain insight into how you can take care of your body for God, ask yourself two questions: *Do I fill my body with things that harm it (drugs, unhealthful foods, chemicals, evil images, or sinful thoughts)? Do I fill my body with things that please God (healthful foods, Scripture, uplifting thoughts)?*

Amy and Gloria asked themselves these two questions, and then made the choice to fill their bodies with things that please God:

Amy: For me to honor God with my temple means that I put good stuff in and keep bad stuff out. I try to read my Bible every day. I say no to R-rated movies and MTV. And I joined the local gym to keep my body strong so that if God asks me to do something, I'll have the physical strength to do it.

Gloria: There are a lot of cracks in my temple, but the foundation is solid. I fill in the cracks with a good makeup concealer and then spiff up my exterior with a daily "paint job." Just as people used exquisite tapestries to cover the flaws in the walls of the stone temples, I wear clothes that hide my figure flaws and colors that make me look vibrant.

No one would mistake me for a brand-new temple, but many see this old temple as beautiful because as my body has *fallen*, my skill in caring for it has *risen*.

Put down this book now and ask the Lord, "What does it look like for me to please You in caring for this temple of Yours?"

TAKE CARE OF YOUR TEMPLE FOR YOURSELF

If you are like most women, you feel overworked, overtired, and under-appreciated. We are so busy taking care of everyone else's needs that we fail to take care of our own. But we have it backward: We must take care of ourselves so that we have the ability to care for others. As the airline safety video clearly states, "In case of an emergency, oxygen masks will drop from above. Secure your own mask first before helping others with theirs."

When we eat healthful meals and exercise regularly, when we get enough sleep, when we wear clothes and colors that look good on us, we naturally feel better about ourselves. These activities directly impact our sexual relationship with our husbands. One woman told us, "I recently lost twenty pounds. I feel so much better about myself. I can be so much more free sexually now that I don't have to position my arm over my stomach to hide the roll of fat."

Ask the Lord, "What do I need to change so that I can take better care of myself?"

TAKE CARE OF YOUR TEMPLE FOR YOUR HUSBAND

Your husband will applaud what we are about to say because it is something he would like to tell you but can't. Listen carefully. As a man, he needs to see you as attractive. He does not need you to have the body of a supermodel. He does not need you to have a face like Helen of Troy that men would go to war over. But he does want you to care about looking good for him and to make an effort to do so.

Several years ago, after Linda had just finished a radio interview, a man called the station and asked to talk with her. He said:

When I married my wife, she was very attractive. After having children, she gained eighty pounds and does nothing to try to lose it. She

hates herself and will hardly go out of the house. I love my wife and am committed to being faithful, but I struggle continually with lustful thoughts of other women. I hate myself for this. Why won't my wife help? Tell me what to do.

God designed men to be stimulated sexually through what they see. If you are irked, irritated, or angry about this, your issue is with God, not your husband. Ask the Lord, "Is there anything You would have me do about my appearance that would bless my husband?" (Although this application has been addressed to wives, it is equally as important for a husband to take care of his temple for his wife.)

As you read our challenge to you about taking care of your body, how did you respond? Did you enthusiastically nod in agreement, saying, "Yes, God! I want to take care of my body for You, for myself, and for my husband"? Or did you find yourself saying "no" to each suggestion because you know what it will cost you in terms of time and discipline and you don't want to put forth the effort? We know that what we've suggested can seem difficult, but life is short. Staying healthy, fit, and attractive is important. This is not something you have to do all on your own. Books, exercise clubs, and programs such as Weight Watchers are available to help you. Ask God to help you — He will! We know it also helps when your husband encourages you, so make sure he reads what follows, because God wants him to be a support to you.

APPLYING THE SONG FOR HUSBANDS

UNDERSTAND THE POWER OF PRAISE

A wise husband understands that when his wife feels insecure about her body, she cannot make love with abandon. The servant lover within him rises to her defense and, with the forcefulness of a sword-wielding Zorro, proclaims:

- I will defend my wife against the lies that assault her mind.
- I will affirm her beauty.
- I will speak words that soothe her insecurities and release the passions within her.

Men down through the centuries have broken the chains of their wives' insecurities by speaking words of praise. Although the words may sound different, the heart to affirm their wife is the same:

- "Oh most beautiful among women, go forth." (Solomon, 2000 BC)
- "Age cannot wither her, nor custom stale her infinite variety." (Shakespeare, AD 1600)
- "Hey, babe, you are hot!" (Jody Dillow and Peter Pintus, 2004, each in reference to his wife)

Husbands, don't ever underestimate the power of your praise! Proverbs 31 describes an intelligent, godly wife who is highly esteemed. She is noble, lovely, diligent, and respected by all. Verse 28 implies that her husband's praise in some way enables her to be who she is, to rise to her potential as a woman of God.

According to Proverbs 15:4, "The tongue that brings healing is a tree of life, but a deceitful tongue crushes the spirit" (NIV). Your words can give life to your wife because they have power:

- Positive words encourage her to be a godly wife.
- Positive words build her up emotionally and spiritually.
- Positive words provide her with a sense of well-being.
- Positive words affirm and heal her.

But beware! Your affirming words will have power only if you speak them with sincerity. God gave females an uncanny ability to sniff out flattery as quickly as a cat smells tuna. If your words are spoken out of duty or insincerity, they will have no value whatsoever. Let your words be genuine, timely, sincere, and specific.

We men sometimes find it challenging to force our words to make the long journey from our minds to our mouths. As one counselor said, "Merely thinking kind thoughts about our wives is not enough. I encourage husbands to direct those thoughts from their brains to their tongues, and then to lovingly articulate the words to their wives."[5]

Johnny Lingo and His Eight-Cow Wife

The story is told of a man named Johnny Lingo, who lived on an island in the South Pacific. Johnny was a wealthy trader respected for his ability to strike a hard bargain — except when it came to securing his wife. In these islands, a man bought his wife from her father by paying from one to six cows. Two or three cows would buy a fair to middling wife; four or five, a breathtaking beauty.

Johnny wanted to marry Sarita, a plain woman who lived on the island of Kiniwata and was scared of her own shadow. For her, Johnny offered the unheard-of sum of eight cows. The residents of Kiniwata smirked that such a successful businessman would pay such an outrageous price for a plain woman. They figured he was a sucker when it came to love.

A woman decided to find out more about Johnny and his wife, so she sailed to the nearby island where Johnny lived and called on his home. When she met his wife, she was amazed to find the most beautiful woman she'd ever seen. When she inquired about what happened, Johnny explained, "Do you ever think what it must mean to a woman to know that her husband has settled on the lowest price for which she can be bought? And then later, when the women talk, they boast of what their husbands paid for them. One says four cows, another maybe six. How does she feel, the woman who was sold for one or two? This could not happen to my Sarita."

"Then you did this just to make your wife happy?" she asked.

"I wanted Sarita to be happy, yes. But I wanted more than that. You say she is different. This is true. Many things can change a woman, but the thing that matters most is what she thinks about herself. In Kiniwata, Sarita believed she was worth nothing. Now she knows she is worth more than any other woman in the islands. She is an eight-cow wife."[6]

Jody understands this dilemma:

> I know Linda needs to be affirmed about her looks, but when she is
> dressed for church, or with a new outfit, I don't notice how she looks.
> It is unbelievable how dense I can be when confronted with the expec-
> tant look on her face that begs for approval. While I often think, *I am
> so fortunate to have a wife who always does her best to look good and who is
> incredibly attractive,* still I must force myself to verbalize to her what I
> am feeling.

Some men never verbalize what they think. Others verbalize their
thoughts when it would have been better if they'd kept their mouths shut, as is
evidenced by the following comments from wives:

- I'm in my fifties, and one day my husband told me, "With a little
  work, those breasts could look like a young woman's."
- I have two children and am a trim size eight, but my husband wants
  me to be a size two. He says, "You are fat and I'm embarrassed to be
  seen with you."
- My husband never compliments me. One time I got into a sexy
  nightgown and he said, "What do you have that thing on for? Are
  you trying to take control or something?"

But not all men are jerks. Many zealously slash away at their wives' insecurities by offering life-giving words, as these women testify:

- I have varicose veins and stretch marks from our four kids. Kyle kisses
  them and says they are beautiful. He calls them my badges of honor.
- I am embarrassed because I have no boobs, but Jason makes it a
  point when we make love to caress them and say, "These are so
  beautiful and satisfying to me."
- He looks at me, starting at my head and working down to my toes,
  then back up, and says, "Hubba, hubba!"

◊ When I was training for a 10K race to lose weight, he encouraged me to keep going toward my goal. "I'm so proud of you," he said over and over. That made me feel good.

Brian, an artist, was scouting for a job in Colorado while his wife, Pam, remained in New Jersey. Every morning he drove a stretch of road with rolling grassland and rocky buttes and mesas. He said, "It was as if Pam were lying under a satin sheet and I was driving my car across the landscape of her body, just like I had done with my fingers and lips many times before." He captured these mental images in a poem he sent to her:

> In your absence, you are everywhere.
> The hills that undulate in the prairie are like your hips when you are lying down.
> There are two mountains that I pass every day that are like your breasts, but I cannot reach out and touch them.
> God certainly made you for me.[7]

Maybe you aren't a poet like Solomon or Brian and you feel inadequate and clumsy every time you open your mouth. Don't let that stop you! Your wife doesn't require eloquent prose or sound bites from *Love Story*. Even your fumbling attempts at praise will delight her.

We men are often clueless about the pressure our wives feel about how they look and how desperately they need our approval, our affirmation. Our praise can go a long way in removing their insecurities. So are you ready? Will you fight for your lover? Will you speak words that honor her and release her feminine beauty? Grab a thesaurus and a dictionary, make a list of words you can use, and then attack.

IMPLEMENT A THIRTY-DAY PRAISE PLAN

The strategy is this: Each day praise your wife in one of the following areas: acts of service, physical attributes, and character attributes. Here are some examples for you to adapt.

Acts of Service:

- ⚶ I really appreciate the way you spent time with Amanda when she was struggling with her homework last night.
- ⚶ I'm proud of you for making meals for friends when they're sick.
- ⚶ It wasn't easy to talk to your parents about some of their health issues. I admire you for your boldness and courage.

Physical Attributes:

- ⚶ The way you're wearing your hair tonight makes you look so soft and sexy.
- ⚶ I've noticed that you are losing weight. You look great! Your commitment to exercise is really paying off.
- ⚶ Your body is as exciting to me today as it was when we first met twelve years ago.

Character Attributes:

- ⚶ The way you served our guests this evening really demonstrated a Christlike heart.
- ⚶ A woman in your Bible study told me you're a gifted teacher and counselor.
- ⚶ One of the things I appreciate most about you is your honesty. I've seen times you could lie because it was easier, but you chose to speak truth.

Supplement your words with actions. Write her a note and leave it by her coffee cup, or write, "Your beauty captures my heart" with soap or a nonpermanent marker on the bathroom mirror. Here are some other creative ways men have affirmed their wives:

- ⚶ I was driving in the car ahead of my wife, Becky, when I came to a tollbooth. I said to the man inside, "Tell the woman in the car behind me that I paid her toll because I think she's beautiful."
- ⚶ I gave her a dozen red roses and wrote a note that said, "These pale in comparison to your beauty."

◊ We were at a party the other night. I was talking with a group of men and women. Carey walked toward us. I put my arm around her and said in front of the entire group, "Do you know that I'm married to the most gorgeous woman in the world?"

If you implement the Thirty-Day Praise Plan, you can become a praise expert like C. J. Mahoney. He writes,

> Recently, my wife and I were shopping while on vacation. We shopped separately at first and set a time to meet up again. As that time drew near, I searched the crowd for Carolyn. Finally, I caught sight of her. She approached and I embraced her. I said, "Love, I just want you to know that whenever I'm searching for you in a crowd, you are the only one who appears to me in color. The rest of the world is black and white to me."[8]

C. J. Mahoney blessed his wife by expressing that he was blind to all others except her. In the story that follows, Ken, who was born blind, shares a vital truth about how we are to "see" our wives.

DEFINE BEAUTY BY YOUR WIFE'S BODY

When Ken asked Delaney to marry him, she said "yes" but admits she was nervous about the wedding night. She says,

> Ken had never "seen" a woman before. His only sight was through the touch of his fingers. I decided to delight his "sight" by embroidering verses from the Song of Solomon in braille on the shoulders of my nightgown. As his fingers moved over my body, he stopped and read the hidden message of love inscribed just for him. "Oh," he exclaimed, yet his ohs became more passionate as the nightgown came off and he "saw" a female body for the first time. He said to me, "So this is what a woman looks like. Oh, how beautiful! How soft!" I was the picture of a beautiful woman to his mind — the only picture he had.

In *Sacred Marriage*, Gary Thomas writes, "On the day I was married, I began praying, 'Lord, help me to define beauty by Lisa's body. Shape my desires so that I am attracted only to her.'"[9]

In the Song, Tirzah feels insecure about her body and God uses her husband to praise away her fears. But the truth is that in the course of a marriage, both husbands and wives will face insecurity issues about their bodies. God desires for our mate to cheer us on, help us embrace His view of our bodies rather than the world's view, and encourage us to maintain a strong, healthy body so we can serve the Lord for many years.

When we allow our mate's body to become our definition of beauty — when we praise our mate's body and make an effort to keep our own bodies healthy for ourselves, for God, and for our mate — God is pleased. He longs to hear from the lips of all who love Him, "I will give thanks to You, for I am fearfully and wonderfully made; wonderful are Your works, and my soul knows it very well" (Psalm 139:14).

SERVANT LOVERS: Express admiration through encouraging words and actions.

SELFISH LOVERS: Tear down their mates with critical looks, words, and actions.

SOLOMON SPEAKS:

"To me, my darling, you are like
My mare among the chariots of Pharaoh.
Your cheeks are lovely with ornaments,
Your neck with strings of beads.
We will make for you ornaments of gold
With beads of silver."

TIRZAH SPEAKS:

"While the king was at his table,
My perfume gave forth its fragrance.
My beloved is to me a pouch of myrrh
Which lies all night between my breasts.
My beloved is to me a cluster of henna blossoms
In the vineyards of Engedi."

SONG OF SOLOMON 1:9-14

❦

chapter four

Offer Sexual Refreshment

"Madison and I rented a cabin in the mountains for our
tenth anniversary. We sipped hot cider and then made love on a
bearskin rug in front of the fire. Afterward, as we lay in each other's arms,
watching the flames dance across the room, I realized I'd never felt closer to
my wife. It was like the rest of the world had disappeared and nothing
mattered but the two of us. I wish we could get away more often,
but juggling two jobs, kids, and church commitments
makes it almost impossible."

Many couples feel they have to get away from home in order to lose themselves in sexual love with their mates. But as Solomon and Tirzah demonstrate,
our intimate encounters can, with a little creativity and imagination, be a place
where we temporarily leave the world behind and bask in the refreshing waters
of sexual love — even if we never venture beyond the bedroom door.

UNDERSTANDING THE SONG

*Solomon to Tirzah: "To me, my darling, you are like my mare
among the chariots of Pharaoh." (1:9)*

Solomon assures his bride that to him she is as beautiful as his horses.
Perhaps you are thinking, *And she didn't slug him?* Believe us, this comparison
was music to Tirzah's ears. At that time in the Ancient Near East, horses were
not beasts of burden; they were the cherished companions of kings. Solomon
loved horses and particularly Egyptian horses; he had fourteen hundred chariots and twelve thousand horsemen (1 Kings 10:26). His mare must have been

the most outstanding of all his horses, so here basically he's telling Tirzah that she's one in a million.

For the first time in the Song, Solomon uses the second Hebrew word for love, *rayah*, which is translated here as "my darling." It means "beloved, darling, companion, i.e., one who is the object of love and affection."[1] While the word can have sexual connotations, as *dod* does, *rayah* seems to emphasize more the idea of friend and companion. By calling Tirzah this, Solomon not only indicates his desire to make love with her but also affirms that she is his intimate partner.

Solomon to Tirzah: "Your cheeks are lovely with ornaments, your neck with strings of beads. We will make for you ornaments of gold with beads of silver." (verses 10-11)

Once again Solomon pours on the praise and tells his beloved that her jewelry is lovely. He assures Tirzah that he plans to have even more costly and luxurious ornaments handcrafted for her.

Tirzah: "While the king was at his table, my perfume gave forth its fragrance."(verse 12)

The table referred to here is likely a divan, a round table where meals were eaten in a reclining fashion.[2] The perfume is probably nard, a very expensive fragrance with which Tirzah has anointed herself. She sees the fragrance wafting from her to the king as an expression of her love reaching out to him while they are reclining at dinner.

Tirzah: "My beloved is to me a pouch of myrrh which lies all night between my breasts." (verse 13)

Tirzah refers to an Ancient Near East custom in which a woman would wear a small sack of myrrh, another delicate perfume, around her neck at night, causing a lovely scent to linger there all the next day. Tirzah likens Solomon to the sachet of myrrh: He brings out whatever beauty and charm she has. His love brings out the fragrance of her beauty all day long. The connotations here are clearly erotic, so perhaps she pictures him laying his head between her breasts like the sack of myrrh.

This is the first of thirty-one times in the Song that Tirzah refers to Solomon as her beloved (*dod*).

Tirzah: "My beloved is to me a cluster of henna blossoms in the vineyards of Engedi." (verse 14)

Tirzah wears myrrh around her neck; Solomon is scented with henna. Note that Tirzah specifies that the henna scent came from the vineyards of Engedi.[3] Engedi is one of the most beautiful places in all of Israel. Situated in a vast wilderness of lifeless rock, Engedi is a lush, verdant oasis formed by a hidden spring that pours forth from a limestone rock at the top of a cliff. Cool water tumbles down an overhang into a wadi canyon, forming a tropical paradise filled with soaring birds and exotic plants. Hidden and private, Engedi is a romantic place where the sweet scent of henna blossoms fills the air. In this verse Tirzah is telling her beloved that he is an oasis, her own personal Engedi. Engedi was a stronghold of safety in early Israel, but the Song of Solomon expands the image of safety to include a hideaway where lovers can discover sexual refreshment.

APPLYING THE SONG FOR COUPLES

We'd like you to imagine walking through a vast wasteland, mile upon mile of nothing but barren rock. As you search the horizon for signs of life, nothing green refreshes your eyes. You see no cool water to soothe your parched throat. Like the earth, your lips are cracked and dry. Your throat cries out for a cool drink and your body for relief from the blazing sun.

After several more hours of wandering, you see something in the distance. You don't know what it is, only that it calls to you. Exhausted, you stumble toward it. Suddenly you are standing at the edge of a cliff. At your feet is a limestone rock from which pours a hidden spring. Water tumbles down the overhang, into a canyon below, creating a lush oasis. Your senses thrill over the verdant trees and exotic flowers, the cool refreshing mists of the waterfall, and birds soaring over the pool below. This is the oasis of Engedi.

God wants your sexual relationship to be an oasis for the two of you. He desires that the two of you find relief from routine and a refuge from stress by splashing around in springs of sexual refreshment. But if you are to discover the refreshment that sexual love can bring, it may require that you make a change in attitude (how you view your intimate times together) as well as changes in your environment (the place where you make love).

First, let's look at your attitude. How do you view your sexual relationship? In order for it to be your own personal Engedi, you need to view your intimacy as a place of *rest,* a place of *refuge,* and a place *renewal.* Let's look at the role each of these plays in your relationship.

OFFER INTIMACY AS A PLACE OF REST

Just the thought of an oasis makes our shoulders relax and our souls sigh. We conjure up images of comfort, peace, and relaxation. We picture a tranquil island of beauty in a barren wasteland. When financial pressure, a rebellious kid, the loss of a job, or the death of a loved one thrusts us into an emotional desert and leaves us drained and exhausted, intimate moments together can become a tropical paradise that offers much-needed rest.

Remember Bathsheba? Her only son had died. Distraught, overcome with sorrow, she had red eyes from crying and lack of sleep. Grief had created within her a cavernous hole that could not be filled. Her husband pulled her into his arms, stroked her hair, and whispered tenderly, "I am here for you." She sobbed against his strong chest. Slowly, their bodies came together. "David comforted Bathsheba his wife, and went in to her and lay with her" (2 Samuel 12:24, NKJV).

Is your mate going through a difficult time? How can you offer comfort? What can you do to offer rest? For most men, sexual release is one of the greatest ways to receive rest. If you want proof of this, just observe how quickly a man falls asleep after making love! For a woman, however, the greatest release sometimes comes not through orgasm but through her husband holding her in his arms and simply letting her cry. Remember, the purpose of Engedi is to give rest, and how this rest looks will vary depending on the needs of your mate.

The key is knowing what your mate needs and offering it at the right time. Peter tells of a time when he did just that:

> Several months ago, Lorraine was emotionally and physically exhausted after a weekend of speaking. I knew she needed a getaway to Engedi, so I decided to create an environment that would help her relax. I told her to rest and then went to work creating an oasis for her. I arranged twenty-five scented candles around the Jacuzzi tub, counter, and windowsills in our master bathroom and put some soft, relaxing music on the CD player. I filled the tub with bubble bath and placed a china plate filled with various cheeses and shrimp and a glass of spiced cider on the ledge. I closed the door and taped on it a one-word sign: Engedi.
>
> Taking Lorraine by the hand, I ushered her to the door and said, "This is a special place, unlike any you have ever been before. This is Engedi. Once you enter here, you are not permitted to think about the world you left behind." I invited her to remove her clothes as a symbolic gesture of leaving her present world, and then I opened the door. The scent of vanilla candles and cinnamon cider beckoned. As she slipped into the tub and allowed the bubbles to engulf her, I saw her visibly relax. I shut the door and prayed that the Lord would use the warmth, smells, food, and music to bring rest to my wife, who poured herself out to so many. He answered that prayer, because after an hour of rest in the tub, she had energy for me!

In a moment we'll talk more about how environment can contribute to creating a place of rest, but for now we want you to focus on your attitude of wanting to give rest to your mate. While other people might provide occasional opportunities for rest, there are certain things only you can do because it occurs within the context of your intimacy. Thoughtfully consider:

᠔ What circumstances trigger a need for rest in my mate (paying bills, an overloaded schedule, a looming deadline, strained relationships)?

- ♦ What kind of touch causes my mate to relax (cuddling, a foot rub, a head massage, sexual stimulation and release)?
- ♦ What words can I use to invite my mate to enjoy an Engedi of rest?

In our hectic, fast-paced world of constant stimulation, we need rest. Servant lovers sense when their mate needs rest and consider how they might give them that rest. They also see their sexual relationship as a place of refuge.

OFFER INTIMACY AS A PLACE OF REFUGE

First Samuel 24:1 speaks of Engedi as David's stronghold, a safe place where he and his men hid from their enemy, Saul. Sometimes we feel as if everything and everyone is against us. We want to run away and hide, but we can't. Still, there is a place where we can run to, a safe place where we can temporarily escape from the assaults of life. We can find refuge in our own personal Engedi.

God intended that a husband and wife's intimate relationship be a safe place where they can be "naked and unashamed" (Genesis 2:25). We are more vulnerable in the sexual relationship than in any other because this is the one place where we bare all. That is why we must make every effort to communicate through touch and words that the place of intimate loving is a place of safety, a place where trust prevails. We will talk more in chapter 7 about how you can make your marriage a safe place, but here we want to go deeper in what it means that your intimacy can be a place of refuge for each other.

What does a safe *place look like?*
- ♦ Unconditional acceptance: "No matter what others say, I think you're terrific."
- ♦ Support: "I may not understand what happened, but I support you."
- ♦ Appreciation: "Let me tell you what I love about you."
- ♦ Sexual sensitivity: "I want to do what pleases you."

This refuge is not built overnight. Usually it is built over time as we grow in acceptance and trust of one another. When trust is broken or harsh words are spoken, sexual intimacy can no longer feel like a refuge. Instead of being a place we run *to*, it becomes a place we run *from*. Rather than helping us feel safe and protected, our sexual relationship becomes just one more place in which we must protect ourselves. When this happens, we shut down emotionally or sexually to prevent more pain from being inflicted upon us.

What does an unsafe *place look like?*

- ⬥ Conditional acceptance: "I'll accept you *if* _____."
- ⬥ Judgmental attitude: "Quit whining — this is your own fault."
- ⬥ Critical spirit: "I hate this about you."
- ⬥ Sexual demands: "Do this, be this, accept this."

If you felt convicted after reading this list — Yes, I have been critical, judgmental, and conditional in my acceptance of my spouse, and these attitudes have not created a safe place in our intimate relationship — we suggest you begin to rebuild trust. How?

- ⬥ Ask God to forgive you for your failings.
- ⬥ Tell your spouse: "Please forgive me for _____ (name your wrong attitudes). I understand why you haven't always felt safe with me, and I am committed to changing that."
- ⬥ Ask your spouse, "What can I do to help you feel safe in our sexual relationship?" Then make every effort to fulfill that wish.

Creating a place of safety can be one of the most loving things we ever do as a husband or wife. Such a place can promote healing. Sometimes the healing is physical, as rest recharges our body. Other times the healing is emotional, such as releasing the poison of pain in a place where we won't be judged. Still other times the healing is sexual, as was the case with Ellen.

> My father sexually abused me when I was between the ages of three and twelve. When I married, I found the whole idea of sex revolting. Certain touches, certain images transported me back to the horror of my childhood. But Rob has been so patient with me. When he knows that I'm having a flashback while we are making love, he'll gently say, "Honey, I

love you. Let me just hold you." Or he'll whisper over and over, "I am your husband who loves you. You can trust me. I will never hurt you."

Rob acted as a servant lover to Ellen, placing her needs above his own. Servant lovers recognize their mate's need for refuge and do everything in their power to make their spouse feel safe in the sexual relationship. They also understand that intimate loving can be a place of renewal.

OFFER INTIMACY AS A PLACE OF RENEWAL

What creates an oasis? Water. It bubbles up from the ground, bringing forth life. Where there is water, trees shoot up. Grass grows. Flowers spring forth. Animals come to drink. If you are traveling through a desert and your throat is parched, you can come to the oasis, drink from the water, and be renewed. Just as cool water brings renewal to a thirsty traveler, intimate loving brings renewal to the couple who has been beaten down and bruised by life.

In Proverbs 5:17-19, we see the description of how a wife's sexual love renews her husband through life-giving water:

> Your spring of water is for you and you only. . . . Bless your fresh-flowing fountain! Enjoy the wife you married as a young man! Lovely as an angel, beautiful as a rose — don't ever quit taking delight in her body. Never take her love for granted! (MSG)

What does it look like to renew our mate with our sexual love? We'll let Kevin tell you:

> I'd been out of work for a year and felt like I could not go on. Do you know how hard it is not to be able to provide for your family? To put yourself out there day after day, only to hear the same words: "Sorry, we can't use you." One day I walked into our house after being rejected yet again. Tori greeted me, and when she saw the look on my face, she didn't ask for the humiliating details. Instead, she said in a bossy voice, "Well, mister, I have a job for you. And the benefits are great. I want you to make love to me now." So I did — right there on the living room

floor. Afterward, as I lay in Tori's arms, relaxed and refreshed, I knew I could go on. Tori's love renewed my strength and filled me with resolve. I'd go to the ends of the earth for this woman.

Engedi is a place where physical needs are satisfied, but it is also a place where emotional and spiritual needs are met. Do you see how your attitude affects your sexual relationship? Maybe you are thinking, *I'd like to create a place of rest, refuge, and renewal for my mate, but where do I begin?* As we've already said, the starting point is your attitude, but your environment also plays a role.

CREATE A BEDROOM SANCTUARY

For most couples, Engedi is lived out in the bedroom. Is your bedroom a place of beauty and rest, or is it the dumping ground for unfolded laundry? Is your bedroom a place you run *to* because it is peaceful, or is it a place you run *from* because it is the hangout of kids and pets? Can your bedroom be described as a place of renewal, or is it more like a depressing den of dirt and disorder?

How your bedroom looks communicates something about how much you value your sexual relationship. Often decorating is an assumed duty for the wife, but in the next chapter we will see that Solomon brought timber from afar to create a special bedroom for his bride. We recommend that husbands contribute in some way to the bedroom decor — although we give permission for their wives to draw the line when it comes to life-size framed race cars! You can use paint, wallpaper, furniture, lighting, and other creative touches to create an ambiance that makes your bedroom conducive to lovemaking. For example:

> *Pete:* "Purple passion" — that's the look Lorraine wanted for our bedroom. So I assembled my handyman tools for the job — paintbrush for applying purple paint, drill to hang pictures and window coverings, and hammer and saw for making shelves for music speakers. As I hung a tapestry over our bed, Lorraine added the finishing touches — silk greenery, recycled throw pillows covered with new fabric, and her wedding veil wrapped around the bedpost so that each morning as I awoke I'd be reminded that she is the bride of my youth. I looked at the total effect. Yes, it was conducive for loving — a great investment, as far as I was concerned.

Jody: I have helped Linda redecorate our bedroom many times in the course of our forty years of marriage. But as I've gotten older, I've gotten wiser. I'm smarter than Pete: When Linda wanted grapevines filled with ivy and berries over the windows, plus a faux painted ceiling, I *hired* it done.

Go into your bedroom and take a long look. Remove what detracts from romance:

◊ Television
◊ Clutter
◊ Dust
◊ Pictures of your mother

Add things that enhance romance:

◊ A bubbling table-top fountain for soothing sounds
◊ A CD player for mood-enhancing music
◊ Satin or 400 thread count sheets for sensuous softness
◊ A bed that makes you want to *stay* in bed
◊ A comforter for snuggling
◊ A lock for the door to ensure privacy
◊ Scented candles for sweet fragrance and soft lighting

Fragrance can also play a key role in lovemaking, as we saw in the case of Tirzah and Solomon.

USE FRAGRANCE TO ENHANCE SEXUAL DESIRE

If you strolled into Solomon and Tirzah's bedroom, powerful scents would overwhelm you. First, you would smell the scented powders sprinkled on their sheets and beautiful linen and on the satin curtains covering the walls. You would also smell their individual scents, personal fragrant lotions designed to delight the other. It's likely that the aroma of burning incense also would fill the bedchamber. (Sounds like overkill for the nasal passage, doesn't it? That much fragrance would probably give you a headache or make your eyes and nose itch and your throat hurt.) But fragrance communicates. As one five-year-old boy said, "Love is when a girl puts on perfume and a boy puts on shaving cologne and they go out and smell each other."

Before you pooh-pooh the importance of scent, read what Dr. Alan R. Hirsch, the neurological director of the Smell and Taste Treatment and Research Foundation, has to say about how our sense of smell affects us: "The quickest way to induce a change in emotions or mood is through smell, because the sense of smell reacts more quickly on the brain than other senses."[4] He reports that "the top odor for putting men in the mood for love was a combination of pumpkin pie and lavender, followed by black licorice and freshly baked doughnuts."[5] (He didn't specify whether men had to eat these!)

Different smells can trigger different responses. The smell of freshly baked cinnamon rolls can stimulate physical hunger, and the fragrance of certain colognes can stimulate sexual hunger. One wife says that her husband always splashes on *Boss!* before they make love, and the hint of that scent automatically shifts her body into sexual gear. How can you use fragrance to increase sexual desire? Here are some ideas:

For the wife: Buy several scented candles and place them around your bedroom. Before you make love with your husband, go around the room and say a prayer as you light each one. At the first candle you might pray, "Lord, light a fire in my *heart* for my husband." At the second say, "Lord, ignite a fire in my *mind* for this man I love." At the third, "Please God, start a fire burning in my *body.*" Continue like this until all of the candles are lit. In doing this, not only do you create a dreamy bedroom environment but you also release the scent of romance within yourself and in the room.

For the husband: Buy a bottle of lavender bath oil and some roses. Select a night this week to pamper your wife. Put some of the roses in a vase on your bedroom dresser. Then, take the petals from two of the roses and drop them on the floor, creating a path toward the bathtub. After dinner, tell her you will do the dishes and put the kids to bed. Instruct her to follow the rose petal path where she will discover a lavender-filled bath waiting to soothe her muscles and soften her skin. After the children are asleep, give her a massage with a scented lotion and discover for yourself how much sense it makes to use scents.

Your bedroom environment can soothe or excite, comfort or delight. Talk together about what would transform your bedroom into your personal Engedi.

God wants your love to be a source of refreshment. He wants you to view your sexual relationship as a place of rest, refuge, and renewal. When the pressure mounts, when the stress of daily living knots your muscles and makes you tense, run to Engedi. Splash around in the life-giving water of oneness. Laugh again. Live again. Revive one another in the streams of Engedi.

SERVANT LOVERS: Seek to make sexual love a place of refreshment for their mate.

SELFISH LOVERS: View their sexual relationship as a place for satisfying their own sexual desire.

SOLOMON TO TIRZAH:
"How beautiful you are, my darling,
How beautiful you are!
Your eyes are like doves."

TIRZAH TO SOLOMON:
"How handsome you are, my beloved,
And so pleasant!
Indeed, our couch is luxuriant!
The beams of our houses are cedars,
Our rafters, cypresses.
I am the rose of Sharon,
The lily of the valleys."

SOLOMON TO TIRZAH:
"Like a lily among the thorns,
So is my darling among the maidens."

TIRZAH TO SOLOMON:
"*Like an apple tree among the trees of the forest,*
So is my beloved among the young men.
In his shade I took great delight and sat down,
And his fruit was sweet to my taste.
He has brought me to his banquet hall,
And his banner over me is love.
Sustain me with raisin cakes,
Refresh me with apples,
Because I am lovesick.
Let his left hand be under my head
And his right hand embrace me."

TIRZAH TO THE CHORUS:
"*I adjure you, O daughters of Jerusalem,*
By the gazelles or by the hinds of the field,
That you do not arouse or awaken my love
Until she pleases."

SONG OF SOLOMON 1:15–2:7

chapter five

Trade Sexual Compliments

"The other night we were in the kitchen and my wife gave me a
suggestive kiss on the lips, so I said, 'Well, do you want to *do it*?' She rolled
her eyes and walked away in a huff. What did I do wrong?"

How do you communicate to your mate that you are interested in an intimate encounter? Are you sensitive, or do you spout off the first unedited thought that comes to mind?

Solomon and Tirzah are masters of intimate language. Skillfully, they weave together compliments that build anticipation and sexual desire. In this passage, we see them playing verbal volleyball. "You are beautiful, my darling," Solomon declares. "And you are handsome, my lover," Tirzah responds. As passion mounts, their praise moves from compliments about appearance to compliments about lovemaking techniques.

UNDERSTANDING THE SONG

Solomon to Tirzah: "How beautiful you are, my darling, how beautiful you are! Your eyes are like doves." (1:15)

Earlier, Tirzah wondered, *Does my husband find me attractive?* Here Solomon again affirms that she is incredibly beautiful to him and that her eyes, so soft and luminous like those of a dove, captivate him.

Tirzah to Solomon: "How handsome you are, my beloved, and so pleasant! Indeed, our couch is luxuriant! The beams of our houses are cedars, our rafters, cypresses." (verses 16-17)

Tirzah returns his compliment, saying that not only is her beloved outstandingly handsome but the bridal chamber he created for her makes her feel cherished. As Tirzah lies on a luxurious couch covered with a beautiful canopy, she comments on Solomon's thoughtfulness in constructing the bridal chamber. It appears that he surprised his new bride by importing wood from her native Lebanon; perhaps he wanted to create a bedroom that would remind her of the open air and the country that she loved. The bedchamber's cedar-beamed ceiling and cypress rafters created a private Engedi, away from the hustle and bustle of palace life and its many responsibilities. We know from other passages of Scripture that much of Solomon's palace was made with cedar beams from Lebanon (see 1 Kings 7:1-12). It appears that Solomon brought in this wood so that his bride would feel at home in their personal hideaway.

Tirzah to Solomon: "I am the rose of Sharon, the lily of the valleys." (2:1)

In previous verses, the lovers declared, "You are beautiful!" Now they speak in more subtle terms, comparing each other and themselves to flowers and fruit. Here Tirzah likens herself to the rose of Sharon, a flesh-colored meadow flower with a leafless stem that blanketed the countryside in the warmer regions of Israel. Like the dandelion, the rose of Sharon is a common, ordinary flower. Tirzah is humbly describing herself as a country maiden alongside the coffered palace beauties in King Solomon's palace.

Solomon to Tirzah: "Like a lily among the thorns, so is my darling among the maidens." (verse 2)

Solomon takes up the comparison and gives it a notable turn, saying that all the other women in Jerusalem are as thorns compared to his bride. This sensitive husband hears the insecurity in his wife's words and seeks to reassure her by telling her that her beauty and nobility of character set her above all the court women who have spent their lives "caring for their own vineyards" (1:6).

Tirzah to Solomon: "Like an apple tree among the trees of the forest, so is my beloved among the young men." (verse 3)

Tirzah responds with a botanical analogy of her own. In essence she says, "Solomon, all the men in Israel are the same — plain green pine trees. But you, my lover, stand out amid the common trees like an apple tree laden down with ripe red fruit." In the East, the apple tree is often used to symbolize sexual love.[1] Tirzah has increased the tempo of their passion by moving beyond words of praise about physical beauty to praising Solomon's skill as a lover.

Tirzah to Solomon: "In his shade I took great delight and sat down, and his fruit was sweet to my taste." (verse 3)

Passion mounts. Solomon and Tirzah are now actively involved in their loveplay. She sits (presumably on cushions in their private bedchamber) beneath Solomon's shade, cast perhaps from a lamp in the room, and delights in "tasting his fruit." Several interpretations have been given for this phrase. Some believe that she is saying that as an apple refreshes a weary traveler,[2] her beloved's presence refreshes her. However, in view of the erotic nature of the symbols (apples, raisin cakes) and the context ("Let his left hand 'fondle' me," in verse 6), we feel that this is unlikely. Others believe she is referring to the sweet taste of Solomon's words and works, which make a positive impression on her.[3]

Still others see the sweet fruit of the apple tree as a symbol of his caresses.[4] In other words, she "tastes" his sexual embrace. In extrabiblical literature, "fruit" is often equated with the male genitals[5] or with semen.[6] Also, there are many balancing parallels in the Song; what is characteristic of her is also characteristic of him. The "fruit" on her "tree" (7:7-8) is her breasts, so the "fruit" on his "tree" suggests his genitals. If this is so, then this phrase may be a veiled and delicate reference to an oral-genital caress.[7] Whatever interpretation you take, Tirzah's words clearly speak of intense sexual pleasure.

Tirzah: "He has brought me to his banquet hall, and his banner over me is love." (verse 4)

The banquet hall refers to the bridal chamber, and the banner, which would be a cloth attached like a flag to a long pole, speaks of the king's protective care.[8] As Tirzah sits in Solomon's shade (his protective care), she immediately associates his banner with his love, because his love provides what she as his wife deeply desires: security, care, and protection.

Solomon introduces the third Hebrew word for love in this verse, *ahabah*. This is the word used of God's love for Israel (see Jeremiah 13:3; Hosea 1:4). While this is a general word for love in the Old Testament, it is the word used for the highest form of love that God asks of us, "And what does the LORD require of you but to do justice and to love kindness" (Micah 6:8).[9] This word is associated with "serving" the one loved.[10] It is the only word for love that applies to God's love for us.[11] It speaks of God's permanent covenant commitment to His people.[12]

Like *dod*, *ahabah* can have powerful sexual connotations,[13] but it carries a higher and sacrificial note. It is the kind of love that seeks the good of the object loved and is willing to love in spite of sin.[14] It is the love of a mother for her son,[15] of a father for his son,[16] and of Ruth for her mother-in-law.[17] *Ahabah* is the word most often translated in the Septuagint as the Greek word *agapao*. *Agape* is the highest form of love and speaks of sacrifice, serving, and seeking only the good of the object loved. It refers to "a spontaneous feeling which impels to self-giving."[18] If *dod* speaks primarily of erotic love in the Song and *rayah* of companionship, then *ahabah*, while it includes the other two, takes us deeper into servant loving that is lifelong or, as Jeremiah put it, "everlasting" (Jeremiah 31:3).[19]

Tirzah to Solomon: "Sustain me with raisin cakes, refresh me with apples, because I am lovesick." (verse 5)

Tirzah confesses that the intensity of her love makes her physically weak. She is overcome with sexual desire for her husband. "She is swooning with desire. She has that ache in the pit of her stomach, she has that loss of appetite which can only be cured by her being 'spread out' with her lover, and by eating and drinking of the delights of lovemaking."[20] Tirzah needs sustenance to alleviate her lovesickness and asks Solomon to bring her raisin cakes and apples, which are symbols of erotic love. Raisin cakes (dried raisins pressed together to form a cake) were thought to be an aphrodisiac.[21] In other words, she asks him to satisfy her sexually.

Tirzah to Solomon: "Let his left hand be under my head and his right hand embrace me." (verse 6)

Here, Tirzah tells her husband exactly how she wants him to hold her. As they lie on the couch, she requests that he place his left hand under her head and that he embrace her with his right hand. The Hebrew word *habaq*, translated here means "to embrace,"[22] "to show close association and affection,"[23] and here has the sense of "to fondle."[24] She is asking her husband to fondle her and stimulate her body sexually.

Tirzah to the Chorus: "I adjure you, O daughters of Jerusalem, by the gazelles or by the hinds of the field, that you do not arouse or awaken my love until she pleases." (verse 7)

Why this abrupt change from passionate embrace to warning? Why would a bride in the midst of lovemaking want to tell other women not to quicken passion until the proper time? Many possible reasons have been suggested, but we believe it is for this reason: She is experiencing the joy and freedom that God desires in her intimacy with Solomon, and she longs for every bride to know this same joy. Perhaps she believes that her present enjoyment is linked to her purity before marriage and so she gives a warning to other young women to remain pure so that they also will experience deep passion, freedom, and joy in marriage.

APPLYING THE SONG FOR COUPLES

The two couples writing this book have a confession to make: We do not talk to one another in poetry. Epithets of love do not flow from our lips. Jody doesn't say to Linda, "Like a lily among the thorns, so are you, dear Linda, among the maidens." Nor does Lorraine tell Peter, "Sustain me with raisin cakes and refresh me with apples because I am lovesick." Nowadays, such words would likely arouse laughter rather than passion. So what words can you use to express admiration or communicate certain sexual desires? How do you tell your mate you are interested in making love? One way is to develop a private sexual language, known only to the two of you.

DEVELOP A SEXUAL LANGUAGE

Unlike Tirzah and Solomon, some couples rarely talk during lovemaking. They are afraid to open their mouths while making love because they feel embarrassed, insecure, or self-conscious. A wife may think, *How can I tell him I want him to touch me* there? A husband may wonder, *What words can I use to excite her?* One wife told us she felt she was making progress when she could finally say, "Ah . . ."

What a contrast to Tirzah, who did not hesitate to tell her husband that he was a stud. Nor did she balk at telling him how to pleasure her while guiding his hands over her body during their lovemaking. And Solomon? He too was no silent lover. Solomon and Tirzah understood that love is expressed not only body to body but also through tender words that speak a language of love all their own. It is important for couples to learn to verbalize their sexual desires during lovemaking because communication deepens emotional oneness. Also, words are a key way for a husband and wife to know how to satisfy each other. None of us qualifies as a mind reader, so how can the ones we love know what pleases us if we don't tell them?

One wife said she was angry with her husband until she realized how unfair her expectations were:

> I don't have a hard time imagining what I want to say. The words describing my wants, my fears, and my feelings come easily, until I open my mouth. But once it's time to speak the words aloud, I become embarrassed, self-conscious, and tongue-tied — all of which leave me feeling ridiculous, more embarrassed, and even angry. *I shouldn't have to tell him this*, I think. *If he loves me, he'll know how I feel, what I want, what feels good and bad.* And therein lies the problem: I have expectations that I don't voice. When those naturally go unmet — how can he meet them

if he doesn't even know about them? — it leaves me feeling upset, sad, or hurt. And in my mind, anyway, it's all his fault. Not very fair, is it?[25]

Linda too struggled early in her marriage to find the words to speak. When Jody asked her to tell him in detail what she was going to do to pleasure him and what she wanted him to do to pleasure her, she gulped, "In detail?" What could she voice out loud without turning bright red? *God, help me! This man I love has asked me to express my passion for him, and I have a choice: I can claim embarrassment and clam up, or I can ask You to enable me to say what I know will please him.* It was difficult at first, but Jody's delight spurred Linda on, and with practice, it became easier.

Don't expect to be able to do this overnight. Developing a sexual language is like learning to speak a foreign language: It takes time and practice. No one takes Spanish 400 without first taking Spanish 101 where common nouns and verbs are learned. Once these are mastered, the student moves to a more advanced level. With years of patience and practice, Spanish can become a language that rolls off the lips with ease. Even so, there are always new words to learn and more to discover within the language.

So it is with developing your private sexual language. Start with the basics — with establishing what words you will use to describe sexual parts of the body and what phrases to speak that will effectively communicate, "Let's make love." Most couples do not use the technical words *penis* and *vagina* in their private love language because they seem too sterile. The language of love is poetic, as we saw in the interchange between Solomon and Tirzah. They used words such as *fruit* and *garden,* words that conjure up images of beauty and pleasure. While you may choose to use these words in your lovemaking, you might also want to invent your own. One wife calls her husband's intimate parts The Lighthouse on the Rocks. As a gift, he gave her a framed picture of a lighthouse. It sits on the nightstand by their bed, a sweet secret shared by them alone (and now the multitudes who will read this book!).

Here are some things other couples say:

§ I call her Little Doe; she calls me Big Buck.

❧ We use our middle names, William and Mary. When he says, "William wants to play with Mary," I understand the message.

❧ I call my wife's garden the Pearl of Great Price.

In addition to creating a sexual vocabulary, you also need to determine what words or phrases you can use to ask each other, "Do you want to make love?" Wives often tell us, "I wish he'd say something other than, 'Well, do you want to *do it* tonight?'"

Let us suggest a fun exercise that will help expand your sexual vocabulary. One night this week when you are alone as a couple, make a list of all the words you can think of for the private areas of both of your bodies. Then write down words or phrases for "making love." Next, each of you talk about the words or phrases you like and the ones that make you uncomfortable. Discuss those images that the two of you enjoy and whether that image might be suitable for your private love language.

Here are some words others have used to say, "Let's make love":

❧ *Engedi* — "Want to go to Engedi tonight?" (See chapter 4 for an explanation of Engedi.)

❧ *Hideaway* — "Let's spend a half hour in our hideaway."

❧ *Fly* — "Would you like to fly with me?"

❧ *Sailing* — "Let's go sailing." (Translation: "Let's enjoy twenty minutes of loving.") Variations include: "I'd enjoy a speedboat ride" (a quickie) or "How about a cruise next weekend?" (long, leisurely loving).

❧ *Frisky* — "I feel frisky tonight, do you?"

❧ *Gardening* — "I'd like to plant some flowers tonight in your garden."

Some couples use signals along with their words to express interest in an intimate connection:

We keep two candles in our bedroom. If one is lit, we consider it an invitation for intimacy. If the second candle is lit, we know our invitation has been accepted. One time, I lit the candle. Later, instead of finding only one other candle, my wife had lit twenty and placed them all around the room.

My husband and I have a rhinoceros Beanie Baby. (I hope the comparison is obvious.) We place it somewhere the other person will see it when one of us is interested in sex. It is silly, but we love it! That Beanie Baby has ended up in some interesting places!

As your sexual language expands, you will feel more comfortable in expressing what you like or don't like in lovemaking and what you are going to do to thrill your lover. Here are some phrases you might try:

- Oh, honey, that feels *so* good!
- Yes, I like it.
- Just a little gentler — oh, yes, that's right.
- Don't stop — it makes me want you.

You get the idea! We can't get much more specific because while we want to be practical and helpful, we don't want to cross any lines.

CREATE A SEXUAL READING LIST

How long has it been since the two of you read a book together? Our suggestion is that you create your own Sexual Reading List and delve into one book on sex each year. Perhaps you would want to take your book of the year with you on your anniversary getaway and begin reading and talking about it. Just think how many books you would have discussed about your sexual intimacy in ten years! Here are the titles of a few books to get you started:

- Song of Solomon
- *Intimacy Ignited* — if you aren't working through the Bible study at the back of this book, begin now. It will reinforce all you are reading and encourage talking.
- *Celebration of Sex*, by Dr. Douglas Rosenau
- *Intended for Pleasure*, by Dr. Ed Wheat

- *52 Ways to Have Fun, Fantastic Sex,* by Dr. Clifford and Joyce Penner
- *The Gift of Sex,* by Clifford and Joyce Penner
- *When Two Become One,* by Christopher and Rachel McCluskey
- A bonus book for wives — *Intimate Issues,* by Linda Dillow and Lorraine Pintus
- A bonus book for husbands — *Every Man's Battle,* by Stephen Arterburn and Fred Stoeker

WATCH YOUR WORDS

As Christians we want to create an intimate vocabulary that honors God and delights our lover. What words are on "God's list"? While Scripture doesn't give a list of specific words to use in lovemaking, other than those used in the Song, it does offer us some principles that we can apply. Consider how Ephesians 4:29 might come into play as you agree on words or phrases for your sexual language:

> Don't use foul or abusive language. Let everything you say be good and helpful, so that your words will be an encouragement to those who hear them. (NLT)

> Watch the way you talk. Let nothing foul or dirty come out of your mouth. Say only what helps, each word a gift. (MSG)

The words *foul* and *dirty* come from the Greek word *sapros,* which literally means spoiled or rotten fish or fruit, i.e., garbage.[26] What words classify as "dirty rotten garbage"? Only the foul four-letter variety? Our answer is found in the second half of the verse, which tells us what kinds of words we should use: words that edify and bring encouragement. These words are a "gift" to our mate. Ask yourself, *Do the words I use during lovemaking encourage and build up my mate? Are the words playful, encouraging, and respectful?* If so, they should be considered. If the words are hurtful, disrespectful, or demeaning, they should be eliminated.

In chapter 14, we will talk more about how to build up your lover. But for now, let us say this. As writers, we are aware that we must be careful about speaking in absolutes, but we are absolutely certain of the following two rules:

- Never, never, never criticize your mate's sexual performance.
- Always, always, always look for ways to affirm your mate's prowess as a lover.

Salt your speech with affirmation, and then pepper it with a sexual tease: "You are such a skillful lover, I'll bet you could make love to me with no hands and do it in such a way that I'll be screaming for relief." See? Now you're talking. You are using sexual language in a way that adds spice to your love life.

Now we need to look at a more serious topic. We've already said that God's Word prohibits certain kinds of words and that we need to avoid these when it comes to developing our sexual language. God also has things to say about our actions. If we are going to honor Him and each other as we communicate how to pleasure each other sexually, we need to know which sexual acts God permits and which He prohibits.

ESTABLISH SEXUAL BOUNDARIES

The Song opens our eyes to the freedom we have to delight one another, but sometimes couples do not fully enter into that freedom because one or both are afraid they will do something of which God disapproves. As a result, they are inhibited and unable to enjoy all that God intends for married couples to experience.

Does God prohibit certain actions in the marriage bed? Yes. We searched Scripture from Genesis to Revelation and found ten sexual acts that He prohibits. These are listed in the appendix. However, you may have questions about sexual activities that are not specifically addressed in Scripture. If you are wondering about *any* sexual practice that Scripture does not address, you might find it helpful to evaluate them in light of these three biblical principles.

Unselfish Love

When a husband and wife make love to each other, the goal should be to please the other person. Consider Philippians 2:3-5 in light of selfless love:

Do nothing out of selfish ambition or vain conceit, but in humility consider others [your husband or wife] better than yourselves. Each of you should look *not only to your own interests,* but also to the interests of others [your mate]. Your attitude should be the same as that of Christ Jesus. (NIV, emphasis added)

Unselfish love must be the motivation behind our behavior toward one another in the bedroom (see 1 Corinthians 13:4-7). Love turns to lust when a husband or wife is obsessed by a particular form of sexual expression, when he or she can no longer be happy without it. We're speaking here about forms of sexual expression other than sexual intercourse, such as oral sex.

THREE IMPORTANT QUESTIONS TO ASK

These questions will help you decide what is appropriate in your sexual relationship.[27]

1. Is it prohibited in Scripture? (Refer to the list in the appendix.)

If not, we may assume it is permitted, based on 1 Corinthians 6:12: "'Everything is permissible for me' — but not everything is beneficial" (NIV).

2. Is it beneficial?

Just because something is permitted does not make it beneficial. Each couple must also ask, Does this practice harm either of us in any way, or does it hinder our sexual relationship? If so, it should be rejected. One couple may say yes to a certain practice, while another couple may say, "No, this is not beneficial."

3. Does it involve anyone else?

Sexual activity is sanctioned by God for husband and wife only. If a sexual practice involves someone else or becomes public, it is wrong, based on Hebrews 13:4, which warns us to keep the marriage bed undefiled. It is important to realize that if you bring someone else into your bedroom on a piece of paper, on a video, in your mind, or in person, you desecrate your one-flesh intimacy. God gives incredible freedom, but this freedom is exclusively for one husband and one wife in private.

Mutual Agreement

Both husband and wife should agree on any sexual act that is a part of their intimacy. Consider Philippians 2:1-2:

> If you have any encouragement from being united with Christ, if any comfort from his love, if any fellowship with the Spirit, if any tenderness and compassion, then make my joy complete by being *like-minded*, having the same love, *being one in spirit and purpose*. (NIV, emphasis added)

If one partner is uncomfortable with something, the other needs to respect that person's feelings. Don't be like one husband, who after hearing a Bible teacher suggest that Song 2:3 might be a reference to oral sex, went home and immediately told his wife, "There! It's in the Bible, so now you have to do it!" This husband totally missed the point. Even if it can be proven that God endorses oral sex (and it can't), this husband was ignoring the importance of mutual agreement.

Mutual Submission

Paul exhorts couples to "submit to one another out of reverence for Christ" (Ephesians 5:21, NIV). This verse applies to every area of our marriages, including the sexual relationship. A husband and wife are not to have a demanding spirit toward one another but rather a yielded spirit that desires the best for the other person. If a wife prefers certain forms of sexual expression and her husband hesitates or doesn't want to do as she asks, he should ask himself, *Is this a legitimate concern, or am I just being stubborn?* Likewise, a wife should prayerfully ask God what mutual submission looks like if she balks at some particular form of sexual expression that her husband enjoys.

In this chapter, we've stressed the importance of developing a sexual language and establishing sexual boundaries that align with God's Word. We urge you to pray together about these areas. Perhaps this seems odd to you. After all, these aren't the kinds of things you normally talk to God about. You secretly wonder, *Can I really talk to God about specific sexual acts? Does He really care about what words I use when we make love?* Yes, you can talk to Him. Yes, He cares! Remember, sex was His idea, and He was quite creative in His design.

So seek Him. Ask Him to give you wisdom and creativity — and fun. Don't forget the fun, because that too is part of His gift to you:

> *Holy God, thank You for caring about our intimate relationship. Thank You for being so specific about sex in Your Word. That amazes us. Lord, we don't ever want to violate sexual boundaries that You have set. Please show us if we are in error. Help us as we seek to develop our own sexual language. Show us what words we can use so we can communicate in a way that honors You and delights each other. Amen.*

SERVANT LOVERS: Develop a sexual language so they can communicate lovingly to one another.

SELFISH LOVERS: Use crude words and inappropriate actions to satisfy their own lustful desires.

TIRZAH TO HERSELF:
"Listen! My beloved!
Behold, he is coming,
Climbing on the mountains,
Leaping on the hills!
My beloved is like a gazelle or a young stag.
Behold, he is standing behind our wall,
He is looking through the windows,
He is peering through the lattice.
My beloved responded and said to me,"

SOLOMON TO TIRZAH:
"Arise, my darling, my beautiful one,
And come along.
For behold, the winter is past,
The rain is over and gone.
The flowers have already appeared in the land;
The time has arrived for pruning the vines,
And the voice of the turtledove has been heard in our land.
The fig tree has ripened its figs,
And the vines in blossom have given forth their fragrance.
Arise, my darling, my beautiful one,
And come along!

SOLOMON TO TIRZAH (CONTINUED):

O my dove, in the clefts of the rock,
In the secret place of the steep pathway,
Let me see your form,
Let me hear your voice;
For your voice is sweet,
And your form is lovely."

TIRZAH:

"Catch the foxes for us,
The little foxes that are ruining the vineyards,
While our vineyards are in blossom.
My beloved is mine, and I am his;
He pastures his flock among the lilies.
Until the cool of the day when the shadows flee away,
Turn, my beloved, and be like a gazelle
Or a young stag on the mountains of Bether."

SONG OF SOLOMON 2:8-17

chapter six

𝄞

Catch the Little Foxes

"When we were in premarital counseling,
our pastor asked each of us to list five habits or personality
traits that we found annoying about the other person. I stared at
my blank piece of paper for a long time and finally said, 'Honestly, nothing
about Kevin annoys me.' Our pastor laughed: 'By this time next year you'll
need a notebook to list everything.' My delusion must have been solid because
even three years into our marriage, I could name only a few things about my
husband that bugged me. However, by year ten, my grievance list had grown,
primarily due to the stress of managing two kids, a demanding job,
a monstrous mortgage, and an incontinent cat. These made me
irritable and zapped my strength, leaving little energy
for my husband — or for sex."

Every couple wishes that the romance and the starry-eyed love could last forever. But at some point, every husband and wife must cross the invisible line between fantasy love and real life, where the majority of a marriage is lived out. Tirzah and Solomon cross that line as problems threaten to erode their intimacy.

UNDERSTANDING THE SONG

Tirzah: "Listen! My beloved! Behold, he is coming, climbing on the mountains, leaping on the hills!" (2:8)

Tirzah's excitement punctuates her sentences, as evidenced by the three exclamation marks in this verse. Her lover is coming! And he is not leisurely walking; he is leaping and bounding over hills. So committed is Solomon to reaching Tirzah, so willing to work hard to overcome all obstacles in his path, he'll even scale mountains to meet with her.

Tirzah: "My beloved is like a gazelle or a young stag. Behold, he is standing behind our wall, he is looking through the windows, he is peering through the lattice." (verse 9)

Gazelles and stags suggest swiftness and often symbolize sexual virility; gazelles also evoke an image of beauty in form and movement. Tirzah says, "My beloved is filled with beauty in his body, in the way he looks and the way he moves." When her lover finally arrives, he beckons to her through the window to join him in the lovely outdoors.

Tirzah: "My beloved responded and said to me,

Solomon: 'Arise, my darling, my beautiful one, and come along. For behold, the winter is past, the rain is over and gone. The flowers have already appeared in the land; the time has arrived for pruning the vines, and the voice of the turtledove has been heard in our land. The fig tree has ripened its figs, and the vines in blossom have given forth their fragrance. Arise, my darling, my beautiful one, and come along!'" (verses 10-13)

Tirzah then recalls Solomon's words. He begins and ends his plea with the same passion-filled phrase, calling her his darling (the Hebrew word here is *dod*, which means lover and has sexual connotations) and his beautiful one. He begs her to come to him — and quickly. As a way of enticing her to leave the warm protection and comfort of home, he paints a joyful, welcoming picture of springtime, "the universal time for love: warmer weather, the fragrance of flowers — a time to go outside, a time for the removal of clothes and intimacy."[1] The message is, "Come to me, my love. Springtime is for loving."

Solomon to Tirzah: "O my dove, in the clefts of the rock, in the secret place of the steep pathway, let me see your form, let me hear your voice; for your voice is sweet, and your form is lovely." (verse 14)

Earlier Tirzah listened for her lover. Now he listens for *her*, longing to hear her sweet voice and see her lovely face, eyes, hair, smile, and body. The implication is that he desires to touch all that he longs to see.

Tirzah to Solomon: "Catch the foxes for us, the little foxes that are ruining the vineyards, while our vineyards are in blossom." (verse 15)

Most interpreters agree that the vineyards in this verse represent Solomon and Tirzah's love, which is in full bloom. Everything seems perfect, except that Tirzah spies some little foxes in their vineyard and warns Solomon of their presence. While seemingly harmless at only fifteen inches tall, these foxes dug holes and passages that loosened the soil around the vines, preventing them from developing a stable root system. Proverbial symbols of destroyers,[2] the little foxes in this passage seem to symbolize the small problems that gnaw at the root of their love. Tirzah sees the problems first and asks Solomon to "catch them," or help work out the small problems that threaten to hinder their love.

Tirzah: "My beloved is mine, and I am his; he pastures his flock among the lilies. Until the cool of day when the shadows flee away, turn, my beloved, and be like a gazelle or a young stag on the mountains of Bether." (verses 16-17)

Tirzah beautifully affirms her joy in belonging to Solomon. She tells him to act swiftly and sensuously, like a gazelle or young stag on the mountains of Bether. Because no one knows of such a place, commentators differ on their interpretations of what is meant by this reference. Some suggest that these mountains are a symbol of the woman herself.[3] Others say that *the mountains of Bether* means "hills of separation" and is a reference to Tirzah's breasts.[4] The root of the word *Bether* is the verb *batar* and means "to cut in pieces"[5] or "to cut in two."[6] This has led others to suggest that the mountains refer to her cleavage and that she is inviting Solomon to play with her breasts,[7] or possibly with her vagina, the other moundlike erogenous zone which is "divided."[8]

Whatever the exact meaning of "mountains of Bether," the lovers' previous game of "Find me" has been replaced by the game of "Love me."

APPLYING THE SONG FOR COUPLES

God wired men and women differently. It's almost as if He installed in women an internal alarm that goes off whenever problems threaten a relationship. Beep. Beep. Beep. Tirzah's alarm sounds and she tells her husband, "We've got problems. Can't you see those little foxes? They are going to ruin everything for us. Do something about this." Solomon, normally a sensitive husband, gives no indication that he sees the foxes. He does not hear an alarm, so he feels no urgency. Tirzah and Solomon remind us of many couples we know.

Here is a typical drill:

> *Wife to husband (with alarm beeping in her head):* "Honey, we have a problem. Please, let's get help."

> *Husband (who hears nothing):* "You're just emotional right now because it's *that* time of the month. Wait a few days, and things will look better."

> Five days later, another blowup.

> *Wife to husband (with alarm shrieking):* "Please! We've got to get help *now!* Can't we see a counselor or talk to our pastor about this?"

> *Husband (who is alarm-deaf):* "You are overreacting. We don't need help. We just need more _____ " (fill in the blank: prayer, patience, self-control, trust).

What happens when a couple continues to ignore the alarm? If they allow the foxes to multiply and take over, one day they wake up and find themselves in a mess. Just ask Bruce and Chrissy. They had been married for twenty years. During that time, numerous foxes had crept into their marriage. Chrissy repeatedly asked Bruce if they could go together to see a counselor. Each time, he refused, saying, "We can work things out on our own." One day they received a call from the high school principal, who told them their teenage son had been suspended from school on serious charges.

As things unfolded, it became clear that their son's problems were directly related to problems in their marriage. Their family was falling apart, and this time, Bruce couldn't deny it. When he finally told Chrissy, "Call that counselor you've been wanting us to go to — we need help," relief flooded her. At last they were getting help, and with help came hope. Guess what was lying in their front yard the day of their first counseling appointment? A dead fox. (Seriously — we did *not* make this up!)

RESOURCES FOR CAPTURING THE FOXES

- Online or at your local Christian bookstore, purchase books that can help you with particular situations.
- Invest a weekend rebuilding your marriage. Family Life marriage conferences are excellent, and they are offered every month all across the country (www.familylife.com).
- Focus on the Family offers outstanding resources on all aspects of marriage (www.fotf.org).
- *Two Becoming One*, published by Christian Family Life, is a time-tested small-group study created to help couples learn the biblical foundations of marriage (www.christianfamilylife.com and www.2becoming1.com).
- If you have serious relationship problems, we beg you to get help. Talk with your pastor, or seek out a Christian counselor and address the issues. Do not wait, or else these foxes will trample on other members of your family.

Watch Out for the Foxes

All marriages have foxes. Often the wife sees the foxes first because of her inborn alarm system, but men see foxes too. Some men cite sex as a fox, so they are grateful for this book that helps to ignite intimacy. Which foxes pester you?

Are your foxes related to people or circumstances?

- ✎ Overwork
- ✎ Kids
- ✎ Finances
- ✎ Pornography
- ✎ Conflicts with relatives
- ✎ Health problems
- ✎ Communication issues
- ✎ Unemployment

Or are your foxes related to attitudes and emotions?

- ✎ Apathy
- ✎ Anger or resentment
- ✎ Shame
- ✎ Grief
- ✎ Depression
- ✎ Other: _____

We must catch the foxes that gnaw at the root of our love because if we don't, they will destroy our desire for sexual intimacy. A recent cover of *Newsweek* shows a husband and wife in bed, dressed in full-length pajamas.[9] He stares blankly at a computer on his lap while she shovels spoonfuls of Häagen-Dazs into her mouth with a zoned-out look on her face. A blaring headline reads: "No Sex, Please, We're Married." The subtitle asks, "Are Stress, Kids and Work Killing Romance?"

The answer? Yes! Stress is eating us alive. One couple quipped that because stressed spelled backward is desserts, they reverse stress by eating lots of chocolate.

Hey, if chocolate works for you (and it certainly has proven effective for the four of us), go ahead and pop a few Milk Duds. As you savor the flavor, let's consider the impact of the "foxes" mentioned in the *Newsweek* article — work and kids — because these are two of the most common intimacy killers for married couples.

Catch the Fox of Work

Work, work, work. A study conducted by the International Labor Organization (ILO) discovered that "Americans added nearly a full week to their work year during the 1990s," and this trend continues leaving Americans with less personal time than in the past.[10]

John works seventy-five hours a week under the guise of providing for his family. Amy's request for him to spend more time at home unleashes strong emotion in them both. He is angry: "Doesn't she understand the pressure I'm under?" She is despondent: "Doesn't he see that he's becoming a stranger to me?"

Men are not the only ones who suffer from overwork. Lynne is a stay-at-home mom. She homeschools five children, manages the household, teaches Sunday school, and sells cosmetics on the side. If you asked Lynne, "How is your sex life?" she'd answer, "Sex — what's that?" Researcher Janet Hyde of the University of Wisconsin points out that

> We've had this kind of myth — this rosy view of homemakers that they kind of sit around and relax all day when in fact, they're working very hard, and they experience sex problems in their marriage. They experience fatigue and so do women who are employed full-time.[11]

It used to be that every year, Americans took a vacation. They retreated to a quaint cabin (with no television) by a mountain lake, where they sipped lemonade, listened to the katydids chirp, and enjoyed the chance to get away from the phone and their daily routine. These days, instead of getting away, we take it all with us. On our last vacation, we each took a cell phone and a laptop. Count it up — between us, five days away with four cell phones, four laptops, two Palm Pilots, and two Day-Timers. God forbid that we should miss an urgent message related to work! We punch a series of numbers or letters and are instantly connected to friends, family, and coworkers. Unfortunately, constant connections with the outside world can leave us disconnected from our mate.

Do the two of you feel overworked? When was the last time you had a long, relaxing lovemaking encounter? Consider how wonderful it would be to soak in the tub together in candlelight, freely enjoying one another with no thoughts about your responsibilities and commitments. One couple admitted that because they were both self-employed, they had not been away together in four years.

In a moment, we'll look at how it's possible to recapture intimacy when work has consumed your life, but first let's look at the other fox — kids — and how it can cripple your sex life.

INTIMACY IS A STRESS RELIEVER[12]

Are you stressed? Sex might help. Here is what doctors have learned about the positive effect sex can have on your health.

Heart Disease — Lovemaking is good aerobic exercise, and couples with active sex lives tend to have fewer heart attacks.

Weight — Sexual intercourse burns about two hundred calories (not bad for a short "workout" and far more fun than a run on the treadmill).

Pain — Endorphins released during orgasm can dull the chronic pain of backaches and arthritis as well as migraines.

Depression — Sexually active couples appear to be less vulnerable to depression and suicide.

Anxiety — Hormones released during arousal can calm anxiety, ease fear, and break down inhibitions.

Immunity — Frequent intercourse may boost levels of key immune cells that help fight off colds and other infections.

Cancer — Early studies hint that oxytocin and the hormone DHEA, both released during orgasm, may prevent breast cancer cells from developing into tumors.

Longevity — Frequent orgasm has been linked to longer life; this may have something to do with sex's beneficial effects on the heart and immune system.

Catch the Fox of Kids

First you married; *then* you had kids. Problems surface when couples reverse this order. We best serve our kids when we make our marriage our first priority. Children, while gifts from God and a source of great joy to parents, require constant care, resulting in diminished opportunities for intimacy. Cassie told us,

> I've got three preschoolers. I'm so exhausted from kids pulling on me all day that by bedtime, I can hardly move. Then my husband wants sex and he wonders why I'm irritated. The last thing I need is another person pulling on my worn-out body.

As someone once said, "Sex makes little kids. Kids make little sex." Comedian Ray Romano, who has four kids — including ten-year-old twins — says: "After kids, everything changes. We're having sex about every three months. If I have sex, I know my quarterly estimated taxes must be due. And if it's multi-orgasmic sex, I know its time to renew my driver's license."[13]

We know that it's not easy to keep intimacy alive when we have daily responsibilities. We understand what it's like to have babies and toddlers and teenagers in the house. But don't give up simply because it's difficult. Jody and Linda tell of a time when persistence paid off:

> Years ago, when our kids were preschoolers, we realized we needed some time alone together as a couple. After years of being pregnant and nursing, Linda was beyond exhausted, so we planned a weekend away. We secured a woman to stay with our children, prepared food for the kids to eat while we were gone, cleaned the house, and purchased gifts for the kids. Everything was in place — and then the babysitter got sick, so we cancelled our plans. A few months later, we tried again. We spent days getting every detail in place, and then Linda got sick. On our third attempt, we thought, *Surely this time it will really happen*, and the car broke down. Our attempts to be alone were just adding more stress to our already stressed-out lives, but we were determined to have some time together without any kids. On the fourth try, we actually had our weekend away and it was glorious, worth fighting for in every way.

We must fight to have time together as a couple. In the last fifty years, our society has shifted from a marriage-oriented society to a kid-oriented society. The temptation to structure all activity and decisions around the children threatens marital oneness. Couples focus on their kids because they want to give them the best, but they fail to understand that what a child wants far more than a big-screen television is parents who love each other and are committed to one another. When the marriage is a priority, it makes for happier kids — and for happier parents.

So what do we do about the foxes of work and kids? How can we catch these foxes and recapture intimacy? We make our marriage our first priority.

PUT YOUR MARRIAGE FIRST

Priorities are revealed through heart disposition and time distribution. You cannot say, "My marriage is the most important relationship in my life," and never spend time with your spouse.

In our busy, stress-filled lives, we race from work to children to marriage, and in our race we end up putting out fires rather than living by priority. One couple described it this way:

> We keep saying that we'll find time for us — that next year will be better, the kids will be older, work commitments will be different. We've been saying these kinds of things for five years, and nothing has changed. We've finally realized that we must find time *today, this week,* not next year.

Perhaps part of the problem is our perspective. It isn't about *finding* time; it's about *making* time.

One researcher concluded that husbands and wives average as little as four minutes a day of meaningful conversation.[14] Four minutes? No wonder marriages are in trouble! Many couples invest less time in their relationship than they do in cooking a hard-boiled egg.

If you are like most people, one reason you have so little time for each other is because you stuff your calendar full of activities. Dennis Rainey, director of Family Life Ministries, admonishes,

If your day planner has a blinking NO VACANCY sign hanging on it, chances are good that everyone else in the home is running on turbo too. You need to examine every activity that takes you away from your spouse (and children) and determine if it is worth the cost. This applies even to ministry activities; we need to be involved in our church and be reaching out to others in our community, but not at the continual expense of our families.[15]

Do you spend only four minutes a day in meaningful conversation with each other? Does your calendar have a blinking NO VACANCY sign on it? We suggest you take the following test to help you determine if your marriage is suffering from low priority.

MARRIAGE MINUTES (MM) TEST[16]

Over a seven-day period, note the number of minutes you spend doing each of the following activities:

1. _____ Talking with your spouse when *no one* else is around.
2. _____ Discussing things related to just the two of you, excluding the kids, your parents, work, money, friends, or daily activities.
3. _____ Spending time just looking at each other.
4. _____ Having fun together, alone, in a mutually enjoyable activity.
5. _____ Making love, kissing, hugging, or touching each other.
6. _____ Talking about the future of your marriage, not about retirement funds, retirement homes, and insurance plans.
7. _____ Discussing world events, politics, or issues of the day. This means two-way talking and listening.
8. _____ Just sitting together doing the same thing or something different, such as reading, listening to music, sewing, and so on. Do not include television watching or computer time.
9. _____ Eating together without interruptions (no kids, no phones).
10. _____ Spending time in prayer, Bible reading, devotional reading, or worship together. Do not include religious services.

_____ TOTAL MARRIAGE MINUTES (MM)

Explanation: Estimated total number of Marriage Minutes (MM) available for relating to each other is 1,800 minutes, or thirty hours per week. Divide your total MM score by the 1,800 available minutes. For example, if you estimated your total MM to be 180, divide the 180 by 1,800 for an MM quotient. This would equate to 10 percent. If your score was near 10 percent, congratulations! In our over-scheduled society, many couples don't even rank above 5 percent.

This tool can give you an indication of where marriage and intimacy fall on your priority list. If marriage is low on your list, how do you go about changing that? How do you find time in a schedule that is already jam-packed? Here are our top ten suggestions for grabbing time to be alone together.

Top Ten Time Grabbers

1. Talk to God. If your heart is not right, you will dismiss even the best suggestions for how to spend more time with each other: "No, I don't want to do that." The place to begin to create time for your mate is to ask God to instill in you a deep desire to make your marriage a top priority. Next to God, your relationship with your spouse is your most important relationship. Pray to Him,

> *Father, thank You for my marriage. I confess that at times I've allowed many things to take priority over our relationship. Show me ways I can honor my spouse by expressing that no one is more important to me and that I will do whatever it takes for us to have time together.*

2. Schedule time on your calendars. Sit down together with your calendars. Across the top of a piece of paper, write the name of each family member, making a column for each. Then list the activities associated with each person and how much time that activity takes each week. Be sure to include transportation time as well as time spent planning or preparing for the activity. Your goal is to review all of your current activities so that you can recover a minimum of two hours a week and one weekend a year that the two of you can devote to time alone together for the purpose of enhancing your marriage relationship. To accomplish this goal, you will need to eliminate or curtail certain activities on your list. Review each activity and ask these questions: *Can this be eliminated from our schedule? If not, how can we minimize its drain on our time?* Discuss how you can grab at least two hours a week to focus on each other, and mark out that time on your schedule. This will enable you to protect your marriage from the fox of overwork or overcommitment. We challenge you to use the extra Marriage Minutes to schedule one simple romantic encounter each month. See chapters 7 and 15 for specific instruction and practical ideas.

3. *Interview an older couple.* Invite one or two older couples whose marriages you respect over for dinner. Ask them questions such as: *When you were younger, how did you keep your marriage a priority? How did you make time for romance and intimacy? What is your most memorable romantic time together? What suggestions do you have for us as a couple? Is there anything you would change about the priority you placed on your relationship?* Their wisdom will inspire you to create Marriage Minutes together.

4. *Brainstorm with couples your age.* Organize a "Potluck with a Purpose" and invite couples who also want time together. Ask every couple to be prepared to share three creative things they have done to grab Marriage Minutes. Compile a master list and ask the couples if they are willing to meet every six months (or year) to update the list.

5. *Fast from television for one week.* We think you will be shocked how much time you will have for romance when you turn off the tube. Try it for one week and see the difference it makes in finding time to enjoy your intimacy.

6. *Hire a babysitter.* Don't waste your babysitting dollars on going to see a movie. Instead, hire a sitter to take your kids to a park Saturday morning for two hours while you spend that time at home — in bed.

7. *Arrange for a kid swap.* Find a couple you trust who is willing to swap kids with you one evening a month. You take their kids from 5:00 to 8:00 PM the first month, and next month they watch yours. Three hours focused on loving each other can revitalize any marriage.

8. *Schedule a motel date.* When curious teenagers fill the house and won't go to bed before midnight, it can short-circuit your love life. Leave your teens with a pizza and a good movie; pack a picnic basket filled with fun food, a CD player, candles, and scented lotion; and go to a motel from 5:00 PM to 11:00 PM. You'll be amazed at how much loving and talking you can do with no

ringing phones! It's cheaper than dinner out and a movie — and more fun!

9. Enjoy a daily devotional. Intimacy is about sex, but it is also about being emotionally and spiritually one with your mate. One of the ways to accomplish this is by praying together and reading Scripture together. Set aside ten minutes every weekday morning. Use four of those days for your written devotion (we recommend *Moments Together for Couples,* by Dennis and Barbara Rainey). Use the fifth day as an intimate devotion, a time of loving one another in the shower or between the sheets.

10. Enjoy the Sabbath rest. God asks us to take a Sabbath rest. Our bodies were made for a day of rest once a week. We encourage you to work and do activities with your kids for six days and then take one day off — no work, no shopping, and no running to sports activities. Instead, set aside the entire day to worship God, take naps, rest, and play together. This is part of intimacy — finding rest in one another, lying in each other's arms, and enjoying the closeness without the stress of life.

Look through the ten time grabbers and pick several that appeal to you. Then implement them.

We pray this chapter has spurred you on to stop, look, and listen to the warning signs of foxes in the vineyard of your marriage. Commit to God and one another to make your marriage a priority, and delight in the joy of your renewed intimate oneness.

SERVANT LOVERS: Work to catch the little foxes that threaten their love.

SELFISH LOVERS: Are unwilling to take the time and effort to work on problems.

TIRZAH TO HERSELF:
"On my bed night after night I sought him
Whom my soul loves;
I sought him but did not find him.
'I must arise now and go about the city;
In the streets and in the squares
I must seek him whom my soul loves.'
I sought him but did not find him.
The watchmen who make the rounds in the city found me,
And I said, 'Have you seen him whom my soul loves?'
Scarcely had I left them
When I found him whom my soul loves;
I held on to him and would not let him go
Until I had brought him to my mother's house,
And into the room of her who conceived me."

TIRZAH TO THE CHORUS:
"I adjure you, O daughters of Jerusalem,
By the gazelles or by the hinds of the field,
That you will not arouse or awaken my love
Until she pleases."

SONG OF SOLOMON 3:1-5

chapter seven

◊

Create a Safe Place for Loving

"I have this horrible recurring dream in which
I open my front door and see a lawyer dressed in a bright red suit,
shoving divorce papers in my face. When I was eleven, my parents divorced.
I was devastated. When Pam and I married, we swore we'd never mention
the 'D' word. Last week we had a horrible fight — the worst we'd ever had —
and she said, 'Maybe we should get a divorce.' I felt like she'd
slugged me in the stomach. I put my face in my hands
and cried, 'No, God. How did this happen?
How did we get here?'"

Maybe you've experienced things in your marriage that you never dreamed would happen. You promised, "We'll always be madly in love; we'll never fight like my parents did." But the truth is, you do. All of us, at some point, experience disappointment with our mate. Disappointment cools our view of the one we love. If disappointment is not dealt with early on, it leads to distance. Distance leads to isolation. Isolation can lead to abandonment.

Is abandonment something you fear in your marriage? Tirzah did. In this next scene, she dreams that Solomon has abandoned her. Fitfully, she clutches the sheets, trying to pull herself out of the nightmare and into the light of reality. Her heart cries out, "Don't leave me! Please, don't leave."

UNDERSTANDING THE SONG

Tirzah: "On my bed night after night I sought him whom my soul loves; I sought him but did not find him." (3:1)

Tirzah is in bed alone. All night she dreams of her husband.[1] Here we see the first of four times in this poem that Tirzah describes Solomon as "the one whom my soul loves" (verses 1,2,3,4).

Tirzah: "I must arise now and go about the city; in the streets and in the squares I must seek him whom my soul loves. I sought him but did not find him. The watchmen who make the rounds in the city found me, and I said, 'Have you seen him whom my soul loves?'" (verses 2-3)

In her dream, Tirzah finds the absence of her lover intolerable. She needs him. Nothing but his presence can satisfy her. She leaves her bed and wanders the streets, seeking her beloved. For the second time, she says, "I've searched and searched, and I can't find him. My heart is broken." Desperation sets in, and then she runs into the watchmen, who are making rounds of the city.

Tirzah: "Scarcely had I left them when I found him whom my soul loves; I held on to him and would not let him go until I had brought him to my mother's house, and into the room of her who conceived me." (verse 4)

After she leaves the watchmen, Tirzah finds Solomon. The *New American Standard Bible* says that Tirzah held him, but the meaning of the Hebrew word suggests that she clutched her beloved and refused to relax her embrace.[2] While we may think it strange that Tirzah would dream of pulling her beloved into her mother's bedroom, in Solomon's time, a mother's bedroom was a place associated with intimacies.[3] This reference also communicates feelings of safety and security.

Earlier in the Song, Tirzah expressed insecurity about her appearance (1:5-7). Now we glimpse another insecurity — fear that Solomon will abandon her. Behind the words in verse 4 are the unspoken questions *Will the one I love leave me? Will he continue to love me?*

Tirzah to the Chorus: "I adjure you, O daughters of Jerusalem, by the gazelles or by the hinds of the field, that you will not arouse or awaken my love until she pleases." (verse 5)

Once again we see the refrain: "Do not arouse or awaken my love until she pleases." Why the admonition for sexual purity here? Many reasons have been suggested. Perhaps Tirzah is saying, "Love is hard enough. Don't add more problems to your relationship by arousing sexual love before the right time and thus bringing baggage into your marriage."

APPLYING THE SONG FOR COUPLES

We don't know anyone who has ever gotten up in the morning and out of the blue decided, *I think I'll chuck my marriage today.* For most people, the decision to leave a marriage is the result of choice after choice to move away from intimacy. Dennis Rainey, in his excellent book *Lonely Husbands, Lonely Wives,* observes,

> Every day each partner in the marriage makes choices that result in oneness or in isolation. Make the right choices and you will know love, warmth, acceptance, and the freedom of true intimacy and genuine oneness as man and wife. Make the wrong choices and you will know the quiet desperation of living together but never really touching one another deeply.[4]

None of us signs up for this! We don't want to live in mediocrity. We marry because we want passion and intimacy. So how does a marriage go from intimacy to abandonment? Most of the time, it's a slow slide into complacency. The couple ignores little problems, and then the little problems become big problems. Of course there are times when abandonment comes as a shock, as when one partner commits adultery or a major incident goes unresolved. But even then, there are usually warning signs. Here are a few:[5]

- ꙮ A feeling that your mate isn't hearing you and doesn't want to understand what you are trying to communicate.
- ꙮ One or both of you have an apathetic attitude, an attitude that says, "Why try?" or "I don't want to work on this marriage."
- ꙮ You seem unable to please your mate or meet your mate's expectations.
- ꙮ You are leading separate lives.

- Your mate is withdrawing from you.
- Your mate refuses to accept responsibility for the marriage: "That's *your* problem, not mine."
- One or both of you believe that avoiding conflict is better than dealing with the pain of reality.

Don't ignore these "foxes," or abandonment could become a possibility! When people hear the word *abandonment*, they often think of physical abandonment, as when one person leaves the relationship. But abandonment can also be sexual or emotional. In these instances, couples live under the same roof, but because they have abandoned the marriage sexually or emotionally, they live separate, unconnected lives.

What does *sexual* abandonment look like? One husband talks about his situation:

> Eleven years ago, my wife stood before me and said, "I will never have sex with you again." Eleven years of living in the same house, yet miles apart. Now we have separate rooms, separate friends, and separate lives. The pain is too deep for words.

Sometimes we mistakenly believe that people who follow Christ are protected from such tragedy, but this man and his wife are both respected leaders in their church. Another couple we know is in a similar crisis. He is a pastor and preaches every Sunday. She sings on the worship team. They haven't had sex in seven years. According to her, "He's not interested." According to him, "She is so critical and disrespectful toward me that I have no desire to touch her." They both admit, "We stay together for the sake of the kids, but there is no relationship. People see us in church and think we are a happy, godly family. If they only knew . . ."

Sexual abandonment is painful. So is *emotional* abandonment. Emotional abandonment occurs when couples either refuse to communicate on a deep level, or they speak in such an abusive way that one of the partners withdraws. Here are two examples of emotional abandonment:

From a wife: I long for tenderness to flow between us and for there to be an intimate connection in our smiles, words, and touch, but instead we are like two pieces of sandpaper rubbing against each other. Sandpaper is abrasive, bruising both the skin and heart. I desperately want us to move out of the defeat of this jarring separateness into the joy of communion in which body, soul, and spirit melt together in true oneness. What do I do? Where do I start to reconnect with him?

From a husband: I feel that I can't even relax in my own home, that I am continually walking on eggshells. I never know what will trigger the hateful comments, the outburst of anger, the look of disgust on her face. She doesn't slap me with her hands, but she does with her words. My home is not a haven but a living hell.

Emotional safety is the one quality upon which all the other qualities we desire in a relationship — intimacy, openness, and passion — depend. "Without emotional safety, a marriage simply will not feel good. When we believe we are threatened, we defend ourselves and once defensiveness enters the picture, the possibility of openness and intimacy is lost."[6]

If you have experienced emotional or sexual abandonment, how do you go about reconnecting with the one who has hurt you? Is it possible for your marriage to be a safe place again? Yes, it is possible. We've witnessed the resurrection of many dead marriages. It happens when couples entrust themselves to the Giver of Life and make a decision to become servant lovers to one another. This requires personal sacrifice and a willingness to regard your mate's needs as more important than your own, but every couple whose marriage has been healed agrees that their sacrifices were worth the love they now enjoy.

If you as a couple want to make your marriage a safe place, the first thing you need to do is erect a security fence around it.

DELETE THE "D" WORD FROM YOUR VOCABULARY

When was the last time you thought or spoke the word *divorce*? This word flashes a warning light to your mate that is equivalent to a level-five security breech. One wife said she feels incapable of working on their marriage because whenever things get really difficult, her husband threatens divorce: "I never feel safe enough to press through to solutions in our marriage because I'm afraid if I press too hard, he'll leave."

Listen up, because what we are about to say is of the utmost importance: The quickest way to destroy emotional safety — and all hopes of intimacy — is to threaten divorce.

Do you want to take what God made holy, smash it, spit on it, and grind it into the ground? Then go ahead. Callously throw around the "D" word like it doesn't matter. Christians have been increasingly lenient about speaking the "D" word. We are of the opinion that every Christian couple ought to delete the "D" word from their dictionaries, from their computers — certainly from their vocabularies. Listen to God's voice:

> You flood the LORD's altar with tears. You weep and wail because he no longer pays attention to your offerings or accepts them with pleasure from your hands. You ask, "Why?" It is because the LORD is acting as the witness between you and the wife of your youth, because you have broken faith with her, though she is your partner, the wife of your marriage covenant.... So guard yourself in your spirit and do not break faith with the wife of your youth. *I hate divorce.* (Malachi 2:13-16, NIV, emphasis added)

Notice that God doesn't say He disapproves of divorce or that it makes Him sad. He says He hates it. Why? Because the marriage covenant is a picture, a reflection, of the covenant God has with each believer. Hebrews 13:5 contains the only triple negative in the New Testament. God emphatically proclaims, "I will never, never, never leave you. I will never, never, never forsake you." God is faithful to keep His covenant to a thousand generations (see Psalm 105:8; we'll talk more about covenants in the next chapter). Of course, our God is a God of grace who extends forgiveness to those who divorce. But to break our marriage covenant with our spouse other than for issues related to adultery is to break God's heart, because our marriage no longer reflects the permanence of His covenant with us.

Another reason God hates divorce is because He sees the ever-expanding rings of pain that circle out when we toss the stone of divorce into the pool of marriage. When we bring divorce into the conversation — even if it's not something we intend to follow through with — we become an unsafe spouse and increase the likelihood that we will end up one day in divorce court. One wife shared that she and her husband thought the word *divorce* long before they actually spoke it out loud. At first they said it to shock each other into action, but now they've said it so often that it's lost its shock value. What was once an unthinkable idea now seems like a viable option.

Author Mike Mason says there is only one way out of marriage. "And the way out is not divorce! No, the way out in marriage (no matter how bad things may get) is simply to put everything we have back on the line, our whole hearts and lives, just as we did the moment we took our vows."[7] (Hmmm. Seems that Mike knows the secret of being a servant lover!)

When we eliminate the "D" word from our vocabularies and recommit to our pledge "I will never leave you," we create a security fence around our marriages. With this boundary in place, we feel safe and able to address the deep issues of what we can do to reconnect with our spouse.

Meet Each Other's Deepest Needs

Nothing makes a husband or wife feel safer than having their greatest need met in the marriage. But what is the greatest need for a man? We could speculate and never reach a consensus because one author will say one thing and another will say something different. What is the greatest need for a woman? Read a hundred different surveys and you will get a hundred different answers. That is why we cannot look to the world for the answer to this question. Instead, we look to the Author of Life, the Creator God, who alone knows the secret because He created male and female.

Scripture doesn't say, "A man's greatest need is . . ." Nor does it say, "A woman's greatest need is . . ." But God does make specific commandments to husbands and wives in Scripture, and we believe that these commands are there to ensure that couples meet each other's deepest needs. He commands, "Husbands, *love* your wife. Wives, *respect* your husband."

Let's look at these two needs and see how love fulfills the greatest need of a wife, while respect satisfies the greatest need of a husband.

APPLYING THE SONG FOR HUSBANDS

LOVE YOUR WIFE

When we want our spouse to hear what we are saying, we often repeat our-selves once, twice, maybe even three times. That is what God does when He speaks to husbands in Ephesians 5. Three times He reinforces His command for a husband to love his wife:

> Husbands, love your wives, just as Christ also loved the church and gave Himself up for her. (verse 25)

> Husbands ought also to love their own wives as their own bodies. (verse 28)

> [A husband must] love his own wife even as himself. (verse 33)

Look again carefully at these three verses. Do any of them offer a dis-claimer? Do any say, "It's not necessary for you to love your wife if she is self-ish or if she doesn't love you in return"? No. In fact, search the entire Bible. You will not find even one exception to the command. Regardless of your wife's actions, God says you are to love her — period.

Okay, but what does love look like? The answer is found in a little-talked-about word closely associated with the command to love: *cherish*. Ephesians 5:28-29 expands on this:

> So husbands ought also to love their own wives as their own bodies. He who loves his own wife loves himself; for no one ever hated his own flesh, but nourishes and *cherishes* it, just as Christ also does the church. (emphasis added)

The Greek word for cherish, *thalpo*, has important nuances not easily translated into English. It literally means "to keep warm, or to soften by heat."[8] We see it used in a beautiful and descriptive way in 1 Thessalonians 2:7: "But we proved to be gentle among you, as a nursing mother tenderly cares for her own children." The word *thalpo* is used here of the tender care that a nursing mother has for her children. Note the tenderness and warmth associated with the metaphor. In the Old Testament, the image used to communicate this concept is that of a mother bird covering her young with her feathers.[9]

Another meaning of the Hebrew equivalent of *thalpo* is "to be of service to."[10] It is used of God's superintending care, as in, "You scrutinize my path and my lying down, and are intimately acquainted with all my ways" (Psalm 139:3). Thus, God is "intimately acquainted" with everything about us. Here's what the word *cherish* means to Jody:

> When I see all the nuances of the word cherish, I have to ask, What does it mean for me to cherish Linda? I am to communicate warmth to her; I am to treat her tenderly like a nursing mother and never be harsh; I am to be thoroughly acquainted with all her needs, emotions, dreams, and hopes; and I am to provide protection just like a mother bird hovers over her young, covering them with her feathers. This is very convicting, and I know I must become a student of my wife to even begin to live out all that loving and cherishing her means.

To cherish your wife is to actively love her.

LET YOUR ACTIONS SPEAK LOVE

While there are many ways you can meet your wife's deep need for love, we want to highlight three that every wife we know will welcome:

- Help her — with the kids, the house, the yard.
- Show her affection — nonsexual touching, such as hugs and tender kisses.
- Listen to her — without interrupting or trying to fix things.

Here are examples of how husbands loved their wives in each of the three ways. First, Jeremy tells us how he loved his wife by *helping* her:

Every time Vicki and I made love, one of the kids would have a nightmare or wake up for no apparent reason, get out of bed, and knock on the bedroom door. I told Vicki to ignore the interruptions, but there was no way she could make love with a baby crying. I grunted with disgust and frustration as she got out of bed to care for little ones. One night it hit me: *Jeremy, why do you assume this is* her *problem? Why do you lie here like a king waiting for her to finish the rounds of mothering?* The next time one of our kids interrupted us, I told Vicki to stay in bed and that I'd take care of things. I suggested that she cuddle under the covers and daydream about how I was going to pleasure her. Her look of disbelief and then delight showed me that my act of loving service was long overdue.

Connor loved his wife through *affection:*

DeDe called me from work and told me she had accidentally backed over the trash can and into the concrete fence in our driveway, denting the car. My first thought was, *Great. Our insurance premiums are going to go through the roof.* I stuffed the thought and muttered a halfhearted, "I'm glad you weren't hurt." I felt badly that I'd sounded so insincere, so when I got home that night, I pulled her into my arms and said, "Honey, I'm sorry your day started so badly. Let's end it right." Then I offered to do what speaks love to her — a half-hour foot massage.

Derek loved his wife by *listening* to her:

I had been away for ten days on a business trip. As I walked through the door, I could smell the aroma of her special lasagna. We had already agreed that dessert would be in bed, so I was eager to be done with the meal! But over dinner, Melissa burst into tears and told me her cat, Tuffy, had died. I thought, *Good riddance to the little hairball,* but she'd had that cat since before we were married, so I listened to her reminisce about this pet that I wasn't particularly fond of. She went on for what seemed like an hour. Finally, the tears and words stopped. Then she looked at me and said, "Thanks for loving me."

Let us say a bit more about the need to listen and dialogue with your wife, because this is one of the primary ways you make her feel emotionally safe. Your wife gives and receives love through words, whereas words are just not as high on most men's priority list. As one husband said, "I just don't get it. When I come home from work, I want quiet, peace, and to veg out in front of the television. My wife wants none of these. She wants to talk, talk, talk. It took me a long time to figure out that listening to her was loving her."

Kevin Leman, author and host of a popular radio program, says that he has yet to meet a man who, after a long day at work, thinks to himself, *What I really need right now is a long, forty-five minute talk with my wife.*[11] But a servant lover understands his wife's need to communicate with him and that regular verbal communication is necessary for her to feel loved and emotionally safe.

GET PERSONAL

Your wife is unique. Although certain attitudes universally communicate love to a woman, some things are unique to your wife. We encourage you to develop a personal profile in a notebook under the heading "Things That Speak Love to My Wife":

- Make a list of every action and attitude that you think communicates love to your wife. Don't rush through this exercise. Take time to list everything you can think of. (Look at 1 Corinthians 13 to spur your thinking.)
- Ask her to write a list of what communicates love to her. Instruct her to include attitudes as well as actions. Tell her to be thorough.
- Combine your list with hers and together create a master profile. Then place this list where you can review it often. Tell her, "Honey, I want to love you more. Please pray for me and be patient with me as I grow in this area."

When a husband loves his wife, he provides an emotionally safe place for her heart and for their lovemaking. All wives need to feel emotionally and physically safe, but this is especially important for the wife who has suffered from sexual abuse. If your wife has been wounded in this way, she likely feels

unsafe and violated. These feelings are deeply woven into her psyche. It is critical that you create emotional safety for her, in and out of bed. She needs you
to be a safe shelter, a place for healing. You may find it helpful for both of you
to read the letter on page 158, "To the One Who Has Been Sexually Abused."

Your wife desperately needs you to love her through your words and
actions. We know that sometimes this can be difficult, but what we are about
to ask her to do for you will be difficult for her as well. No one ever said being
a servant lover is easy, only that loving sacrificially can help a marriage flourish.

APPLYING THE SONG FOR WIVES

RESPECT YOUR HUSBAND

Your husband craves your respect. If you don't believe us, do what one
woman did. On an evening when her husband was relaxed and had nothing
in particular going on, she said three simple sentences before leaving the
room: "I was thinking of you today. I was thinking of the things I respect
about you. I want you to know that I respect you." As she turned to leave the
room, her husband yelled, "Wait! Come back! What things?" He was so loud
that their children came running into the room. After the kids left, the wife
again started to leave, and in a loud whisper he said, "Wait. Wait. Come back!
What things?" He was riveted on her. After she had told him several things
that she respected about him, he said, "Wow, can I take you and the family
out to dinner?"[12]

Does it surprise you that your husband's deepest need is for respect, not
love? Of course a husband wants love and a wife wants respect. But when God
created the first man and woman, He wired subtle differences in their male-
ness and femaleness as to their basic needs. God wove into the fabric of a
man's being a basic need for respect. Authors of the book *Rocking the Roles* say,

> My wife longs to hear me say, "I love you." I say it often because I know
> it means so much to her. But the phrase that has comparable value to
> me from her is not "I love you" but "I'm proud of you." Respect and
> admiration are special ingredients to a husband's happiness.[13]

Every husband yearns for the respect of his wife. He desperately needs to know she thinks he is important, that in her eyes he has value. The apostle Paul and the apostle Peter understood this truth. That's why both of them ended their teaching on marriage with this instruction for wives: Respect your husband. Paul wrote in Ephesians 5:33,

> Nevertheless, each individual among you also is to love his own wife even as himself, and the wife must see to it that she *respects her husband.* (emphasis added)

Peter wrote in 1 Peter 3:1-2,

> Wives, be submissive to your own husbands so that even if any of them are disobedient to the word, they may be won without a word by the behavior of their wives, as they observe your chaste and *respectful behavior.* (emphasis added)

The Greek word *phobos,* translated here as "respect," carries the meaning of "reverential fear."[14] The best description we have found of this reverential fear is in the *Amplified Bible,* which offers an expanded definition of respect:

> Let the wife see that she respects and reverences her husband [that she notices him, regards him, honors him, prefers him, venerates and esteems him; and that she defers to him, praises him, and loves and admires him exceedingly]. (Ephesians 5:33)

Who knew that respect encompassed so many ideas? *Notice, regard, honor, PREFER . . . praise and admire EXCEEDINGLY?* Is this really what God says to wives? Yes!

Look carefully at these verses on respect. Not one offers a disclaimer. None says, "You don't have to respect your husband if he is selfish or if he doesn't respect you in return." No. Search the entire Bible. Look cover to cover. You will not find even one exception to this command.

In fact, Peter tells a wife that her respectful spirit will be used to change her husband. What does respect look like in everyday life? Let's consider some ways you can actively respect your husband: honor and esteem him, support him, and respond sexually to him.

HONOR HIM

A man's masculinity is more fragile than a woman's femininity. The view a man has of himself (whether good or bad) is usually a reflection from two sources: his work and his woman. A wife's ongoing responsiveness to her husband should be a well from which he can draw respect for himself. His self-respect is, in many ways, her respect reborn in him.[15]

The book of Proverbs speaks of the importance of a wife's respecting her husband. The wife in Proverbs 31 esteemed her husband in public: "Her husband is respected at the city gate, where he takes his seat among the elders of the land" (Proverbs 31:23, NIV). We believe the idea here is that because this wife publicly honors her husband with her words, others respect him.

How do we honor our husbands? Through the words we speak privately and publicly to him and about him. If the only thing people knew about your husband was what you say about him, would they respect him? If others (your mother, mother-in-law, friends) could listen in on the way you speak to him in private, what would their opinion of him be? Do you honor your husband by the words you speak?

SUPPORT HIM

A wife's words and actions communicate to her husband either "I support you" or "I compete with you." Dr. Laura Schlessinger, in her book *The Proper Care and Feeding of Husbands*, relates what competition looks like in the average home. A woman had called her, wanting a way to convince her husband that she was right in her desire to have another cat.

DR. LAURA: What? He doesn't have the right to his position?

CALLER: Yes, of course he does. It's just that I don't see any good reason not to have another cat.

DR. LAURA: A good reason is that he doesn't want to live with multiple animals. Why isn't that a good enough reason?

CALLER: Can't I keep pushing him to specify his reasons? I just want to know why he feels that way.

DR. LAURA: No, you don't. You are not really interested in understanding his position. You want to know his arguments so you can shoot them down so you can have another cat. You don't want to understand; you want to manipulate.

CALLER: Yeah, I guess that's so. But I really want this other cat!

DR. LAURA: Obviously, you want that cat more than you want to show your husband respect.[16]

Do you support your husband, or do you compete with him? Do you support him in his roles as a provider, a father, a Christian, and a man, or are you more concerned with getting your own way?

Here are some examples of how wives we've talked with support their husbands.

In his role as a provider:

- Even though I was petrified that we would suffer financially when he went out on his own as a financial consultant, I prayed for him, reorganized his office, and often entertained future business clients and their wives.
- I support him by editing and typing all his papers and correspondence.
- When he is traveling for an extended period of time, I take over everything at home (and then don't detail all the "tragedies" that have happened while he was gone).

In his role as a father:

- Because it is hard for him to know how to talk to a three-year-old, I write out questions for him to ask our daughter when they go to McDonald's on their date.

◊ I constantly tell our daughters, "Don't ever marry a man unless he is as wonderful as your father."

In his role as a husband:

◊ For his fortieth birthday, I wrote out forty reasons why I thought he was a terrific husband. I framed this, and now it is on his desk, where he sees it every day.

◊ Once a month, I make his arrival home from work really special by having his slippers waiting at the door, cooking his favorite meal, and keeping the kids occupied for several hours.

In his role as a lover and friend:

◊ When he was fired from his job, I encouraged him with emotional support (hours of listening), physical support (hours of sex), and practical support (hours of sending out résumés).

Not only do our husbands need us to honor and support them but they also need us to notice them physically.

RESPOND SEXUALLY TO HIM

Your husband wants you to desire him. Why? Because sexual intimacy affirms his masculinity. That's how God created him. One honest man said, "For me, respect is spelled S-E-X." It is important to understand that sex not only meets a *physical* need in your husband but that it also meets an *emotional* need. This revelation changed the way Kasey viewed sex:

> In the past, I dismissed Trevor's need for sex because I viewed sex as a physical need, and for me, a mom of three preschoolers, there was no time for my physical needs. If I were hungry, I overlooked it. If I had a headache, I ignored it. So I thought if Trevor had an urge for sex but I wasn't in the mood, it wouldn't kill him to wait another day. But then I learned that sex was more than a physical need for Trevor — it was a way he connected *emotionally* to me. That changed things because emotional needs are important to me!

Another wife said,

> It may sound stupid, but I want to make sure he gets what he wants. He's too wonderful and I love him too much to disappoint him. That's how I respect my husband: communication, understanding, support, great chocolate chip cookies, and great sex!

A servant lover willingly does these things in order to meet her husband's deep need for respect. She also seeks to build him up in other ways that will be meaningful to him.

GET PERSONAL

Your husband is unique. Although certain attitudes universally communicate respect to a man, certain ways will be unique to your husband. We encourage you to develop a personal profile in a notebook under the heading "Things That Speak Respect to My Husband":

- Review Ephesians 5:33 in the *Amplified Bible*. Consider each of the words listed in this definition of respect, and then make a list of what you do that you feel communicates respect to your husband.
- Ask your husband to write a list of what actions communicate respect to him. Tell him not to leave anything out.
- Combine your list with his and together create a master profile. Then place this list where you can review it often. Tell him, "Honey, I want to show respect to you. Please pray for me and be patient with me as I grow in this area."

When wives respect their husbands and husbands love their wives, they create a safe place for loving. Listen to these wise words from author Tommy Nelson:

> Show me a woman who feels that her husband deals with her tenderly — with kindness, good manners, generosity, genuine affection, and understanding — and I'll show you a happily married woman,

regardless of external circumstances that may come against their union as a family.

Show me a husband who feels that his wife deals with him with respect — admiration, appreciation, upholding his dignity as a man, thankful for his protection and provision — and I'll show you a happily married man, regardless of the stress he may feel from the outside world.[17]

SERVANT LOVERS: Make their marriage a safe place by meeting each other's deep needs for love and respect.

SELFISH LOVERS: Make their marriage an unsafe place through unloving actions and disrespectful words.

THE CHORUS:
"What is this coming up from the wilderness
Like columns of smoke,
Perfumed with myrrh and frankincense,
With all scented powders of the merchant?
Behold, it is the traveling couch of Solomon;
Sixty mighty men around it,
Of the mighty men of Israel.
All of them are wielders of the sword,
Expert in war;
Each man has his sword at his side,
Guarding against the terrors of the night.
King Solomon has made for himself a sedan chair
From the timber of Lebanon.
He made its posts of silver,
Its back of gold
And its seat of purple fabric,
With its interior lovingly fitted out
By the daughters of Jerusalem.
Go forth, O daughters of Zion,
And gaze on King Solomon with the crown
With which his mother has crowned him
On the day of his wedding,
And on the day of his gladness of heart."

SONG OF SOLOMON 3:6-11

chapter eight

◊

Remember Your Vows

"When the pastor asked, 'Do you promise to love, honor,
and respect Peter for as long as you both shall live?' I shouted, 'I do!' so
loudly that everyone in the church started laughing. But I meant it.
What greater cause could there be for my life than to love, serve,
and start a family with this incredible man?"

At a wedding, the bride and groom say goodbye to singleness and "I do" to loving one another as a married couple. We invite you to join us in viewing this significant event in the life of Solomon and Tirzah.

UNDERSTANDING THE SONG

Welcome to Solomon and Tirzah's wedding. Perhaps you're thinking, *But aren't they already married?* Yes, but remember, this Hebrew poetry describes scenes that are not always in chronological order. In this chapter, we'll view the wedding procession, and in the next two chapters, we'll learn about their wedding night. Certain scenes are rated "H" for "hot," but they are also holy. God encourages us to pay attention because through this couple, we learn valuable principles about loving our mate in intimate and unselfish ways.

The Chorus: "What is this coming up from the wilderness like columns of smoke, perfumed with myrrh and frankincense, with all scented powders of the merchant?" (3:6)

In verses 6 through 11, the chorus comments on the wedding procession as it makes its way along the roads toward Jerusalem. Presumably, Solomon followed traditional Hebrew custom and sent a wedding entourage to escort his bride from her home in Lebanon to the palace in Jerusalem, where the wedding ceremony would take place. Here the chorus is observing that the ever-present cloud, which looks like a pillar of smoke, did not cloak the rich fragrances that emanated from the bride and her procession. The myrrh and frankincense perfume, which Solomon had given to Tirzah, were not native to Israel; they came from faraway places, such as Arabia and India. Solomon had said he longed to shower her with gifts (see 1:11), and these fragrant offerings made his beloved feel elegantly special. He chose the very best, frankincense and myrrh, the same gifts given to the baby Jesus by the wise men.

The Chorus: "Behold, it is the traveling couch of Solomon." (verse 7)

The bride traveled on Solomon's own couch, which would have been covered. The legs of the couch were attached to two long poles, allowing four to six men to carry it on their shoulders.

The Chorus: "Sixty mighty men around it, of the mighty men of Israel. All of them are wielders of the sword, expert in war; each man has his sword at his side, guarding against the terrors of the night." (verses 7-8)

King David had thirty warriors who served as his private bodyguards, but Solomon's bride had *double* this number. These men were the elite corps. Only the best could guard the king's beloved against possible attacks from animals, thieves, or kidnappers on the long journey from Lebanon to Jerusalem.

The Chorus: "King Solomon has made for himself a sedan chair from the timber of Lebanon." (verse 9)

Imagine Tirzah's elation as she lifts her eyes and sees her groom and his attendants coming to meet her. Solomon approaches her in grand style, carried on a chair especially designed for the occasion. It was a couch long enough for its rider to recline, covered with a canopy resting on four pillars at the corners. Curtains protected the rider from the sun, and doors on each side, made of lattice, provided a means of entry and exit.[1] As Tirzah approached Solomon's sedan chair, she climbed in and joined him, and together they traveled to the palace.

The Chorus: "He made its posts of silver, its back of gold and its seat of purple fabric, with its interior lovingly fitted out by the daughters of Jerusalem. Go forth, O daughters of Zion, and gaze on King Solomon with the crown with which his mother has crowned him on the day of his wedding, and on the day of his gladness of heart." (verses 10-11)

Solomon's crown was not a physical crown but a garland of fresh flowers of the kind worn on festive occasions, especially weddings.[2] Can you picture the smile on his mother's face as she placed the wreath on his head? Can you imagine Solomon's anticipation and delight in this moment? His heart is overwhelmed with joy and gladness.

APPLYING THE SONG FOR COUPLES

This is Solomon and Tirzah's wedding day, a day of rejoicing. The procession has arrived, a parade of pomp and ceremony. People from all over have come to be part of this glorious celebration, to witness Solomon and Tirzah's marriage. The fact that their wedding is tucked into the middle of the Song, after we've already seen many snapshots of them together as a married couple, is significant. It's almost as if Solomon is saying, "Let's stop for a moment and go back to the beginning, back to where our love started as husband and wife."

Remembering has value. It serves as a time-out from the craziness of life to reflect on what really matters, a checkpoint to make sure we haven't strayed from our values or our vows. Take a moment now and think back on your wedding day. Can you picture the place where you got married? Do you remember what you were wearing? Who were your attendants? Do you remember speaking your vows? What did you promise? Who witnessed your words? Do you remember the announcement "I now pronounce you man and wife. What God has joined together, let no man separate"?

REFLECT ON YOUR VOWS

Too often when couples speak their vows, their attitude communicates a promise to love one another for BETTER or for WORSE, for RICHER or for POORER, in SICKNESS and in HEALTH. They focus only on the good words, but marriage is also about the difficult words. Sometimes couples agree to marry for better or worse, but not for good. They view marriage as a contract rather than as a covenant. What is the difference? A contract is what you sign for your cell phone or to lease office space. Contracts can be broken without devastating consequences. But a covenant is different than a contract. How?

A covenant is made in the presence of God. Most marriage ceremonies begin, "We are gathered together here in the sight of God." The thought is that God is present to approve and bless the marriage, which is why most weddings take place in a church, commonly referred to as "the house of God."

A covenant is a binding agreement made for life. You and your spouse spoke words of a *verba solemnia,* a solemn vow, and entered into a covenant with God and your mate. In a covenant agreement, we don't have the option of loving and cherishing our mate only as long as he or she loves and cherishes us. There is no quid pro quo.[3] Your vows did not include the words "as long as we both feel like it"; they included words such as "as long as we both shall live."

A covenant has witnesses. A marriage covenant has three levels of witnesses: God Himself, the wedding party who stands with the bride and groom because of their relationship to them, and the congregation of family and friends. These witnesses serve to testify, "These are the vows you made — we heard you speak them," in the event that one of the parties involved encounters a temporary memory lapse.

A covenant involves the exchange of seals or signs. In two separate ceremonies, the bride and groom exchange signs or seals as part of their covenant. First, in a public ceremony, they give rings to one another as a sign of the vows they have made. Later, they seal their covenant vows through the joining of their bodies in a private ceremony. Sex not only is part of the covenant of marriage, sex is the divine seal.[4] Each time a husband and wife celebrate their sexual oneness, they affirm their covenant with one another and with God.

What vows did you make on your wedding day? You probably didn't say, "I promise to be the perfect husband/wife." Nor did you vow, "I will always meet your every need" or "I will never change." The longer we are married, the more apparent it becomes that we are not perfect, we will fail to meet the needs of our mate, and we will change. Our wedding vows were promises of *commitment*, not *contentment*. The big idea is this: "I may fall short of what I want to be for you. But I promise to love you always. No matter what we come up against in our lives, we'll face it together because I am in this until the end."

The psalmist asks, "How can I repay the LORD for all his goodness to me?" (116:12, NIV). The answer is given, "I will fulfill my vows to the LORD" (verse 14, NIV). Marriage is a sacred covenant in which you made a vow to your mate and to God. Fulfill it. Reflect upon it. Revisit your words so that you do not forget what you promised. How can you remember your vows?

- If you have an audiotape or videotape of your wedding, set aside time to thoughtfully watch (or listen) to it together. Pay special attention to the vows you made.
- Spend an evening looking at your wedding pictures and sharing reflections about the vows you each made. How has your knowledge about the depth of your vows changed over the years?
- Celebrate significant anniversaries by renewing your vows to each other. You could do this privately as a couple or invite family and friends to witness your renewal of vows.
- Have a Wedding Reflection Party. Invite several couples for dinner. Ask each to bring their wedding pictures and share one vow they made at their wedding and how they are currently trying to honor that vow in their marriage. Seeing your friends in their wedding glory is fun! End the evening by praying for each other's marriages and committing to holding one another accountable to living the vows they made at their wedding.

As you reflect upon your wedding, it will likely cause you to relive strong emotions: the joy of friends and family as they surrounded you, the awe of a ceremony wrapped in beauty and pageantry, and the passion of the night when you made love as husband and wife for the first time.

REFLECT ON YOUR PASSION

Do you remember the first days of lavish loving, when you couldn't seem to get enough of each other? Free from the responsibility of kids, you could flow with the call of passion. But as the years pass, time and the pressures of life often diminish the intensity of passion, even in happy marriages. How can you recapture tantalizing times together?

Revelation 2:3-5 speaks to this very issue. Although this passage was written to the church of Ephesus and addresses their waning love for Christ, the message also provides sound marital advice, as it relates to rekindling the fire of love between a husband and wife. God's words are strong:

> "You have perseverance and have endured for My name's sake, and have not grown weary. But I have this against you, that you have left your first love. Therefore remember from where you have fallen, and repent and do the deeds you did at first."

Here is our paraphrase of this passage as it relates to marriage:

> Hey, you've done good! You've faced some tough issues, but you haven't given up. Excellent! But you have one problem. You've lost the passion of the love you had when you met. How can you recapture the fire of first love? Do three things. First, *remember.* Think about how intense that love was at first. Second, *repent.* Tell your mate you are sorry for being lazy and letting the fire of your love cool. Third, *return.* Do the thoughtful, tender, creative things you did when you were first married.

What did you do when you were first married? Make a list and then commit to keep doing those things. Here are some examples from other husbands and wives about what they did as newlyweds:

For wives:

- ◊ I studied recipes and experimented to find different meals that would please him.
- ◊ I washed and waxed his car.
- ◊ I freshened up and put on perfume before we saw each other in the evening.
- ◊ I tucked little notes in his computer case that said, "You are the greatest lover in the world."
- ◊ When he opened the door after work, I stopped what I was doing, ran to him, and gave him a heartfelt kiss.

For husbands:

- ◊ I called her on the phone to say, "I've been thinking of you."
- ◊ I surprised her by filling up her car with gas and having it washed and waxed.
- ◊ I bought her favorite candy bar and hid it under her pillow.
- ◊ I bought her jewelry and little gifts.
- ◊ I told her how excited she made me feel.

You might plan a night away together and then share how you've grown as lovers since your wedding day by demonstrating in tangible ways all you've learned. One couple we know recaptures the passion by playing the song they first danced to at their wedding. They know all the words by heart. Singing and dancing to that song helps bring back the memory of their wonderful wedding day and the passion of their wedding night.

Pete offers another idea you might try:

> We spent a weekend reliving our wedding at a really nice hotel. First we went through our wedding pictures, read cards and notes from people we had not thought about for years, and snacked on the kinds of appetizers served at the reception. In the evening, Lorraine dressed in a white nightgown complete with her wedding veil. The rest of the evening — well, it was better than our honeymoon!

Passion and intimacy are important not only to us but also to God. Many people do not realize that He actually commanded husbands to take time away from their normal work during the first year of their marriages in order to learn how to please their wives. We are guessing that this is one command many were delighted to obey.

APPLYING THE SONG TO HUSBANDS

COMMIT TO A YEAR OF SEXUAL DELIGHT

A verse in Deuteronomy makes it clear that the first year of marriage is a time to concentrate on building a deep, passionate love affair with each other: "When a man takes a new wife, he shall not go out with the army, nor be charged with any duty; he shall be free at home one year and shall give happiness to his wife whom he has taken" (24:5). The Hebrew word *samach*,[5] translated here as "give happiness," carries the idea of "to gladden, make someone merry." Dr. Howard Hendricks says that this "expression encompasses happiness in all areas but certainly includes sexual delight."[6]

Husbands, if you failed to "give happiness" to your wife during the first year of your marriage, commit now to discovering what delights her sexually. Study her. Pay attention to her. Learn what lights her up and what turns her off.

God is serious about this. First Peter 3:7 says, "You husbands in the same way, live with your wives in an understanding way, . . . so that your prayers will not be hindered." The verb translated "live with" is consistently translated in the Septuagint, the Greek translation of the Old Testament, as "have sexual intercourse with" (see Deuteronomy 22:13; 24:1; 21:13; 22:22; 25:5; Isaiah 62:5; Genesis 20:3). The phrase "an understanding way" implies acquiring knowledge and insight through a process of personal investigation. So an interpretive and expanded paraphrase of this verse might read,

> Likewise, you husbands have sexual intercourse with your wives in a way that is based upon insight gathered from personal investigation of her needs. If you do this, your prayers will not be hindered.

The Almighty God says to husbands, "Spend the first year of marriage learning to satisfy your new wife sexually. Discover what pleases and delights her. If you do this, I will answer your prayers." Will you commit to taking God's instruction seriously?

As we studied this passage on the wedding procession, one idea in particular jumped out at us as husbands about the meaning of our vows: our responsibility to protect our wives.

PROTECT YOUR BRIDE

Solomon arranged for "sixty mighty men" to guard and protect Tirzah (see 3:7). While this may sound like overkill to our ears, to her it sent a comforting message: "I will protect you." When a husband provides protection for his wife, he tells her that he places high value on her and he helps meet her need for security. Let's look at three ways modern-day Solomons can protect their wives.

Provide Physical Protection

While you don't need to hire sixty mighty men with swords to shield your wife from danger, you do need to have the following:

- Secure locks on doors and windows
- Working fire alarms
- AAA or a cell phone should your wife get a flat tire and you are not around to change it for her
- A list of people your wife could call if you were out of town and something broke

It is important that you make every effort to create an environment in which your wife feels safe and secure. If you travel frequently, your wife will feel safer if you take extra precautions to protect her: getting a watchdog, putting up motion-detector lights outside the house, and calling home every night to reassure her that should anything happen, you are only a phone call away.

Provide Emotional Protection

What kind of emotional stress is your wife under? Are you aware of what she does all day and how it affects her? If you don't know, make a point to find out. Jody gives us an example:

> During the first years of our marriage, I was more of a selfish lover than a servant lover. Linda had to ride herd all day long on our zoo of three under three, and often I was oblivious to how much energy and effort she was exerting. We affectionately called the period between 4:00 and 7:00 PM "the pit." By this time Linda was completely exhausted, and the children were demanding, tired, and fussy. One night, as I saw her slipping into total exhaustion, I realized I needed to do something, so I arranged a babysitter and took her out to dinner.
>
> While we ate, I told her that I needed to better understand the emotional pressure she was under. I got out some paper and asked Linda to list her weekly responsibilities. She quickly reeled off ten items. I kept pressing, "What else?" An hour later, I had a list of sixty-three items (I still have it in my file after thirty-three years). *No wonder she's tired,* I thought, *I would be in a hospital if I felt responsible for all that.*
>
> Each day, I made a choice to switch into servant-lover mode on the drive home from work. Two miles from our house there was a stop sign. As I passed it on my way home from work, I placed all the concerns of the office and ministry on the stop sign and spent the next five minutes praying for my wife and planning how I could absorb the shock of the "pit." Instead of coming in the door and relaxing and watching the news, I came in with one objective: taking pressure off my wife. Instead of sitting in front of the television, I set the table, played with our kids, did the dishes, and helped put our children to bed.

Ask yourself the following questions to figure out if you are providing emotional protection for your wife:[7]

§ Do I protect her from attacks of disrespect from our children and other family members?

- Do I provide objective feedback in decision making and help my wife set boundaries by encouraging her to say no when saying yes would not be in her best interest or serve our common purposes?
- Am I free of addictive behaviors, such as viewing pornography, abusing drugs, and gambling? And sin patterns such as jealousy and outbursts of anger? If not, am I getting help and working on ways, right now, to eliminate or control the behaviors so they do not negatively impact my wife and our kids?

Tell your wife, "Honey, I want to better understand the stresses in your life. Please sit down with me and list everything you feel responsible for, and then we can talk together about how I might help you." This is the heart of a servant lover. If you do this with an attitude of humility, it will refuel the fire of passion.

Provide Financial Protection

These questions might help you determine if you are providing protection for your wife in the financial area:[8]

- Do we have adequate life, health, and car insurance?
- Do we have an up-to-date will? (If you are married, you need a will, even if you are only in your twenties. Calamity comes to people of all ages.)
- Do we have a savings plan or a retirement program in place?

Sit down with your wife and ask her, "Do you feel I'm protecting you in the financial area? What else can I do?"

Jody: Several years after Linda and I were married, a close friend in his thirties died of a heart attack. He had no life insurance and left his wife and child destitute. I knew I needed to protect Linda against future financial uncertainty should anything happen to me. If she suddenly became a widow, she would have enough to deal with between my death and managing the home and kids. In the event something happened to me, I didn't want her to have to deal with financial pressure. I secured a good life-insurance policy, a savings plan, and a retirement program.

Peter: When we were first married, I gave Lorraine a brief overview of our financial situation. Whenever she asked for more information, I assured her, "Honey, don't worry about that. Everything is taken care of." It wasn't until a few years later that I learned she needed more specifics. Bottom line: She did not feel protected. So I typed up a master list that contained the location of our legal papers; pertinent information about our checking, savings, and retirement accounts; and a list of people she could call in case something happened to me. This is stored in a strongbox and updated every year. Now that she knows what specifics are in place, she has a sense of peace.

ADD A NEW WEDDING VOW

In this chapter, we've talked about the importance of *reflection* and *protection*. We want to end by challenging you to make an addition to your wedding vows. Actually, this vow is not *new*, because it was spoken hundreds of years ago in the Anglican church, but it will probably be new for the two of you. Unlike the vows you spoke in public, this vow is spoken in private. We encourage you to schedule a private ceremony where you speak this vow to one other and seal it with your actions:

> With my body I thee worship
> My body will adore you
> Your body alone will I cherish
> I will with my body declare your worth.[9]

SERVANT LOVERS: Honor their wedding vows daily.
SELFISH LOVERS: Never think about the vows they made.

SOLOMON TO TIRZAH:
"How beautiful you are, my darling,
How beautiful you are!
Your eyes are like doves behind your veil;
Your hair is like a flock of goats
That have descended from Mount Gilead.
Your teeth are like a flock of newly shorn ewes
Which have come up from their washing,
All of which bear twins,
And not one among them has lost her young.
Your lips are like a scarlet thread,
And your mouth is lovely.
Your temples are like a slice of a pomegranate
Behind your veil.
Your neck is like the tower of David,
Built with rows of stones
On which are hung a thousand shields,
All the round shields of the mighty men.

Your two breasts are like two fawns,
Twins of a gazelle
Which feed among the lilies.
Until the cool of the day
When the shadows flee away,
I will go my way to the mountain of myrrh
And to the hill of frankincense.
You are altogether beautiful, my darling,
And there is no blemish in you.
Come with me from Lebanon, my bride,
May you come with me from Lebanon.
Journey down from the summit of Amana,
From the summit of Senir and Hermon,
From the dens of lions,
From the mountains of leopards."

SONG OF SOLOMON 4:1-8

chapter nine

ۿ

Be Romantic In and Out of Bed

*"My wife is always saying she wants me to be
more romantic, but frankly, beyond flowers and candy,
I don't know what that looks like."*

It would be impossible to explore all of the nuances of sexual love without also including a discussion on romance. Who better to give us lessons than Solomon? We have seen his flair for romance in previous chapters, and we will see more examples in the future. In this scene, his sensitivity and romantic gestures to his wife are an inspiration to us all.

UNDERSTANDING THE SONG

This is Solomon and Tirzah's wedding night. It is amazing and gracious of God to allow us to partake of the beauty and holiness of this sexual union. He does this for our understanding. Through the medium of poetry, God found the perfect balance. The Song is specific enough to be helpful, but sensitive enough not to offend. These words of love are a masterpiece and the best sex manual we will ever find. Enter in as we see this extended description (it will take two chapters) of Solomon and Tirzah's lovemaking on their wedding night.

Solomon to Tirzah: "How beautiful you are, my darling, how beautiful you are! Your eyes are like doves behind your veil." (4:1)

Presumably, Solomon and his bride, on the couch in the bridal chamber, have initiated their loveplay. Overwhelmed by the beauty of his bride, Solomon praises her charms as his eyes caress her body. He again calls Tirzah

"my darling," an endearment that speaks of her companionship as both intimate and sexual.

Scholars are divided about what Tirzah's veil represents. Some believe it
refers to the way her long black hair cascaded around her face and shoulders
like a veil. Others believe that she was still wearing her wedding veil. But whatever form the veil takes, it seems likely that it evokes an aspect of mystery that
simultaneously allured Tirzah's husband and heightened his desire for her. As
he looks through the veil and into her eyes, he compares them to the dove, a
bird known for its intense loyalty and that often served as a symbol of purity
and innocence.

Verses 1-7 make up the first of four occurrences in the Song of what
Arabic love poetry labels a *wasf*, a poem of praise in which one of the lovers
describes the beauty of the other, beginning with the head and moving down
the body. The *wasf* is intended to describe and express emotions in a way that
evokes the reader's own emotions.[1]

*Solomon to Tirzah: "Your hair is like a flock of goats that have
descended from Mount Gilead. Your teeth are like a flock of newly
shorn ewes which have come up from their washing, all of which bear
twins, and not one among them has lost her young." (verses 1-2)*

Having eyes like doves is one thing, but what wife wants her husband to
tell her that her hair looks like goat's hair or that she has all her teeth? Today
such a husband would either be met with tears or a purse thrown directly at
his empty head! Solomon was not stupid, so obviously he is telling Tirzah
something that escapes those of us living in the twenty-first century.

In this verse, Solomon is referring to black goats, whose long, silky hair
glistened in the sun. As they wound their way homeward, coming down the
gentle slopes of Gilead, they looked like a graceful stream flowing down the
hills. Solomon is saying that Tirzah evokes within him a similar picture of
tranquil beauty. As he looks at her hair, a sense of serenity envelops him. He
loves to take in what he sees.

While we can see the romance behind Solomon's compliments about his
bride's hair, why the compliment about her teeth? Remember, this couple lived

in a time when oral hygiene was nonexistent and root canals and crowns were an impossibility. So it must have been very rare for Tirzah to possess all her teeth and for them to be glistening white. No wonder he found her beautiful!

Solomon to Tirzah: "Your lips are like a scarlet thread, and your mouth is lovely. Your temples are like a slice of a pomegranate behind your veil." (verse 3)

Whether Tirzah's lips were scarlet naturally or due to cosmetics, the meaning is clear: Her lips are delectable and Solomon desires to kiss her; her mouth is filled with delight and he longs to possess it. When he speaks of her temples as being like a slice of pomegranate, he is comparing them to the rosy, blush color that is unique to this delicacy when it becomes ripe.

It is unlikely that Solomon stood across the room when he recited this poem to his new bride. It's much more probable that as he mentions each part of her body, he kisses and caresses it. So we assume that he starts his lovemaking by kissing and stroking her hair, lips, and mouth. Next he kisses and caresses her cheeks and neck.

Solomon to Tirzah: "Your neck is like the tower of David, built with rows of stones on which are hung a thousand shields, all the round shields of the mighty men." (verse 4)

Once again Solomon seems insensitive. What bride wants her neck compared to a solid, thick tower weighted down with heavy metal shields? The image of the muscular, bulging neck of a professional wrestler fills our minds. Yet we don't think Solomon had Hulk Hogan in mind. Some commentators believe that Solomon wasn't complimenting the appearance of her neck; rather he was saying that it was strong and dignified.[2] Her neck spoke of her erect and queenly carriage and symbolized what she was to her husband: a source of strength and encouragement.

Solomon to Tirzah: "Your two breasts are like two fawns, twins of a gazelle which feed among the lilies." (verse 5)

Solomon then compares his wife's breasts to two small young animals that are soft to the touch and display lightness and playfulness. Their texture and softness are invitations to "come, caress, and fondle."[3] This word picture suggests sexual playfulness.

Next he describes her breasts as "twins of a gazelle which feed among the lilies." One commentator believes that this hints of Solomon's intimate kissing of her breasts, because in Song 5:13, the bride refers to *his* lips as lilies. Tirzah's breasts are the most powerful, visible expression of her femininity, and she wants to share that aspect of herself with her lover.[4]

Are you surprised that God's Word discusses breasts in such an erotic way? Sadly, not all Christians down through the centuries have seen the beauty in the imagery in the Song, and they have allowed their cultural preconditioning to reject the obvious meaning of some of the passages of the Song. For example, one well-known German exegete of the last century wrote this about verse 5: The one "who supposes a particular reference in the young gazelles to the dark-colored nipples of her breasts as their especial charm, and in the lilies to the snowy whiteness of her bosom is inadmissible, and leads to what is a violation of good taste or to what is obscene."[5] But because God has included it in Scripture, and He is holy, this description cannot be obscene.

Still, some Christians believe that mentioning the words *breasts* and *the Bible* in the same sentence seems sacrilegious. But as we shall see, the Song refers to Tirzah's breasts many times. The book of Proverbs also proclaims that a wife's breasts are to satisfy her husband at all times (see 5:19).

Solomon to Tirzah: "Until the cool of the day when the shadows flee away, I will go to the mountain of myrrh and to the hill of frankincense." (verse 6)

This appears to be synonymous parallelism — the first item (mountain of myrrh) is synonymous with the second (hill of frankincense). Thus the mountain of myrrh and the hill of frankincense refer to the same thing. But what do they represent? Both Song 4:12-14 and 4:16–5:1 use a garden to symbolically refer to the female genitals.[6] In both passages, myrrh and frankincense are described as characteristic scents of Tirzah's "garden."

Thus, when Solomon says he will go "to the mountain of myrrh and the hill of frankincense," he speaks of his desire for intercourse. This interpretation is reinforced by the fact that Solomon's praises and caresses start at his wife's head and work downward. Note the sequence:

- eyes — like doves
- hair — long and black
- teeth — white and smooth
- lips — red and lovely
- cheeks — red
- neck — erect
- breasts — full and youthful
- "garden"—erotically scented

Solomon now sums up the beauty of his bride.

Solomon to Tirzah: "You are altogether beautiful, my darling, and there is no blemish in you." (verse 7)

It is as if Solomon steps back and reflects on the whole package, this wonderful gift from God that is his wife. He exclaims, "From head to toe, my Tirzah is sublime." Some commentators have suggested that Solomon is not summarizing his bride's appearance here but her character. It is likely both assessments are valid, because inner beauty often manifests itself in outer beauty.

Solomon to Tirzah: "Come with me from Lebanon, my bride, may you come with me from Lebanon. Journey down from the summit of Amana, from the summit of Senir and Hermon, from the dens of lions, from the mountains of leopards." (verse 8)

This is quite a switch. What is going on? Aren't they in a bridal chamber in Jerusalem? It is obvious from the previous verses that Solomon's praise was accelerating the pace of their lovemaking, but with this verse it looks as if he puts on the brakes by changing the topic of conversation. This seems odd and extremely unromantic given that this was their wedding night. What groom wants to pause in the midst of passion?

Scholars throughout the ages have disagreed about the meaning of this passage. Is Solomon asking his bride to "come away *with* him to Lebanon" or "come *from* the heights of Lebanon"? The original Hebrew is obscure; no preposition is provided. Also, it isn't clear if Solomon is speaking here in sexual imagery or if he is speaking of an actual geographic location.

Those who believe that this is sexual imagery suggest that the passage is a clear description of sexual climax — moving higher and higher to the greatest physical ecstasy possible.[7] According to this view, a modern translation of Solomon's words might be, "Come away with me and together we will scale the heights of passion, see things we've never seen before, and experience the wild and erotic."

There is another way of viewing the passage, however, that seems to us to make more sense. Tirzah is not, of course, literally in Lebanon but is nostalgically thinking of the country home she left. The contrast between where she was raised and the events of the past days must have been striking. We would not be speculating too much if we imagined that she felt somewhat out of place and insecure in her new surroundings. Solomon is sensitively aware of her thoughts. He invites her to set them aside and come with him into his loving embrace.

APPLYING THE SONG TO COUPLES

Once again, Solomon piles on the praise. Does Tirzah ever tire of hearing how wonderful she is? We doubt it. The fact that praise is a repeated pattern in the Song speaks to us about the significant role praise should play in a marriage relationship. However, because we dealt extensively with the subject of praise in chapter 2, here we want to focus on the mood created by Solomon's praise — the mood of romance.

Solomon wins the prize for the most romantic husband of the year. Remember, this is his wedding night. No doubt he is eager to make love to his wife's body, but first he makes love to her soul by sensitively meeting her emotional needs. Step into Tirzah's bejeweled slippers for a moment. Less than a month ago she had been walking barefoot in the vineyards near her home in the mountains of Lebanon. In the past week she had been transported south in a gala wedding procession, been placed in the splendid palace, and officiated at a wedding banquet, and now she finds herself alone with her new husband, the king. Wedding jitters and the magnitude of becoming a wife would be enough to make any bride anxious, but Tirzah had other concerns as well. We know she felt insecure about her appearance (see 1:5-6; 2:1-2) and it's likely that this country girl was overwhelmed by her new position as queen, as evidenced by her daydreams about her home in Lebanon.

Solomon is aware of Tirzah's misgivings. First, he invites her to forsake her musings about her country home and come "with me," that is, into the safety of his embrace. Then, he assures her that she is beautiful (see 4:1-7) and desirable. Their loveplay is relaxed and unrushed. This king knows how to be a servant lover! He longs to be intimate with his new bride, yet he sets aside his own desires in order to meet the heart needs of his wife.

Wow Your Mate with Romance

Sex is not an event — it's an environment. It's not an act — it's an atmosphere. Romance creates the atmosphere for intoxicating sex. Dennis and Barbara Rainey define romance this way: "Romance is not the foundation of a marriage. It is the fire in the fireplace."[8] The Song defines the atmosphere of romantic love for us in tangible ways. But before we talk about what romance is, let us first explain what it is not.

Romance is not Elmer.[9] Elmer arrives home from work, nods briefly to the kids, grunts to his wife, asks if there was anything in the mail, and then lets his mind be stimulated by blankly staring at the six o'clock news.

"Shhh," his wife says to the children, "don't make any noise. Daddy is trying to watch television."

At exactly the right time, his wife tiptoes into the den and says, "Dear, dinner is ready." (Elmer gets very upset when his dinner isn't ready on time.) He shares the latest moves in the office games, and she describes struggles with her part-time job and the children's misbehaviors. Wow! Exciting evening. Elmer burps his way through dinner and then leaves his wife to clean up the kitchen, diaper the baby, do the laundry, vacuum the house, and write an e-mail to his parents. She falls asleep totally exhausted about 10:00 PM. In the meantime, Elmer dozes off in front of "Tuesday Night at the Movies."

Suddenly, about 1:00 AM Elmer is jolted awake by a blaring commercial. He turns off the television set, dons his Roman toga, puts on a crown of ivy leaves, crashes into the bedroom and shouts, "Let the games begin." Elmer wants "play-time" before he goes "nite-nite." And of course his wife's supposed to be aroused and excited. Being very considerate, Elmer may even give her sixty seconds before favoring her with his "Let's get down to business" virility. Elmer just can't understand why his wife isn't passionately responding to his every initiative!

Nor is romance Thelma. It's Wednesday. Thelma grudgingly responds to her husband's overtures with a sigh, *Oh, brother, I can't believe he wants sex again.* She puts on her favorite flannel shirt with the rip under the left arm. They kiss for exactly 2.2 seconds while she forces herself not to think about the release form she forgot to sign for their daughter's field trip. Mechanically, she touches him using the same motions she always uses. He rubs her in the same spot, using pre-dictable pressure as she inwardly moans, *How long is this going to take?* Two moves later, they are in position. One minute more and she rolls over and turns out the light. She sarcastically mutters under her breath loud enough for her husband to hear, "Another exciting evening of romance at the Toziers' house."

Romance is Solomon. He romanced Tirzah with the *unexpected,* the *imprac-tical,* and the *intentional.* Let's look at each of these concepts and consider ways we can apply them today to enhance romance in our marriages.

ROMANCE EACH OTHER WITH THE UNEXPECTED

Solomon surprised his wife with a lavish bedroom constructed with cedars from Lebanon (see 1:16-17). The message this sent to her was, "You have sacrificed your home for me, so I am bringing a bit of your home to you." He placed romance as a priority when he left his demanding responsibilities in order to have a romantic rendezvous with his wife in the country (see 7:11). Today a hus-band can romance his wife by offering her a single long-stemmed rose for no reason, other than "I love you." A wife can romance her husband by surprising him with a new transparent, low-cut teddy after the kids have gone to bed.

Darryl used the unexpected to redeem an evening that was headed for dis-aster. He and Kit were dressing to go to a friend's wedding when they had what they describe as a knock-down, drag-out fight (fortunately, only words were hurled, no pots and pans). Darryl stomped out of the bedroom in a huff. As Kit slipped into her beautiful dress, she thought, *This is the* last *man on earth I want to be with right now.* About fifteen minutes later, the doorbell rang. When she opened the door, surprise! There stood Darryl dressed in a tux, holding a bouquet of roses. But he looked different; he had on a hat and sunglasses. And he talked differently — with an Italian accent. The rose bearer announced, "My name is Ramon. I received news that your pigheaded husband was a brute to you, so I have come to escort you to the wedding in his place. Come, my Precious Rose, and on the way you can talk to me about this imbecile you are married to." "Ramon" took Kit to the wedding. They laughed and danced, and later they made passionate love. Darryl awoke with a smile on his face.

Several years ago, Jody unexpectedly surprised Linda. They were on their way to Europe to speak at a conference. During the plane ride, he handed her a sealed envelope containing a poem and tickets to two musicals in London. Instead of going straight to the conference, Jody was whisking his beloved away for two nights of romance and love.

Mark put together a group of men who were determined to love their wives sacrificially. They called themselves Men of the Titanic. For six months, the men planned every detail of a special surprise evening for their wives. First, the wives received hand-written invitations. Then, on the special night, limousines arrived and the wives were taken to a banquet hall the men had rented. Harp music greeted the ladies as they were escorted to their seats, where an embroidered napkin and flower awaited each one. Then, their husbands served them a six-course meal — an exact replica of the first-class dining menu on the *Titanic*. The men even sang love songs to their wives between the courses! Afterward, the men each read aloud a love letter they wrote to their wives. They are now planning another special adventure involving medieval romance.[10]

Surprises don't have to be a big production, such as showing up at a wedding using a different personality, seeing plays in London, or reenacting a meal on the Titanic. Sometimes the little things mean the most. One night, Brandon laid his head on the pillow and discovered that his wife had used glow-in-the-dark stars to write him a love message on their bedroom ceiling. The words glowed, "You are my lover and my friend."

ROMANCE EACH OTHER WITH THE IMPRACTICAL

Not only did Solomon romance his bride with the unexpected but he was also at times extravagant and impractical. It must have been very expensive for him to bring cedars from Lebanon to build their bedroom sanctuary. He could have used a local wood, but that wouldn't have sent Tirzah as powerful a message of his love for her. He also lavished her with gifts of jewelry (see 1:11) and gifts of time. How did a busy king have time to frolic through the vineyards with his wife (see 7:11)?

The classic story of *The Gift of the Magi* illustrates the kind of impractical romance we are advocating. Here's the story: Della, the wife, sacrificially cuts her beautiful, long hair in order to buy Jim, her husband, a gold chain for his watch for Christmas. Meanwhile, he has sold his watch to buy combs for her hair. What they did was impractical, yet their actions demonstrate what it means to be a servant lover. And even though Della no longer needed the combs and Jim no longer needed the gold chain, we have no trouble imagining how loved each of them felt.

Have you ever done something romantic for your spouse that was extravagant? Or does your desire to be practical get in the way? Maybe you tend to think that it's not a strategic way to spend money, that you're too old for that sort of thing, or that you should wait until you've fulfilled all of your other responsibilities.

If so, we encourage you to be willing to take a risk. Please understand. We are not advocating irresponsibility. We aren't encouraging you to take out a second mortgage so that you can surprise your spouse with a trip to Europe or to go into credit card debt to buy a special gift. (Remember, Solomon had the money to purchase those cedars and ship them to Jerusalem!) We're simply pointing out that it's possible to be so practical that romance gets squelched. Your husband may need a new drill to the point of desperation or your wife's blender may have mixed its last protein drink. While drills and blenders are practical gifts, they do not make the needle on the romance meter soar. Save your money and buy the necklace she longs to possess or the golf clubs of his dreams.

What can you give from your time, love, hard work, or savings that would make your mate feel as cherished? Is it redoing your bedroom to create a romantic mood? Is it a night under the stars together? Or maybe helping your mate

achieve a dream that's always seemed out of reach? Put on your thinking cap —
we know you can come up with just the right thing. Here's what Peter did:

> Lorraine and I had been married five years and were saving every spare
> penny to purchase our first home. Going out for dinner? Never! (Unless
> it were McDonald's.) We shopped at garage sales and clipped coupons.
> We pledged never to spend more than fifty dollars without consulting the
> other. But it was our anniversary, and it was time to be impractical. "Dress
> up really nice, darlin', 'cause I have plans." I drove Lorraine to Long Beach
> Harbor in Southern California where we boarded the HMS *Queen Mary*
> ship. We were seated at Sir Winston Churchill Restaurant, a five-star din-
> ing experience overlooking the harbor lights. I knew Lorraine gulped
> inwardly, thinking, *How can we afford this?* I handed her an anniversary
> card. Inside were messages of my undying love for her and an entertain-
> ment coupon for a "two-for-one dining experience on the Queen Mary."
> She was thrilled. Yes, our evening was impractical but not undoable, and I
> could tell by the fact that her foot was stroking my leg under the table that
> she would relish every moment of being pampered like a queen.

Larry and Renee had dreamed for years about going to an exotic tropical
island together, but other priorities surfaced. The washing machine broke.
One child needed speech therapy, while the other needed braces. Meanwhile,
Larry received a modest raise at work and secretly began putting away fifty
dollars a month in a separate account so he could take Renee to her dream
island. Two months before their departure date, Larry told Renee, "We are
going away for a week, so please mark these days on your calendar. Every
Saturday morning, you will receive one clue about where we are going." In
large letters, Larry wrote on a sheet of paper, "Look under our bed for all the
details." Then he cut the paper into six puzzle pieces. Each week, he gave
Renee a "puzzle piece." On the sixth week, after putting all the pieces together,
she ran to the bedroom, looked under the bed, and discovered a box filled with
brochures, airplane tickets, and even a suggested itinerary. Larry says, "Yeah,
we spent a wad. But we fulfilled a dream, and it was worth every penny."

ROMANCE EACH OTHER WITH THE INTENTIONAL

Wise man that he was, Solomon understood that sometimes even the unexpected and the impractical must be planned. Solomon was intentional in his love for Tirzah. He planned a date (see Song 2:8-17) and cleared his schedule for a vacation so they could spend time loving one another (see 7:11–8:14). When she felt insecure about herself, he was intentional with his words, praising every part of her body (see 4:1-8).

Of course, romance can be spontaneous, such as embracing under a full moon and enjoying the sweetness of a kiss that makes your bones ache, or walking hand in hand by the seashore. When such moments occur, we need to pause and drink them in. But the majority of romantic moments in marriage are the result of intention. In other words, we schedule, we prepare, and we implement. In our hectic lives, romance will get crowded out unless we are intentional about it.

It's not intentional (or romantic) when a husband tosses the newspaper at his wife while he's flipping through the television channels and says, "Honey, why don't you see if there is anything on at the movies and call and get a babysitter?" If a husband wants to romance his wife, *he* needs to plan the evening, line up the babysitter, and take her to the movie, just as he did *before* they were married — just the two of them. Going out with another couple is great, but it is not romantic, nor is it a date. A date is one husband and one wife, not a crowd. When couples go out with other couples, the wives spend the evening talking to one another and the husbands do the same. This is going out with friends, not going out on a date.

Even though *intentional* means "planned," it can look spontaneous. For instance, let's say a husband and his wife are out window shopping downtown one evening. He casually says, "Why don't we stop in this store for a moment and look?" If she doesn't faint when he says this, she may faint when the clerk behind the counter says, "Excuse me, are you Mrs. Jones? I have a little gift for you." Her husband had purchased her a gift the day before, had it wrapped, and asked the salesperson to join in on his romantic plan.

Or adapt this idea for dinner. You just happen to go by your favorite restaurant, which is always packed, and you say, "Let's see if they have a table." She is hesitant, but you convince her. As expected, twenty-five people are waiting to be seated, and the hostess informs you it will be about an hour and a half before you can get a table. Just at that moment, the headwaiter arrives and says, "Good evening, Mr. Jones. We have your table for two right over here, overlooking the lights of the city." That's romance! That's planning that appears spontaneous.

Are you thinking that neither of you is good at coming up with creative dates? You are in luck, because we surveyed thousands of couples and included some of their most creative ideas in chapter 15. *Ten Great Dates,* by David and Claudia Arp, also offers date suggestions as well as communication exercises. But if you want an entire year's worth of creative date ideas in one box, try *Simply Romantic Nights,* a product Linda and Lorraine helped create with Family Life Today. This boxed product includes a book; "His and Her Romance Inventories," which will help you know how your mate spells romance; and a series of sealed envelopes — twelve for him and twelve for her. Inside each envelope is everything you need for creating a romantic night (or day) for your mate. Some of the dates are sexual ("Sex in a Shoebox"); others are romantic ("As You Wish"). All can help put fun and romance back into your intimacy. (You can order *Simply Romantic Nights* online at www.intimateissues.com.)

We hope this chapter has inspired you to nurture the romance in your marriage. Romance is one of the sparks that will ignite intimacy and keep the flame of your love burning. For that reason, we encourage you to take a few minutes to do the following:

- ⚭ Each of you write out your own definition of romance.
- ⚭ List two romantic things your spouse has done for you in the past.
- ⚭ List two romantic things you would enjoy for your spouse to do in the future.

Now it's time to put what you have read into practice. Take action! Romance is the fire in the fireplace of your marriage. So venture out and romance one another. Do the unexpected. Be impractical. Be intentional. What you reap in your intimacy will be well worth your effort!

SERVANT LOVERS: Are romantic, in and out of bed.

SELFISH LOVERS: Are unwilling to invest the time, energy, and effort to romance their mate.

SOLOMON TO TIRZAH:
"You have made my heart beat faster, my sister, my bride;
You have made my heart beat faster
with a single glance of your eyes,
With a single strand of your necklace.
How beautiful is your love, my sister, my bride!
How much better is your love than wine,
And the fragrance of your oils
Than all kinds of spices!
Your lips, my bride, drip honey;
Honey and milk are under your tongue,
And the fragrance of your garments is like
the fragrance of Lebanon.
A garden locked is my sister, my bride,
A rock garden locked, a spring sealed up.
Your shoots are an orchard of pomegranates
With choice fruits, henna with nard plants,
Nard and saffron, calamus and cinnamon,
With all the trees of frankincense,
Myrrh and aloes, along with all the finest spices.
You are a garden spring,
A well of fresh water,
And streams flowing from Lebanon."

TIRZAH TO SOLOMON:
"Awake, O north wind,
And come, wind of the south;
Make my garden breathe out fragrance,
Let its spices be wafted abroad.
May my beloved come into his garden
And eat its choice fruits!"

SOLOMON TO TIRZAH:
"I have come into my garden, my sister, my bride;
I have gathered my myrrh along with my balsam.
I have eaten my honeycomb and my honey;
I have drunk my wine and my milk."

GOD TO THE COUPLE:
"Eat, friends;
Drink and imbibe deeply, O lovers."

SONG OF SOLOMON 4:9–5:1

chapter ten

Give Your Body as a Gift

*"Our God, who is spirit, can be found behind the very
physical panting, sweating, and pleasurable entangling of limbs and
body parts. He doesn't turn away. He wants us to run into sex but to do so
with his presence, priorities, and virtues marking our pursuit."*[1]

In the last scene, we left Solomon and Tirzah in the heat of the moment. Solomon had just awakened desire in his bride. As we reenter the bridal chamber, we see a lot of pleasurable entangling going on. The sexual temperature is near the boiling point and . . . well, we'll let you see for yourself.

UNDERSTANDING THE SONG

Solomon to Tirzah: "You have made my heart beat faster, my sister, my bride; you have made my heart beat faster with a single glance of your eyes, with a single strand of your necklace." (4:9)

The king's heart is pumping! That enticing look of hers is driving him wild. Solomon literally says, "You have inflamed every cell of my body with desire, and I want you so badly I'm about to explode."

Solomon to Tirzah: "How beautiful is your love, my sister, my bride!" (verse 10)

In the Western world, a husband would not call his wife his sister, but to Tirzah's ears, this was a term of endearment.[2] The *New Living Translation* paraphrase reads, "How sweet is your love, my treasure, my bride!"

Solomon to Tirzah: "*How much better is your love than wine, and the fragrance of your oils than all kinds of spices!*" *(verse 10)*

The word *love* (*dod*) refers to Tirzah's skill in sexual love. Specifically, it refers to her sexual passion for Solomon: It is better to him than wine.[3] In Song 1:2, Tirzah says that Solomon's lovemaking is sweeter than wine, and in this verse he says the same about her skill as a lover. Her caresses, embraces, and sensuous touch intoxicate him more than any wine. And her oils, those she naturally produces, are more fragrant to him than the world's storehouse of frankincense and myrrh. The contrast here seems to be between naturally produced "oils" (the moisture associated with feminine passion) and manufactured perfumes. As you can see, things are heating up!

Solomon to Tirzah: "*Your lips, my bride, drip honey; honey and milk are under your tongue, and the fragrance of your garments is like the fragrance of Lebanon.*" *(verse 11)*

Here, Solomon compliments his bride on the sweetness of her kisses. Some mistakenly believe that a certain kind of kissing originated in France; however, Solomon discovered milk and honey (words suggesting abundant pleasure) under his bride's tongue long before the French named the kiss.

The way the garment displayed Tirzah's body took Solomon's breath away. It seems to have been created from a *very* transparent fabric, because her adoring husband clearly described every part of her body, including her breasts and private "garden."

The verses that follow are some of the most important of the Song, and they lead up to the climax of the book, the consummation of the sexual union.

Solomon to Tirzah: "*A garden locked is my sister, my bride, a rock garden locked, a spring sealed up. Your shoots are an orchard of pomegranates with choice fruits, henna with nard plants, nard and saffron, calamus and cinnamon, with all the trees of frankincense, myrrh and aloes, along with all the finest spices. You are a garden spring, a well of fresh water, and streams flowing from Lebanon.*" *(verses 12-15)*

Solomon is growing ever more excited as he describes in poetic imagery the most intimate part of Tirzah's body as "a locked garden" and "a garden paradise."

A locked garden: This image praises Tirzah's virginity. In Palestine, rock walls surrounded gardens and vineyards in order to prevent strangers from intruding. Only the lawful owner of the garden could enter, and Solomon is this privileged one.

As pointed out earlier, the word *garden* is a reference to Tirzah's vagina.[4] This word usage is full of poetic and symbolic beauty. The Hebrew word *gan,* which is translated here as "garden," refers to "a plot of ground protected by a wall or hedge."[5] These areas were irrigated and used to cultivate flowers, fruit, and vegetables. The phrase is ripe with double entendre. Gardens in biblical times were generally walled enclosures that were frequently irrigated (see Isaiah 58:11); they were rich with canals of running water, fountains, sweet-smelling herbs, aromatic blossoms, and convenient places in which to sit and enjoy the ambiance.[6]

To the Hebrews, a garden was a lovely place of shade and refreshment. Only one who has traveled for days in a dry, glaring desert country (such as surrounds Palestine) and has come upon a beautiful shaded garden can appreciate how similar to paradise these gardens can appear. Thus to describe Tirzah's vagina as a garden is to say it is beautiful to behold, like the flowered gardens of Engedi. It is for Solomon an oasis of sexual refreshment.

Tirzah's "garden" is locked, sealed up. Because water was scarce in the East, owners of fountains sealed them with clay that quickly hardened in the sun. Thus, a sealed spring was protected from becoming impure; no one could drink of its water except the rightful owner. Solomon was about to remove the seal from his bride's "garden" and drink deeply of the cool refreshing water.

Solomon rejoiced that Tirzah had kept herself sexually pure. He was confident that her "garden" would remain, throughout their marriage, a "spring sealed up" for only the "rightful owner," her husband. Each of these metaphors conveys the message that Tirzah's sole allegiance is to Solomon. Before marriage, she saved herself for him, and throughout their marriage, she will keep her "garden" closed to all but him. She is exclusively his.

A garden paradise. This locked garden that is for Solomon alone is truly an exotic wonderland. In verse 13, when he says that shoots compose her garden, Solomon uses a different Hebrew word for garden, *pardes* — a word that leads to our English term *paradise.*[7] This "garden paradise" is filled with the choicest fruits and spices.

Tirzah has eagerly taken in all her husband's praise, and with every word he utters, her own desire rises to match his. Up to this point, every recorded word of their wedding night has come from Solomon, but his sensuous imagery has created a sexual ache within her that cries out to be satisfied. Her words now burst forth in invitation.

Tirzah to Solomon: "Awake, O north wind, and come, wind of the south." (verse 16)

The word *awake* in "awake, north wind" is the same as that used in the refrain to the daughters of Jerusalem, "Do not awaken love until it pleases." Previously the warning was do not awaken love, but the time has come to release the floodgate of passion. Abandon restraint! Express fully what has been held back for so long.

Tirzah calls out to the winds of passion, the winds of the north and south to blow upon her "garden." In Palestine, the north wind brings clear weather and removes clouds, and the south wind brings warmth and moisture. When these winds blow across a garden, the combination of sun, rain, and warmth promotes growth. In this verse, Tirzah is asking Solomon to send the winds of passion, to stimulate her "garden" with caresses to promote the growth of her sexual passion.

Tirzah to Solomon: "Make my garden breathe out fragrance, let its spices be wafted abroad." (verse 16)

Another version reads, "Blow on my garden and waft its lovely perfume to my lover" (NLT). "The verb *blow* in reference to the wind is also used in 2:17 and 4:6 in a romantic setting. As the 'winds' blow through her 'garden,' first from one direction and then from another, Tirzah's sexual passion grows and grows until all the fragrance of the garden rises in waves to become a sea of incense."[8] Tirzah completely accepts her femininity and is anxious that Solomon fully experience what she has to offer. She relishes that he is highly aroused by the sight of her "garden" and by caressing it. Fully aroused, Tirzah urges her lover onward.

Tirzah to Solomon: "May my beloved come into his garden and eat its choice fruits!" (verse 16)

Tirzah is anything but passive. Here she eagerly invites Solomon to possess her body. ("The use of the verb *to come into* is a standard Hebrew metaphor for sexual intercourse.")[9] His heart leapt with joy! This banquet of luscious fruit was for him alone. While no one knows just how literally to take the verb *to eat* (and also the verb *to blow)*, there is no doubt that Tirzah is inviting Solomon to sexual union of the most intimate type.[10]

Solomon to Tirzah: "I have come into my garden, my sister, my bride; I have gathered my myrrh along with my balsam. I have eaten my honeycomb and my honey; I have drunk my wine and my milk." (5:1)

Solomon is beside himself. "I have come," "I have gathered," "I have eaten," "I have drunk." He is satiated with pleasure. Nine times he uses the possessive *my*: my garden, my sister, my bride, my myrrh, my balsam, my honeycomb, my honey, my wine, my milk. The delights of his bride's "garden" are overwhelming and exclusively his to enjoy.

This scene is holy and erotic. A husband and wife enjoy the intimate oneness of their first lovemaking experience together. As they lie in each other's arms, wrapped in the afterglow of their love, another presence enters the room, and the scene is momentarily suspended. For the first time in the Song, someone addresses both Solomon and Tirzah together. We want to say, "No! This is private. No visitors allowed," therefore the presence cannot be that of the daughters of Jerusalem. Who could have the status to call the king and the queen "friends" (*rayah*) and "lovers" (*dod*)? Who could encourage the king and queen of Israel to take full pleasure in their erotic love? Who but the Holy

One could be present at their wedding night? It is as if God Himself walks over to the bed and stretches out His hand in a benediction that expresses His delight and affirmation of their union.

> *God to the Couple: "Eat, friends; drink and imbibe deeply, O lovers."* [11] (5:1)

The Hebrew is very strong and carries the thought of intoxication. Imagine! Our Holy God says, "Be intoxicated with your sexual love! What you are doing is good, wholesome, and right. I approve and endorse your abandonment in giving yourselves freely to one another." Our gracious God desires for every married couple to be intoxicated with sexual love, to revel with delight in the gift He has given.

APPLYING THE SONG FOR COUPLES

What a joy for Solomon and Tirzah to know from the onset of their marriage that God wanted them to intoxicate each another with their sexual love. How glorious for them to feel God's hand of blessing on their intimacy.

Has God put a blessing upon your sexual union as a couple? Yes, He has. But have you received it?

RECEIVE GOD'S BLESSING

People who were raised in a strict environment where it was inappropriate to speak of God and sex in the same sentence often separate their sexuality from their spirituality. They find it difficult to believe that a holy God would bless something as "earthy" as sex. In fact, one woman said she has a picture of Jesus hanging by her bed and that before she and her husband make love, they turn the picture to face the wall so that Jesus can't watch what they are doing!

Those who have been sexually traumatized through an event in their pasts or through sexual abuse also might feel hesitant about receiving God's blessing on their intimacy. It is difficult to receive blessing when it is connected to an area of your life that has resulted in much pain. Other couples fail to ask God's blessing on their sexual relationship because they feel they don't deserve it.

That was true for Alec and Rachel. They told us,

> Before we were married, we'd each had several sexual partners. When we received Christ's forgiveness for our sins, we knew God forgave our sexual mistakes as well, but for some reason we still felt guilty — as though God didn't approve. This caused us to feel restrained and inhibited in our lovemaking. When we read that God gave permission for us to be "intoxicated with delight" in our lovemaking, we could hardly believe it! We want this kind of freedom, but we don't know how to make it a reality.

God makes all things new. He wants to bless *your* sexual intimacy; all you have to do is ask Him. But first you must believe that this blessing is for *you*. Will you believe? Will you stop thinking that God's promise is for others but not for you? God gives *you* permission to be intoxicated with delight. Will you give yourself permission? Will you receive the blessing God eagerly desires to give?

If so, then we suggest you follow the advice we gave to Alec and Rachel. The next time you make love, after you have enjoyed being "one" and are still wrapped in one another's arms, close your eyes and pray, *God, please bless our intimacy.* Then visualize Him standing by your bed. See Him lift His hand over you. Hear the words He speaks to you: "Eat friends; drink and imbibe deeply, O lovers."

What we are about to share next is one of the most important concepts in this book because it directly impacts your ability to embrace intimacy as God intended. Read carefully. Read slowly. Ask God to awaken your heart to all that is involved in giving your body as a gift to your mate.

GIVE YOUR BODY AS A GIFT

Do you remember the table piled high with gifts at your wedding reception? Those gifts were expressions of love, a way for family and friends to bless your new life together as husband and wife. God also gave you a gift, but it wasn't wrapped in a big box with a silver bow. Instead, He put His gift inside a package called "you." God gave you and your mate the gift of sexual desire for one another.

God's gift came with a set of instructions that, when followed, would provide maximum pleasure. What is God's plan? On the wedding night, a husband and wife are to participate in a "gift exchange."[12] In this gift exchange, a husband gives the gift of his body to his wife, and a wife gives the gift of her body to her husband. Sound fun? It is! And it's exciting — the best gift you can open. God means for you to enjoy His gift, but giving the gift, as we see in this verse, also means giving authority of your body to your mate:

> The wife does not have authority over her own body, but the husband does; and likewise also the husband does not have authority over his own body, but the wife does. (1 Corinthians 7:4)

The word *authority*, which means "to rule or have control over," evokes a variety of reactions among husbands and wives. Some couples find it easy to give authority of their body to their mate. These couples tell us that the mutual trust that exists between them enables them to experience great freedom and fun in their sexual relationship. They flow with one another because they focus on pleasing the other person rather than on pleasing themselves, which, as you already know, is at the heart of becoming a servant lover.

However, others find it challenging to give their spouse authority over their body. Although the reasons for this vary among husbands and wives, the result is the same. Both can give their bodies through sex, but something prevents them from giving complete authority to their mate and, as a result, they withhold a small part of themselves. Let's examine this problem — and the solution — first from a wife's point of view and then from the husband's.

APPLYING THE SONG FOR WIVES

For a wife to give authority of her body to her husband is to say:

◊ I entrust my body to you — it is no longer mine but yours.

◊ I yield my body freely as a vessel to give and receive love.

◊ I am forever only yours — all of me.

But for some women, not only is this difficult but it can initially be frightening. Lorraine tells her story:

For years, the words *authority* and *submit* made me cringe inside, even though I didn't know why. Then one day, God and I had a conversation about I Corinthians 7:4 that went something like this:

"I don't like this verse, God. I don't want to give authority of my body to Peter."

Why not? You love him, don't you?

"Yes, I love him. And I give him my body through sex. But does he have to *own* it as well?"

Silence.

"God, I want to obey you, but this is a lot to ask. I want to give authority of my body to Peter, but it's just that, well, I'm afraid."

Why are you afraid?

Now it was my turn for silence, because I really didn't know.

Are you afraid of Peter?

"No."

Then what?

It was a few moments before I could answer, but when I did, the truth of my words rocked me.

"I don't want to give Peter authority of my body because then I'll no longer be in control."

Fear. I was afraid to give up control. Why? Not because of Peter but because of something else. Suddenly, my mind raced back through the years and pulled out a scene I'd stuffed into a locked closet in my mind: a seventeen-year-old boy on top of me, intent on raping me. My fists pounded his chest. *Get off me!* Screams. Terror. Helplessness. *Stop! I can't make him stop!*

God saved me from the worst, but the damage was still done. I saw myself as I was then: a frightened teen with a look of steel on my face that declared, *No one will ever have control over me again.*

"Oh God, oh God, it was so scary," I sobbed.

Yes, dear one, but Peter is not *that boy.*

"I know."

He wants to love you, not to harm you.

"Yes."

Will you love him as I've asked?

I knew that the freedom I longed for in our sexual relationship was connected to giving authority of my body to Peter. Giving him authority wasn't something that happened overnight, but through a series of choices, I gave more and more of myself until finally he had all of me. Am I ever tempted to be selfish and take back control? Yes. But I've discovered that since crossing the line into obedience, there is new freedom and joy in our intimacy.

LETTER TO THE ONE WHO HAS BEEN SEXUALLY ABUSED

Dear Friend,

We can only imagine the pain and heartache that your abuse has brought to your lovemaking, and we are so, so sorry. We cling to Jesus and His promise that He is a God of healing and hope. He wants you to heal so that you can put the past behind and wholly enjoy the gift of sex. Forgiveness is a process and does not happen overnight — we realize this — and it is God who brings healing in His time and in His way.

As you read these next few chapters, please know that we are in no way trying to minimize the grievous wounds you have experienced. God aches for your pain and He cries with you. We also know that sexual abuse makes intimacy difficult and seemingly impossible at times. This is where tenderness, sensitivity, and much, much prayer are needed. God can use the pain of your past to draw you not only closer to each other but also closer to Him.

Our prayer is that together you will stand against the evil that was done to you personally and to your marriage. We pray you will seek the help of a wise mentor, pastor, or trained professional, or read sensitively written books such as The Wounded Heart, by Dan Allender. Please do not give up. You can be healed. Go forward and claim the freedom that God wants for you in your sexual relationship.

With love and prayers,

Linda, Jody, Peter, and Lorraine

While some women withhold a part of themselves because of sexual abuse and rape, others do so because they feel guilty over choices they made in the past. As a college student, Kathy had given her body to her boyfriend. Kathy was a Christian and knew that sex before marriage was wrong, but she had engaged in it anyway. Guilt climbed on her back and refused to leave. Several years later, Kathy met and married Jake. He forgave Kathy for her past. She knew God had forgiven her as well, but the forgiveness in her head hadn't reached her heart. She knew she needed help because she didn't enjoy sex and it was causing a strain on her relationship with her husband. Linda relays what happened:

> When Kathy told me her situation, I asked her, "Is it possible that you fail to enter fully into the enjoyment of sex because by withholding pleasure, you are proving to God how sorry you are for what you did before you married?"
>
> She thought for a moment and then said, "I've never thought about that before, but I think you are right."
>
> "Kathy," I continued, "I think the forgiveness you understand in your mind will sink down into your emotions if you take a significant action toward loving your husband as God says he is to be loved." I opened my Bible to 1 Corinthians 7:4. As we looked at the verse together, I explained that it was God's plan that on the wedding night, a husband and wife were to participate in a "gift exchange" by giving authority of their bodies to one another.
>
> "Based on this verse, what action do you think God would want you to take toward Jake?"
>
> "Well, Valentine's Day is next Saturday. I can't think of a better gift to give him."
>
> Kathy called me a week later and said, "Linda, I copied pages of my journal about my Valentine's night with Jake for you because I think what happened to me may help other women."
>
> Here is what Kathy wrote:
>
> "February 14: Tonight is the night I give my body to my husband. Honestly, I'm nervous. Why? This is what You desire of me, God. Why am I so nervous?

"February 15: Last night was a sweet evening. I told Jake when I gave my body to him that I never really fully gave my body when we were married. There were lots of ifs and nos. Depending on my mood, I would give a little of my body or all of my body but always it was *my* decision for it was *my* body. So with a ribbon on and nothing else, I stood before him and offered myself. He wept. Do I feel different? Yes! It is a constant reminder that I am his, a visual memory that this body belongs to him."

This past Valentine's Day, Kathy told us that her choice to stand before Jake clad in her bow was the beginning of a new sexual relationship. The action of giving authority of her body to Jake in a creative way released her to walk in forgiveness and freed her to enjoy sexual intimacy with her husband. We've told Kathy's story at various Intimate Issues conferences around the country, and it's inspired creative responses from thousands of women. Here's an example:

I knew I had to do the bow thing soon or I would chicken out, so I decided that night was the night. I couldn't find any ribbon in the house, but I did find a package of stick-on bows and figured they could do the job.

Later that evening, dressed in only my birthday suit, I stuck bows all over my body in appropriate places. Attired in only bows, I sat beside my husband on the edge of the bed and explained what I had learned from 1 Corinthians 7. I told him that I'd never given authority of my body to him and that I was doing that now. My body was my gift to him. Then I invited him to "unwrap" me. He reached for a sticky bow. He tugged and tugged, but the bows would not come off! We rolled around on the bed, laughing until we both cried. I'll never forget that night. Not only was it a significant moment for us because it deepened our oneness, but it felt so good to laugh together.

Dear wife, have you given your body as a gift to your husband? If not, what would God want you to do?

APPLYING THE SONG FOR HUSBANDS

While the bow idea appeals to wives — and to their husbands — very few men are inclined to don a bow.

We asked the men in our field-test *Intimacy Ignited* Bible study what it meant for them to hand over authority of their body to their wife. Most admitted they hadn't given it much thought, but as we discussed the matter, Terry verbalized what many seemed to believe:

> I don't think men struggle with giving authority of their body to their wives. You want authority? Take it. It's yours. Do whatever you want, once, twice. Given the chance, we would gladly submit authority of our bodies to our wives in the morning, afternoon, evening, and middle of the night and twice on Sunday, Tuesday, and Thursday. I think this is one of the mysteries that men battle with. Why don't women have this same attitude?

For most men, the issue is not the "giving over" part but rather the idea of "giving up." To give authority of your body to your wife involves sacrifice. Some husbands feel that after they are married they should never have to exercise self-restraint again because, after all, they now have a wife who is supposed to satisfy their sexual needs. But giving authority of your body to your wife means there will be times you must deny your own sexual desire so you can serve her. Here's a case in point:

> After my wife's hysterectomy, the doctor told her, "Your body needs to heal. No sex for six weeks." Instead of empathizing with Martha about the operation, I whined inside, *Six weeks without sex? I'll turn into a serial killer.* But then a voice inside me whispered, "Bill, this is your opportunity to give control of your body to Martha." *What do you mean, Lord? I don't understand.* The Lord reminded me of the many times Martha had spoken my love language — sex — even when she wasn't up to it. Now it was my turn to speak her love language — service. For the next six weeks, I picked up after the kids, drove them to their activities,

vacuumed the house, gave Martha foot rubs, and even did the laundry. (Most of my underwear is now pink.) In all honesty, I was often tempted to take sexual matters into my own hands, so to speak, but I knew this wasn't the answer. God was teaching me self-discipline. I went to Him often and prayed that He would replace my sexual desire with a desire to serve my wife. He did because He is faithful — and so was I.

Jesus said, "If anyone wishes to come after Me, he must deny himself, and take up his cross and follow Me" (Mark 8:34). At times, following Jesus and being a servant lover means denying your sexual needs in order to serve your wife.

Keep Your Eyes on Your Wife

Giving authority of your body also means committing to lifetime exclusivity.

We like this quote from Aristotle: "Now a virtuous wife is best honored when she sees that her husband is faithful to her and has no preference for another woman but before all others loves and trusts her and holds her as his own." Husbands, your body belongs to only your wife. You, in turn, are to look at *only* her, think of *only* her, and be sexually satisfied by her love *only*.

To give authority is to say to your wife:

  ◊ I will make a covenant with my eyes never to look lustfully at another woman, whether in the flesh, in my mind, on a piece of paper, or on a computer screen.

  ◊ I will turn to only you to meet my sexual needs.

  ◊ I will be sexually faithful to you.

To give your wife authority over your body means she is to possess all of you, even your eyes. Job 31:1 says, "I made a covenant with my eyes not to look lustfully at a girl" (NIV). Here's Jody's take on it:

> Like Job, I made a covenant with my eyes because not only does Linda need to know that I notice her, she needs to know that I do not notice other women, at least not beyond a casual glance. I was inspired to make this covenant after reading the resolutions of Jonathan Edwards.

I realized one way I could honor Linda was to adopt Edwards' practice, to make a resolution that I would never be unfaithful to her in thought or deed. It has been surprisingly easy to keep once my mind was set.

Making a covenant is one way to manage your eyes. The authors of *Every Man's Battle* suggest two other practical possibilities:

- *Bounce the eyes* — this is the process of training your eyes to immediately "bounce" away from sights of pretty women or sensual images. They say if you can "bounce your eyes" for six weeks, you can win the battle of sexual temptation.
- *Starve the eyes* — this is a conscious choice not to expose yourself to any image or activity that might produce sexual gratification outside of marriage.[13]

Joel, a missionary, practiced none of these techniques. He had roving eyes. His lovely wife, Colleen, couldn't help but notice. Where was he looking now? What busty blonde were his eyes glued to today? Colleen repeatedly told her husband that his wandering eyes made her feel unloved and angry, but he laughed off her comments, telling her that he was faithful to her, so what did it matter? Wasn't his fidelity enough? When he heard us teach that for a husband to give authority of his body to his wife means that his eyes belong to her, Joel realized that he had been selfish and wrong. He wrote the following to his wife:

> Colleen, today, February 4, 2004, I give my body to you. I give every part — including my eyes. From this day forward, I will look only at you.

Proverbs says that a man is to be delighted sexually by *only* his wife. His eyes, mind, heart, and body are to be refreshed by her love alone:

> Drink water from your own cistern
> And fresh water from your own well.
> Should your springs be dispersed abroad,
> Streams of water in the streets?

Let them be yours alone
And not for strangers with you.
Let your fountain be blessed
And rejoice in the wife of your youth.
As a loving hind and a graceful doe,
Let her breasts satisfy you at all times;
Be exhilarated always with her love. (5:15-19)

God desires that a couple be exhilarated with one another's love. Solomon and Tirzah understood this from the beginning. God is gracious to allow us to share in the joy of their wedding night and see the beauty of their gift exchange so that we might have an example to follow.

How do servant lovers respond to the images of the blessing of God and the gift exchange? Servant lovers say, "Yes, God. We acknowledge that You want to bless our intimacy and we gratefully receive Your blessing. We see the beauty of the gift exchange and desire to give authority of our bodies to each other." Servant lovers want to please God, and they want to delight one another. A willing spirit can ignite intimacy in your marriage and open you up to new delights and possibilities.

In other chapters, we've asked you to pray about some issue we've raised. But this time, *we want to pray for you.* We extend our hand of blessing over you and pray,

> *Lord, bless this couple. Bless their intimate moments. Infuse them with your Holy Spirit so they may obey Your Word and be servant lovers to one another. Lord, where there is hurt, bring healing. Where there is discouragement, bring hope. Let them love freely, honestly, passionately, completely. May the flame of their love burn strong and bright so that they might be a reflection of You. Amen.*

SERVANT LOVERS: Give the gift of their body to their mate.

SELFISH LOVERS: Say, "My body is my own and I'll give it when it suits me."

Keep the Flame Burning

TIRZAH TO CHORUS:
"I was asleep but my heart was awake.
A voice! My beloved was knocking."

SOLOMON TO TIRZAH:
"Open to me, my sister, my darling,
My dove, my perfect one!
For my head is drenched with dew,
My locks with the damp of the night."

TIRZAH TO SOLOMON:
"I have taken off my dress,
How can I put it on again?
I have washed my feet,
How can I dirty them again?"

TIRZAH TO CHORUS:
"*My beloved extended his hand through the opening,*
And my feelings were aroused for him.
I arose to open to my beloved;
And my hands dripped with myrrh,
And my fingers with liquid myrrh,
On the handles of the bolt.
I opened to my beloved,
But my beloved had turned away and had gone!
My heart went out to him as he spoke.
I searched for him but I did not find him;
I called him but he did not answer me.
The watchmen who make the rounds in the city found me,
They struck me and wounded me;
The guardsmen of the walls took away my shawl from me.
I adjure you, O daughters of Jerusalem,
If you find my beloved,
As to what you will tell him:
For I am lovesick."

SONG OF SOLOMON 5:2-8

chapter eleven

Stamp Out Selfishness

"Josey has a cute body and it drives me crazy. But she says she doesn't want sex.
It's been months since we've had intercourse. Finally, I put my foot down and
told her something had to change. Is it so wrong to want to be
intimate with my wife and have fun with her?"

But Josey has a different perspective: "Franklin does nothing all day to help
me around the house or with the kids. On the weekend, he leaves me home
to mow the yard while he goes to a football game with the guys.
He hardly says two words to me, except when he wants sex.
Well, I have two words for him: *No way*."

God does not sugarcoat the subject of sex in His Word. He knows that along
with the delight of sexual intimacy also comes difficulties. Up to this point, the
Song has shown us the ideal of marriage, but here we see the reality of married
love. This chapter deals with sexual selfishness, and selfishness, as we will soon
discover, is one of the greatest enemies of intimacy.

If we want to live as servant lovers and forge a vital marriage despite problems and challenges, we must continue to make sacrificial choices. Here, and
in the four chapters that follow, we will see a progression of brushstrokes that
contribute to the portrait of a servant lover. With each page we turn, we will
discover even more clearly what it looks like to be a servant lover to our mate.

UNDERSTANDING THE SONG

*Tirzah: "I was asleep but my heart was awake. A voice! My beloved
was knocking." (5:2)*

To say, "I was asleep, but my heart was awake," is an idiomatic way of saying, "I had a dream." Often when poets want to imply that someone is troubled about something, they will cast the difficulty in the context of a dream rather than describe it directly. The assumption is that we tend to dream about things that we think upon often or, in this case, that deeply trouble us.[1] In this scene, Tirzah dreams about two recurring problems in their relationship: Solomon demanding sex and her sexual rejection.

Tirzah dreams of a time when Solomon knocked on her bedroom door. In Solomon's time, husbands and wives often had separate bedchambers, particularly if they were royals. Solomon's knock is not a timid bid for entrance. The root of the Hebrew word means to "drive hard or push"[2] or to "beat" on the door.[3] He has one thing on his mind.

Solomon: "Open to me, my sister, my darling, my dove, my perfect one! For my head is drenched with dew, my locks with the damp of the night." (verse 2)

Solomon pours on the sweet talk, calling his beloved his four favorite names for her. He wants entrance, not only to her room but also to the warmth of her embrace. He asks Tirzah to open her door, both literally and figuratively. He wants her to open the door to her bedroom and also the door of her "garden."[4]

The morning dew is already beginning to form, so we know that Solomon has been out late, possibly occupied with affairs of the state. During some months in Palestine, morning dew forms so copiously that it saturates the clothes like rain (see Judges 6:38). Solomon selfishly approaches his wife to make love after midnight. He is insistent, even though he is probably aware that she is asleep. No wonder Tirzah is not interested. She offers him two excuses.

Tirzah: "I have taken off my dress, how can I put it on again? I have washed my feet, how can I dirty them again?" (verse 3)

These may strike you as lame reasons; we see them that way too. Tirzah says she would have to get up, go to the *huge* effort of putting on her dress, walk to the door, and open it. In effect, she is saying, "Really, Solomon, you are *so* insensitive coming to make love after midnight. Can't it wait? Can't you see I'm asleep?"

Then she gives her second excuse, and this time she gets religious about it! She tells her husband, "If I get up to let you in to make love, I'll get my feet dirty walking across the floor and have to go to all the trouble of rewashing them!" In Israel, dirty feet symbolized moral contamination from the petty transgressions of everyday life. Often at night, the Jewish people would wash their feet ceremonially to represent their need for daily cleansing from sin, just as Jesus illustrated to His disciples in John 13:10.[5] A similar response from a wife today might be, "Honey, don't you understand? I just took a shower. If we make love, I'll have to get back in the shower again." The message behind both excuses is "Lovemaking is inconvenient and not worth the effort."

Tirzah: "My beloved extended his hand through the opening, and my feelings were aroused for him." (verse 4)

Undeterred, Solomon tries to force open the door, which was likely secured with a crossbar or bolt fastened with a little button or pin.[6] The upper part of the door may have had a round hole through which a person could thrust his arm and remove the bar, unless the hole had been sealed.

Tirzah realizes how ardently Solomon desires her. His persistence declares, "I want you and I want you now!" His urgency arouses sexual feelings in her, and she climbs out of bed to open the door.

Tirzah: "I arose to open to my beloved; and my hands dripped with myrrh, and my fingers with liquid myrrh, on the handles of the bolt." (verse 5)

Each step Tirzah takes toward her lover increases her sexual longing. By the time she reaches the door, her body has readied itself for lovemaking, as revealed through the image of liquid myrrh. The references to liquid myrrh and fingers on the "bolt" may well be double entendre again, because taken literally, the text makes no sense. Certainly her hands are not "dripping" with myrrh. Myrrh was a common aphrodisiac (see Proverbs 7:17). We believe this is a continuation of the metaphor for her sexual excitement as she thinks of opening the "door" for him.⁷ The mention of the sweet-smelling liquid adds to the erotic atmosphere.

> *Tirzah: "I opened to my beloved, but my beloved had turned away and had gone! My heart went out to him as he spoke. I searched for him but I did not find him; I called him but he did not answer me."* (verse 6)

Expectant, Tirzah opens the door. Her heart falls — her lover is not there. The Hebrew can be rendered, "I nearly died when I found he had gone."⁸ Tirzah's sadness was more than disappointment that Solomon had left; she's racked with guilt that she had sent him away. Frantic, she searches for him.

> *Tirzah: "The watchmen who make the rounds in the city found me, they struck me and wounded me; the guardsmen of the walls took away my shawl from me."* (verse 7)

As the dream progresses, Tirzah finds herself in the streets of Jerusalem, searching for her lover so she can make amends. Obviously, the watchmen would not lay a hand on Solomon's queen, but this is a dream, and it may be another reflection of the guilt she feels over rejecting her husband. In effect, she is beating herself up over her actions.

> *Tirzah to Chorus: "I adjure you, O daughters of Jerusalem, if you find my beloved, as to what you will tell him: for I am lovesick."* (verse 8)

Unable to find her beloved, Tirzah turns to the daughters of Jerusalem to aid her in her search. If they find him, they must promise to give Solomon the following message: "I am sick with love." This is the same word used in Song 2:5 and carries the notion of being highly aroused sexually. Tirzah wants her husband to know that she desires him sexually.⁹

APPLYING THE SONG FOR COUPLES

This scene exposes the problem of selfishness in a marriage. Solomon was being selfishly insensitive when he demanded sex: "I don't care if you are asleep, I want sex now!" But Tirzah's rejection of her husband's overtures was also selfish: "I'd have to put my dress on" and "I'd have to rewash my feet." Both of these responses — sex on demand and sexual rejection — are selfish. We'll look at both of these problems, beginning with sexual rejection.

Problem 1: Sexual Rejection

If the following letter is true, it seems wives in the twenty-first century are almost as adept as Tirzah when it comes to excuse giving:

> To my dear wife,
>
> During the past year I have tried to make love to you 365 times. I have succeeded only 36 times; this is an average of once every 10 days. The following is a list of why I did not succeed more often:

It will wake the children	17 times
It's too late	45 times
It's too early	23 times
Pretended to be asleep	18 times
Headache	23 times
Backache	9 times
Toothache	4 times
Too full	12 times
Giggles	2 times
Baby is crying	15 times
Company in next room	8 times
Windows are open ("neighbors will hear")	9 times
You had to go to the bathroom	12 times
Gained weight ("don't touch my new cellulite")	6 times
Too hot	15 times
Too cold	7 times

There's a good movie on	15 times
Not in the mood	89 times
Total	329 times

During the thirty-six times I did succeed, the activity was not entirely satisfactory due to the following:

You chewed gum the whole time	6 times
You watched TV the whole time	5 times
You said, "Hurry up and get this over with."	17 times
You fell asleep	6 times
You never moved and I thought you were dead	2 times

> Honey, it's no wonder I'm so irritable!
> Your loving husband[10]

The exaggerated excuses in this letter are supposed to make us laugh, but they may not be so amusing to the one living with a mate who continually rejects offers of intimacy. Listen to one husband's pain:

Arlene and I have been married for thirty years. I am an elder in the church and she teaches women's Bible studies. I love Arlene deeply, but our sexual relationship is terrible. She thinks being intimate once a month is fine. I don't. I've talked to her about this on many occasions. After our talks, things improve for a few days, but then she lapses back into indifference. I will be faithful, but it is hard. I tell her that I don't want sex — sex is something you buy on the street from a professional. I say I want to make love to her and enjoy her the way a husband ought to enjoy his wife. The strain on our sexual relationship is causing other aspects of our marriage to suffer. I just can't understand her unwillingness to want to improve this portion of our relationship.

Sometimes we stereotype and suggest that the wife is always the one with the headache and the husband is always raring to go. But as we travel around the country and talk with couples, we find that about 15 to 20 percent of couples have the opposite problem. The wife desires sex, but her husband says he needs Tylenol. Just last week, we received this letter from a wife:

> If I hear one more woman gripe about her husband nagging her for sex, I think I'll scream. She should be glad he wants her and finds her desirable. I've tried everything to get Mike interested in me — sexy nighties, creative encounters, finding the "G" spot, heaping praise on him — but he just ignores me. It's a knife in my heart. There's a guy at work who has been flirting with me. I'm so vulnerable, I fear I might do something terrible. Help!

Sexual rejection deeply wounds our mate and opens him or her up to sexual temptation. But what about the other issue of selfishness raised in this chapter — the situation where one partner selfishly demands sex from his or her mate?

PROBLEM 2: SEX ON DEMAND

Sex on demand is a common problem, one that can create great heartache, as this wife candidly shares:

> Cliff demands sex three times a day: in the morning, before bed, and in the middle of the night at 2:00 AM. The middle-of-the-night version isn't just a quickie but a marathon that involves lights, mirrors, games, and fun. He goes back to sleep at 3 AM, but I can't. I want to respond, but his need for sex has placed me in a permanent state of exhaustion.

Obviously, Cliff's case is extreme. Demanding sex three times a day indicates he suffers not from a physical need but from a deep emotional need that would be better addressed with counseling. If your mate has a sexual addiction, we recommend you seek help. As we said in the beginning of this book, we are not addressing addictions or abuse. Instead, we want to address the issue of a selfish attitude that insists, "I want sex, and I want it now."

It's time for honesty. Where does sexual selfishness show up in you? Do you ever reject your mate, whether directly or indirectly? Do you ever have a demanding spirit toward your mate?

What should your response be when selfishness gains a foothold in your intimate relationship? Is there anything you can do? Yes, you look up, look out, and look in.

LOOK UP

Whenever we have an issue we aren't sure how to address, we must first look up — to God. We must seek His wisdom and open His Word to see what He says about the subject. You have seen that God does not shrink back from addressing sexual issues. He speaks of the joys of sexual love and also the problems. He speaks to the issue of sexual rejection with very specific and strong language. There is no gray area, nor does He offer squirm room when it comes to saying "no" to intimacy:

> Stop depriving one another, except by agreement for a time, that you may devote yourselves to prayer, and come together again lest Satan tempt you because of your lack of self-control. (1 Corinthians 7:5)

We learn several things in this verse:

◊ We are commanded to stop saying "no."
◊ If we abstain from sex, it is because both agree.
◊ Prayer is the *only* reason to abstain.
◊ We must come together sexually again.
◊ Sexual rejection opens a door to Satan.

The person looking for a legitimate excuse for not making love won't find much in God's Word. God says, "Stop saying no." Now obviously there are times when sexual intercourse may not be possible due to health issues or a recent surgery, but the intent of the passage is clear: *Think about your mate's needs and respond accordingly.* Tirzah did not do this.

We can think up scores of reasons for not having sex. God gives only one: prayer. This is not a quick prayer thrown to the heavens: "God, make my wife make love with me *now.*" Instead, it is referring to devoting yourselves to prayer in a concentrated way (several days of prayer and fasting).

Perhaps the question for many of us is not do we abstain from sex because of deep intensive prayer, but do we ever pray about our sexual intimacy? Couples have said to us, "It just feels plain weird to pray about sex! God is spiritual and sex is so, well, earthy." God is for "earthiness," and you can bring anything about your sexual intimacy to Him. In fact, it pleases Him when you do.

Ask yourself two questions:

- ◊ When was the last time I talked to God about how to delight my mate sexually?
- ◊ When was the last time I asked God to help me be less selfish toward my mate?

If it has been a while, why don't you put this book down and talk honestly to Him right now?

We've seen what God's Word says about Tirzah's selfishness of rejecting her husband's sexual advances. Now let's look at Solomon, the infamous midnight Romeo. Was this husband right to insist upon sex even though he likely knew his wife was already asleep? What does God's Word say to the one who selfishly wants sex on demand? Our answer is found in Philippians 2:3, the theme verse of the servant lover. Here is our paraphrase as it applies to sexual intimacy:

> In your sexual relationship, don't let selfishness rule. God asks you to be humble and think of your mate as more important than yourself. So think about what your mate desires and how you can please him or her.

The heart of this passage is clear: *Think about your mate's needs and respond accordingly.* Solomon did not do this.

The solution to the problem of selfishness isn't identifying who is right or wrong. The solution is found in our willingness to consider our mate's needs as more important than our own. Servant loving always involves placing your mate's needs *first* and continually looking for ways to be sensitive and look at life through his or her eyes.

ATTITUDE OF A SERVANT LOVER

Sex is about physical touch, to be sure, but it is about far more than physical touch. It is about what is going on *inside* us. Developing a fulfilling sex life means I concern myself more with bringing generosity and service to bed than with bringing washboard abdomens. It means I see my wife as a holy temple of God, not just as a tantalizing human body. It even means that sex becomes a form of physical prayer — a picture of a heavenly intimacy that rivals the *shekinah* glory of old.

— GARY THOMAS, *SACRED MARRIAGE*[11]

We need God's truth from His Word. We also need His *power* to wage war against our selfishness and declare war against our enemy, Satan.

LOOK OUT!

Recently while eating dinner in a restaurant in Denver, a woman saw a group of people at another table praying. As she was leaving the restaurant, she stopped by the table and said, "I noticed earlier that you were praying. You must be Christians." The man at the head of the table replied, "No, we are Satanists. And we are committed to praying for the destruction of Christian marriages."[12]

This is frightening! Someone is praying *against* us! We must be praying *for* our marriage. We need God's power flowing through our lives and marriages to defeat the Evil One. First Peter 5:8 warns,

> Be vigilant and cautious at all times; for that enemy of yours, the devil,
> roams around like a lion, roaring [in fierce hunger], seeking someone
> to seize upon and devour. (AMP)

Perhaps you know this verse, but have you ever personalized it? Do you see Satan as *your* enemy? Are you keenly aware that he wants to devour *you* and to destroy *your* marriage?

When there's tension in your sexual relationship, have you ever thought,

Why are we fighting? It feels like something a whole lot bigger is going on, like there's a powerful force intent on tearing us apart.

Do you see yourself in any of these scenarios?

- Last night you made love in the same bed. This morning you can't stand to be in the same room together. What happened? *A force is at work.*
- You talk but say nothing. You touch, but it feels rote. Lately you feel like strangers. *A force is at work.*
- You knew she wanted to make love, but you didn't care. You got into a huge fight. You know you hurt her, but it didn't even matter. *A force is at work.*

This force has a name: Satan. Satan's key strategy is to get you to see your mate — rather than him — as your enemy. If Satan can keep you fighting with each other, you won't have energy to fight against him. Has your enemy been effective? Do you see your mate as your enemy? Let us repeat. Your spouse is *not* your enemy; Satan is your enemy. God wants you to stop your quarreling and to turn and fight together against the Devil.

Satan is preoccupied with sex. (You'll see why in the epilogue.) One of his most destructive tools is to take the beauty of sex as God intended and twist it so that it becomes something God never intended:

- God made sex pure; Satan uses it for perversion.
- God created sex for oneness; Satan uses it to bring division.
- God designed sex to produce life; Satan uses it to bring death.

If there is selfishness, division, and death in your sexual relationship, consider the source. Refuse to see your spouse as the enemy, and instead pray together against your true enemy, Satan.

When Satan comes at you and tries to use your selfishness to create discord in your sexual relationship, do what Jesus did in the wilderness when Satan came at Him (see Matthew 4:1-10). Wield the sword of the Word by quoting Scripture directly to your enemy.

How do you use the Word of God as your sword? When Satan says, "Say no to sex — he's been a jerk all day," you take the servant lover verses (Philippians 2:3-4) and throw them in his face: "Get behind me, Satan! I will think more highly of my husband and his needs rather than my own." When Satan says, "Your wife owes you sex — it's your right to have it whenever you want," throw the love passage (1 Corinthians 13) at him: "Get behind me, Satan! Love does not demand its own way."

Defeat your enemy. Pray. Wield the sword of the Word; and see your mate as your ally, not your enemy.

Let's review. In issues related to sex, we need to *look up* to God and His Word. We also need to *look out* because our enemy wants to destroy our sexual oneness. In addition, we need to *look in*, to examine honestly our attitude as it relates to sex with our mate.

Look In

Each of us is acutely aware of selfishness — our mate's selfishness, that is. We have a much harder time seeing it in ourselves, but when we invite God's light to look within us, we can see our crummy, stinking, "I, me, my, mine" attitude.

Look carefully at the following four words and the monument they build:

I

M e

M i n e

M y s e l f

These words build an altar, with "I" on the top as an idol. Are you a selfish lover?

Gary Thomas, in his excellent book *Sacred Marriage,* suggests that you ask yourself these important questions:[13]

- ◊ Is sex something I'm giving to my spouse, or withholding?
- ◊ Is sex something I am demanding, or offering?

- Is sex something I am using as a tool of manipulation, or as an expression of generous love?
- If God looked at nothing other than my sexuality, would I be known as a mature Christian, or as a near pagan?

That last question is a doozy. Put another way, we might ask ourselves, *If my mate looked at my role as a lover and nothing else, would he or she think I was a servant or a selfish slob?*

In what areas of your relationship are you prone to selfishness? Are you prone to any of the following?

- Sexual rejection
- Demanding spirit
- Insensitivity
- An unloving attitude
- A discouraging attitude
- A critical attitude

More marriages die from selfishness than for any other reason. James 4:1-2 says: "What causes fights and quarrels among you? Don't they come from your desires that battle within you? You want something but don't get it" (NIV).

Selfishness is the internal enemy of intimacy; Satan is the external enemy of intimacy. He laughs when he sees selfishness in your intimate encounters. He thinks he's won. Fight Satan. Fight selfishness. How? By becoming a servant lover. Servant lovers are givers — those who regard their spouses as more important than themselves; selfish lovers are takers — those who demand their own way.

If a wife is beyond exhaustion, what is the loving thing for her husband to do? If a husband is under great stress and needs space, what is the loving thing for a wife to do? Our selfishness needs to be replaced by sacrifice and selflessness. "Whether sexuality becomes a celebration of service or a point of contention depends largely on one or both partners' selflessness."[14]

We love the rendition of 1 Corinthians 7:4 in *The Message:* "Marriage is a decision to serve the other, whether in bed or out." God's Word says, "Serve,

serve, serve," but we think, *Self, self, self.* We must fight our inner demands to have our own way. We must battle our selfish nature that insists, "My way or the highway." Solomon and Tirzah had slipped into selfishness. But as you continue to turn the pages of the Song of Solomon, you will discover that they moved from selfishness to sacrifice. The solution involved assuming personal responsibility for their error rather than focusing on their partner's error.

In the next four scenes from the Song, you will find much wisdom and practical truth about how to assume personal responsibility for becoming a servant lover. You will see specifically what you can do to counteract your self-ishness. We pray that God will speak to your heart as you read.

SERVANT LOVERS: Admit their selfishness and learn from it.
SELFISH LOVERS: Do not admit error or learn from mistakes.

THE CHORUS TO TIRZAH:
"What kind of beloved is your beloved,
O most beautiful among women?
What kind of beloved is your beloved,
That thus you adjure us?"

TIRZAH TO THE CHORUS:
"My beloved is dazzling and ruddy,
Outstanding among ten thousand.
His head is like gold, pure gold;
His locks are like clusters of dates
And black as a raven.
His eyes are like doves
Beside streams of water,
Bathed in milk,
And reposed in their setting.
His cheeks are like a bed of balsam,
Banks of sweet-scented herbs;
His lips are lilies
Dripping with liquid myrrh.
His hands are rods of gold
Set with beryl;
His abdomen is carved ivory
Inlaid with sapphires.

TIRZAH TO THE CHORUS (CONTINUED):
His legs are pillars of alabaster
Set on pedestals of pure gold;
His appearance is like Lebanon
Choice as the cedars.
His mouth is full of sweetness.
And he is wholly desirable.
This is my beloved and this is my friend,
O daughters of Jerusalem."

THE CHORUS:
"Where has your beloved gone,
O most beautiful among women?
Where has your beloved turned,
That we may seek him with you?"

TIRZAH:
"My beloved has gone down to his garden,
To the beds of balsam,
To pasture his flock in the gardens
And gather lilies.
I am my beloved's and my beloved is mine,
He who pastures his flock among the lilies."

SONG OF SOLOMON 5:9–6:3

chapter twelve

Be Free in Your Mind

"I'm to the point where I don't even want to make love.
Every time I do, a videotape of women I was with before I got married
parades across my mind. I feel like I'm committing adultery
while I'm making love with my wife. Help!"

None of us wants junk like this in our minds. This chapter will show you how you can free your mind of the things that hinder your intimacy so that you can use it creatively in your sexual relationship with your mate.

UNDERSTANDING THE SONG

In the last scene, selfishness prevailed. Solomon was an insensitive midnight Romeo, and Tirzah's self-centered protestations were hollow and unconvincing. Both made wrong choices. Now she makes a right choice, the choice to put her husband's needs before her own. We're about to look inside Tirzah's head and discover that she is very free in her thinking. No restraints! Because of this, she is able to use her thoughts to shift her body into sexual gear.

> *The Chorus to Tirzah: "What kind of beloved is your beloved, O most beautiful among women? What kind of beloved is your beloved, that thus you adjure us?" (5:9)*

The chorus asks Tirzah, "What's so special about Solomon?" This question seems to be specifically designed to lead Tirzah away from focusing on her husband's weaknesses and help her focus on his many good points. She answers by describing her beloved from head to toe. This poem praising her beloved is the second *wasf* in the Song (5:10-16).

In the last scene, Tirzah was dreaming; in this scene she is daydreaming. She is alone in the palace and her thoughts of her husband are intensely erotic.

Tirzah to the Chorus: "My beloved is dazzling and ruddy, outstanding among ten thousand." (verse 10)

Tirzah begins her praise by calling Solomon *my* lover — he is exclusively hers, and she delights in that fact. In her dream, she did not want him as her lover, but when she wakes up, she reflects on his body, and her attitude changes. His ruddy complexion makes him look radiant. The Hebrew word translated as "ruddy" can also imply the idea of manliness.[1] Her husband is so masculine and magnificent that no other man compares with him. Earlier, Tirzah had said that he stood out like an apple tree among a forest of evergreens (see 2:3). Now she declares that if ten thousand or more men were lined up beside her beloved, he would outshine them all.

Tirzah: "His head is like gold, pure gold; his locks are like clusters of dates and black as a raven." (verse 11)

In essence, Tirzah is saying, "My lover is tall, dark, and handsome." Solomon's features are exquisitely sculpted, his complexion a golden tan,[2] and his hair dark and curly.

Tirzah: "His eyes are like doves beside streams of water, bathed in milk, and reposed in their setting." (verse 12)

In Song 4:1, Solomon said that Tirzah's eyes were like doves, and now she returns the compliment. Doves are loyal to their mates throughout life, and as Tirzah thinks about her husband's eyes, she reflects on his faithfulness to her.

Tirzah: "His cheeks are like a bed of balsam, banks of sweet-scented herbs; his lips are lilies dripping with liquid myrrh." (verse 13)

This reference to his cheeks is likely a reference to Solomon's beard, as beards were the custom in Israel during this time period.[3] Tirzah emphasizes its aroma by comparing it to a fragrant garden of spices. She also says that she longs to experience again the glorious taste of his lips. In the Song, lilies are metaphors with some undertone of sexual activity.[4]

Tirzah: "His hands are rods of gold set with beryl; his abdomen is carved ivory inlaid with sapphires." (verse 14)

As she continues to daydream about her beloved, Tirzah's thoughts move down his body. She imagines his strong yet gentle hands caressing her. Then she says that his belly is like carved ivory. While most translations translate the Hebrew word *me eh* as "belly," this rendering makes little sense here because *me eh* is often used to describe reproductive organs.[5] One commentator explains the verse this way:

> It is conceivable that the verse simply is referring to the fact that his stomach is as smooth as a slab of ivory. However, the words are too suggestive for me to settle on that approach. When one thinks of ivory, one thinks of a tusk of ivory, an object that could easily have erotic connotations. The decoration with lapis, a precious stone blue in color, simply would highlight the object's preciousness. In such an erotic poem, the line at the least is suggestive of, if not explicitly referring to, the man's member.[6]

Are you surprised that Scripture presents a wife imagining her husband's naked body in an aroused sexual state? We are. But we are so grateful, because through it, God is saying, "It is right and good to dwell on *your husband's* body. It is right and good to use your mind to shift your body into sexual gear."

Tirzah: "His legs are pillars of alabaster set on pedestals of gold; his appearance is like Lebanon choice as the cedars." (verse 15)

In her daydreaming, Tirzah continues to lower her gaze and describes the strength of Solomon's legs. His entire appearance is solid — immovable, firm, and steadfast, like the Lebanon mountains. Like the most majestic of trees, the cedars of Lebanon, her beloved is the most excellent of men.

Tirzah: "*His mouth is full of sweetness. And he is wholly desirable. This is my beloved and this is my friend, O daughters of Jerusalem.*" (verse 16)

Tirzah has already imagined her lover's kisses, and here she reflects on his tender speech. His words of praise touch her heart in a way nothing else can.

As she thinks about his sterling qualities, she realizes anew that everything about his body is desirable. Oh, how she wants him! How could she have rejected him? She wants him physically, but she also longs for the sweet whispers of love that flow from his mouth.

In this verse, we see sexual love (*dod*) and friendship love (*rayah*) blended together. The one she desires is the perfect combination; he is her lover (*dod*) and her best friend (*rayah*). She aches for his body to be pressed against hers, but she also longs for his close companionship. To share soul to soul as well as body to body is truly the purest joy of marriage. Blessed is the husband or wife whose mate is not only lover but also best friend.

The Chorus: "*Where has your beloved gone, O most beautiful among women? Where has your beloved turned, that we may seek him with you?*" (6:1)

This scene began with the chorus asking Tirzah to explain why her beloved was so special that they should promise to look for him. Her sensuous description of her lover and friend has convinced them that he is truly a man worth finding. But they want to know where he is.

Tirzah: "*My beloved has gone down to his garden, to the beds of balsam, to pasture his flock in the gardens and gather lilies.*" (verse 2)

Tirzah replies that her husband has gone to his garden. She has been searching for Solomon (see Song 5:8), but now she seems to know where he is.

Apparently, she did not find him; he found her. The literary device of the Chorus asking where he is provides an occasion for her to express the fact that they are united again.

Commentators differ on just what this verse means, as the wording suggests a sexual connotation. Previous scenes have used *garden, beds of balsam, pasturing his flock in the garden,* and *lilies* to express sexual images (e.g., her breasts in 4:5). Elsewhere, the "garden" of the woman refers to her sexuality in general and her vagina in particular (see 4:12,15; 5:1). So it seems likely that Tirzah is saying, "We found each other and have enjoyed intimacy together." Solomon has "gone down to the garden," that is, he is intimately united with his wife. The garden is no ordinary garden, but a garden of sweet-smelling spices.[7]

Tirzah: "I am my beloved's and my beloved is mine, he who pastures his flock among the lilies." (verse 3)

What a glorious declaration of love — "I belong to Solomon and he belongs to me"! Tirzah is at peace. She is the king's wife, and she confidently asserts her belief in his love for her. It is as if she shouts, "Yes, yes, he is mine and I am his!" When she focused on her husband's shortcomings (insensitively coming to her for late-night sex), she did not have the right perspective. Of course he had weaknesses, but by dwelling on his beauty and strength, she took a step toward resolving the sexual conflict between them.

GROWING AS A SERVANT LOVER

DESIRE: I want to be free in my mind.

OBSTACLE: Wrong thoughts are in my mind.

SOLUTION: Remove the wrong thinking and replace it with God's Word.

OUTCOME: I can use my mind to enjoy sex as God intended.

APPLYING THE SONG FOR COUPLES

We want to talk to the wives for just a moment, but husbands, don't tune out. Even though the message is directed toward your wife, the principles of freedom and exclusivity, which we address next, also apply to you.

DON'T SHUT DOWN YOUR MIND

Wives, how do you respond to the idea of doing what Tirzah did? Do you give yourself permission to daydream about your husband's naked body? Or does the very thought cause you to blush or roll your eyes and think, *No way! I could never do that!*

Where do you get the idea that fantasizing about your husband's body is wrong? We think it comes from what you see in the world. For example, a man ogles two young women as they walk by him, or a group of teenage girls at a pool giggle and talk about what the hunk on the diving board would look like *sans* suit. Such actions constitute lust. You know God's Word, and you know lust is wrong, wrong, wrong!

Yet, the Song records Tirzah's sexual fantasies about her husband, and we are telling you right, right, right. Your mind can't make that leap. Why would God say it's okay for a wife to have sexual daydreams about her husband? Isn't that lust?

The distinction happens with two words: *husband* and *wife*. God gives permission for a *wife* to sexually daydream about her *husband*, and for a *husband* to daydream sexually about his *wife*. God urges, "Ponder, dwell, delight in the gift of your *spouse's* body for you. Allow yourself to become sexually aroused so you can enjoy ecstasy with your *spouse*."

For you to fantasize sexually about *anyone* else — the dynamic pastor at church, the witty and kind neighbor down the street, the charming ex-boyfriend — is a sin. But your husband is part of you. God sees the two of you as one. In this oneness is freedom.

As we have been saying over and over throughout this book, God wants married couples to be abandoned sexually, to indulge in unrestrained joy and passion, and to intoxicate one another with delight. His one boundary: *one husband and one wife, in private, for life.* Within the context of this marriage relationship, God gives you permission to:

Be free with your words.

Be free with your body.

Be free in your mind.

Exclusively, with your mate.

Every couple we know wants to experience sexual freedom with each other, but many are unable to because their minds are filled with junk. Listen to what one couple told us.

> *Beth:* I can't even imagine what being free in my mind looks like. I had several sexual partners before I married Max. If I tried to do what Tirzah did, I'm afraid images of other men would flood my mind. That, combined with the guilt I feel over having had two abortions, keeps me from really enjoying sex. To me, sex equals pain. So I just don't think about it.

> *Max:* Beth's not the only one who shuts down her mind. It's the only way I can function. When I was ten years old, a friend showed me some porn magazines. I came into marriage with a mind stuffed full of images of naked women. Although porn is not a part of my life now, every time Beth and I make love, I see page 63 or the centerfold from June. We became Christians after we married, and the more I see God's holiness, the more disgusted I am with what floods my mind. I just don't know how to get rid of the junk. Like Beth, I shut down. I could never let my mind go and be free, because I don't trust where my mind would go.

Please, Beth and Max, don't shut down your minds to sex. God has a better way. He says, "Be transformed by the renewing of your mind" (Romans 12:2). The Greek word for transformed in this passage is *metamorphousthe*, from which we get our English word *metamorphosis*. It involves total change, from the inside out. So we are talking about a mind that is brand-spanking new, like nothing you've seen before — a mind that has been so completely changed, it is barely recognizable. Beth and Max, you can have a new mind. You can be free!

What about you? Do you believe God can renew your mind? Maybe you were sexually abused and you believe the images from the past will *always* haunt you and hinder your sexual expression. Wrong! Perhaps you did something, saw something, heard something, and it imbedded itself so deeply in your psyche that you are convinced your view of sex will *always* be tainted. Wrong! Or possibly you were raised in a strict environment where you were constantly told, "Restrain yourself. Deny sexual passion." You feel these years of conditioning make it impossible for you to ever be wild and abandoned. Wrong, wrong, wrong!

Christ came to set us free: "You will know the truth and the truth will set you free" (John 8:32, NIV). The truth is, Christ wants to give you a new mind. How? Read on.

Your mind is like a computer. When you were born, God installed a directory called Sex. Early on, the directory was empty, but over time, files were added to the directory. Certain files were good — things you learned from God's Word, examples of loving marriages, positive teaching from godly parents or leaders. Other files were corrupted — immoral messages or images, perverted acts contrary to God's Word. Good files produced right thinking; corrupted files produced wrong thinking. Over the years, the accumulation of these files developed attitudes that form your current views about sex.

Everything you have been told about sex, everything you've seen, heard, done — or that has been done to you — all of it is stored in your mind. If sex is tainted in your mind, if freedom seems impossible, it is because the corrupted files keep your mind from functioning as God intended. The way to get your mind working properly is similar to the steps involved in fixing a sluggish computer: inventory the system, identify and remove corrupted files, and install new programs that will protect the system and increase performance.

TAKE INVENTORY

The exercise we are about to suggest will help you only if you do it. It will take time. It may be painful, but if you are serious about renewing your mind, you must do this. We pray that you will be willing because what you are about to do can change your marriage forever.

Beth's Inventory

Inventory (Age)	Good Files	Results	Corrupt Files	Results
1-10 Years	My parents had a good marriage.	Touching looked fun.		
11-20 Years			Sexually abused by a family friend, an elder of the church we attended. I didn't tell anyone. Who would believe me, anyway?	Developed a poor self-image. Felt guilty for being part of the abuse. Was it my fault?
21-30 Years	Married Max at age twenty-eight. Great honeymoon!	I know sex can be good when my mind is right.	Became sexually promiscuous with men before marriage. I didn't care.	I had two abortions. I felt intense guilt and could not experience intimate pleasure with Max. Felt this was God's punishment for past sexual sins.
31-40 Years	Attended an Intimate Issues conference, where I learned how to receive forgiveness for my past.	Asked God for a complete healing of my past. He told me I had to tell Max and ask his forgiveness. I felt an enormous stone lifted off me when I did. I now experience joy in my times of intimacy with Max. When the guilt tries to come back, Max prays with me and for me.		
41-50 Years				
51-60 Years				

Max's Inventory

Inventory (Age)	Good Files	Results	Corrupt Files	Results
1-10 Years			Neighbor boy introduced me to pornographic magazines. Older brother showed me manual on different sexual positions.	Developed an intense curiosity about girls and their bodies. Experienced arousal, even though I didn't understand what I was feeling.
11-20 Years			Parents divorced; dad moved in with girlfriend. I attended a summer camp at fifteen. Had sex for the first time with an older girl from another campsite. Continued to have sex throughout college.	Became sexually promiscuous and viewed girls with little respect. I had sexual needs, and girls were supposed to meet them. Developed a warped macho image.
21-30 Years	Married Beth at age twenty-eight. Became a Christian at age twenty-nine.	Read the entire Bible. Became involved in a men's group, but there was no accountability.	Secretly looked at pornographic computer sites at work and home.	I lied to Beth about my lustful habits toward other women. When I was intimate with her, I often pretended that Beth was a different woman.
31-40 Years	Asked God to show me all of the things that influenced my perspective of sex and marital intimacy and ways that I had hurt Beth. Confessed to Him and asked Him to purify my heart and mind.	Confessed my complete past to Beth and asked her forgiveness. I made a new covenant with her and asked for her help in times of temptation.		
41-50 Years				
51-60 Years				

Study Max and Beth's inventories on pages 193-194. It will serve as your guideline. Get a piece of paper and a pen and draw three columns. On the left, vertically list the time periods of your life in increments of ten years. Horizontally, at the top of each column, list three headlines: Good Files, Corrupt Files, and Results. Now go through your life, decade by decade, and write down every image, every thought, and every deed that God brings to mind. List the positive recollections in the column called Good Files and then the corresponding Result. List every negative image under Corrupt Files with its corresponding Result. As you write, pray,

> *Holy Spirit, I ask You to bring to mind the actions and images You want me to review for this period of my life. I give You permission to reveal anything I've suppressed or previously been unwilling to acknowledge. Search my heart. Expose what is hidden. I trust You to do this so I may be set free.*

Here is how Max and Beth felt about taking their inventories.

Max: As I wrote my inventory, I saw clearly for the first time the connection between the negative images in the past and my wrong attitudes in the present. In the name of pornography, I'd broken promises, been dishonest with Beth and with myself, lusted, and developed a view of women that did not honor God. I hated the choices I'd made and who I was because of them. It took me a week to fully inventory my mind. Then one day, I felt as though the Lord said, "It is finished."

Beth: When I had the abortions, I felt no remorse. Guilt showed up ten years later, after our daughter was born. When it did, it was in the form of outbursts of anger and depression. As our daughter grew older, I mentally calculated the ages of my aborted children and went deeper into despair. As for sex, it was something I did because Max needed it, not because I enjoyed it. I allowed myself to feel some pleasure but stopped before I got too carried away. I think it was my way of punishing myself for being so free before marriage. Doing the inventory exercise convicted me because I realized that all these years I'd not only punished myself, I'd also punished Max.

The purpose of taking inventory of your mind is to set you free. In *Freedom from Your Past*, Jimmy Evans, a pastor and counselor, says,

> Like a surgeon who wishes he could cure a terrible disease with simple medication, I wish I could help people overcome terrible pain and scars in their past without talking about them and bringing them to light, but I can't. Even though painful experiences and memories shouldn't be glorified or prolonged, they do need to be honestly admitted and dealt with.[8]

Welcome conviction. Embrace truth. Allow each to do its work in your heart. Paul admonishes, "Now I rejoice, not that you were made sorry, but that your sorrow led to repentance" (2 Corinthians 7:9). If you have erred in the past, tell God you are sorry — deeply sorry — for your wrong choices.

Perhaps your issue is not what you did but something someone else did to you. If you were wounded sexually, or if someone filled your head with misinformation or wrong images, you need to begin the process of forgiving them. Whether the corrupted files in your mind are the result of something you did or something someone did to you, the process of removing the files is the same: Go to God. He, and He alone, can remove the junk and make your mind new.

ASK GOD TO REMOVE YOUR CORRUPTED FILES

God is the only One who can permanently delete corrupted files in the mind. Read how he did this for Max and Beth.

> *Max:* I sat in my torn leather office chair with my inventory in my lap, feeling nauseated. The summary of my life: I'd been selfish and lustful. I'd treated Beth like a sex object whose duty was to please me, rather than as a beautiful, thinking, feeling woman who loved me. Those corrupted files were death to me. I bowed my head and cried out loud, "God, how could I have been so stupid? So blind? Please, God. Please, Jesus. Forgive me. Take it all away. Make me clean. Please, please, please . . ."

> *Beth:* God kept adding things to my inventory that I had not thought about in years. I was sitting in church when the fullness of my sin

engulfed me. We were singing "I Stand Amazed":

> *I see the nails*
> *Piercing your skin*
> *My wicked heart*
> *Driving them in.*[9]

It hit me — hard. *My* sexual sin crucified Christ. *My* decision to abort drove the nails into His hands. *I* pounded the nails each time I gave my body to a man that was not my husband. When I finally understood this, I ran to the bathroom and cried for five minutes really, really hard. I whispered over and over, "I'm sorry, Jesus. Forgive me. I killed my babies. I violated my body. I was so very wrong. Remove the corruption, God."

The Holy Spirit revealed to Max and Beth what they needed to know in order for God to clean up their minds. What about you? We've asked you to make an inventory because this is the first step in gaining freedom in your mind. Have you done this? If not, bow your head now. Ask Him to remove the junk. He delights in doing this for you. Oh, the joy of a mind made new!

GET RID OF PORN

PORNOGRAPHY IS DANGEROUS

- Researchers now link changes in [sexual] behavior to the startling discovery that when people indulge in pornography, they release powerful chemicals that actually change the structure of the brain and body, creating a physical addiction. This addiction is so powerful it is being likened to cocaine, alcohol, and heroin.[10]
- In a special report on love in marriage, *Time* magazine calls the Internet "the crack cocaine of sexual addiction."[11]
- Porn is transforming sexuality and relationships for the worse, according to psychologists and sociologists.[12]

PORNOGRAPHY IS A GROWING PROBLEM

- Porn revenue is larger than all combined revenues of professional football, baseball, and basketball franchises.[13]

- In the United States, porn revenue exceeds the combined revenues of ABC, CBS, and NBC (6.2 billion).[14]
- Pornography generates $57 billion worldwide and $12 billion in the United States.[15]
- Forty million adults regularly visit pornographic Internet websites.[16]
- Richard Barry, president of the American Academy of Matrimonial Lawyers, said, "Pornography had an almost nonexistent role in divorce just seven or eight years ago." Now, according to two-thirds of the 350 divorce lawyers at a 2003 meeting of the American Academy of Matrimonial Lawyers, Internet pornography "played a significant role in divorces in the past year, with excessive interest in online porn contributing to more than half of such cases."[17]

HELP FOR PORNOGRAPHY ADDICTION IS AVAILABLE

Books and Articles:

Arterburn, Stephen, Fred Stoeker, and Mike Yorkey. *Every Man's Battle: Winning the War on Sexual Temptation One Victory at a Time.* Colorado Springs, Colo.: WaterBrook, 2000.

Fehlauer, Mike. *Finding Freedom from the Shame of the Past.* Lake Mary, Fla.: Creation House, 1999.

Hall, Laurie. *An Affair of the Mind.* Colorado Springs, Colo.: Focus on the Family, 1996.

Sper, David, ed. *When a Man's Eye Wanders.* Grand Rapids, Mich.: RBC Ministries, 1999, http://www.gospelcom.net/rbc/ds/cb991/cb991.html.

Websites:

PureIntimacy at www.pureintimacy.org (Focus on the Family)

Renewing Intimacy at www.renewingintimacy.com

Faithful and True Ministries at www.faithfulandtrueministries.com

National Council on Sexual Addiction and Compulsivity at www.ncsac.org

American Association of Christian Counselors at www.aacc.net

Setting Captives Free at www.settingcaptivesfree.com

ACTIVATE NEW PROGRAMS

Now that the corrupted files are gone, it's time to install two programs: an operating system (the Word of God) and a virus protection program (reliance on the Holy Spirit). These two programs are designed to infuse your mind with new possibilities with your mate and protect you from past and future viruses. You have always had God's Word, and the moment you received Christ as your Savior, the Holy Spirit came to live in you. But when it comes to sexuality, often you have not applied God's Word or relied on the Holy Spirit. So we ask you to cling to God's Word, to His Spirit.

When we put God's Word into our minds, they are made new. This results in transformed thinking, which leads to transformed actions. Two important steps are involved in this transformation process: *memorization* and *meditation*.

When you memorize Scripture about God's view of sex, you increase the Holy Spirit's vocabulary in your life and change your sexual mindset. If you haven't already done so, we urge you to memorize Philippians 2:3-4:

Do nothing out of selfish ambition or vain conceit, but in humility consider others better than yourselves. Each of you should look not only to your own interests, but also to the interests of others. (NIV)

After you have memorized Philippians 2:3-4, meditate on it. "Meditation is a dynamic process that changes your thought life as the first step in changing the rest of your life."[18] It sends the roots of Scripture down deep as you personalize what you've memorized and pray it back to God.

Meditation is more than merely reciting the words of a verse; it involves talking to God about the message of the verse and praying it back to Him. One husband personalized Philippians 2:3-4 by writing this prayer:

God, I don't really like this verse. It says that I am to "do nothing selfish" and to "think more highly of my wife" than of myself. I'm not doing well here, God. Help me. I want to think of her interests — what pleases her — and look at sex through her eyes. Please show me what all this means and how I can serve her rather than myself.

Maybe you're thinking, *I already know this. Every book I read that talks about transforming the mind says that I should memorize and meditate on God's Word.* Yes, you know it, but have you done it? This *is* what changes you! From personal experience, we know this to be true. Others also verify that their minds were renewed and healed when they immersed themselves in God's Word and committed it to memory. Listen to how this worked for Serena:

> Six months ago, after my husband left for work, a man broke into my home and brutally raped me. I tried to make love with my husband, but the sights, the sounds, of the horror continued to run across my mind like a fast-forwarded videotape. I met Linda at a conference. I told her what happened. She prayed for God to pull the violation from my mind. Then she said, "Serena, I want you to memorize one Scripture verse each week for the next four weeks about the beauty of your sexual relationship with your husband. Meditate on each verse and pray it back to God, daily asking Him to transform your mind. After four weeks, e-mail me and tell me what God has done."
>
> I did this for four weeks but knew I needed more time. Six weeks later, I wrote Linda: "I did what you said, and last night we made love. For the first time in eight months, I didn't have any flashbacks!"

The Word of God can reprogram our minds and make them new!

Once you have installed God's Word as your new operating system, you need to rely on the Holy Spirit as your virus protection program. He can alert you with a warning in your spirit when a virus is about to enter your mind. In that moment, you have a choice. You can quarantine files and later delete them so they do not affect your system, or you can ignore the warning and suffer the consequences.

Messages assault you daily. The menu box flashes, *Quarantine: Yes or no?* "Yes" will keep your mind free from infection; "no" will open your mind to corruption. What will you choose?

SCRIPTURES TO MEMORIZE

FOR WIVES:

- As a loving hind and a graceful doe, let [my] breasts satisfy you at all times; be exhilarated always with [my] love. (Proverbs 5:19)
- His mouth is full of sweetness. And he is wholly desirable. This is my beloved and this is my friend. (Song of Solomon 5:16)
- I am my beloved's, and his desire is for me. (Song of Solomon 7:10)
- Let the wife see that she respects and reverences her husband [that she notices him, regards him, honors him, prefers him, venerates, and esteems him; and that she defers to him, praises him, and loves and admires him exceedingly]. (Ephesians 5:33, AMP)

FOR HUSBANDS:

- How delightful is your love, my sister, my bride! How much more pleasing is your love than wine, and the fragrance of your perfume than any spice! (Song of Solomon 4:10, NIV)
- Let your fountain be blessed, and rejoice in the wife of your youth. (Proverbs 5:18)
- As a loving hind and a graceful doe, let her breasts satisfy you at all times. Be exhilarated always with her love. (Proverbs 5:19)
- Husbands, love your wives, just as Christ also loved the church and gave Himself up for her. (Ephesians 5:25)

FOR THE COUPLE:

- Put me like a seal over your heart, like a seal on your arm. For love is as strong as death, jealousy is as severe as Sheol; its flashes are flashes of fire, the very flame of the LORD. (Song of Solomon 8:6)
- Eat, friends; drink and imbibe deeply, O lovers. (Song of Solomon 5:1)
- Do nothing out of selfish ambition or vain conceit, but in humility consider others better than yourselves. Each of you should look not only to your own interests, but also to the interests of others. (Philippians 2:3-4, NIV)

Once you have installed the Word of God in your mind and given the Holy Spirit control over your thinking, you are ready for exciting possibilities. Freedom awaits you! In the joy of that freedom, you will learn a secret: You can use your mind to shift your body into sexual gear.

SHIFT INTO SEXUAL GEAR

Our friend Gayle was diagnosed with advanced stage-three breast cancer at age forty. For the next ten months, she endured every kind of cancer treatment offered — five rounds of high dose chemo, stem cell replacement, mastectomy, and radiation. As a result of all the treatment, she was menopausal and had one breast, no ovaries, and no uterus. Afterward, the cancer was gone, and so was her sex drive:

> I couldn't believe that God would heal my body but then leave me in a condition in which I felt nothing sexually. But with God's help, I have learned how to shift my mind into sexual gear and now can ready my body for my husband. I have a deep passion for him that I never have had before. I find my desire is frequent if I am willing to shift my mind into gear. If this works for me, I know it can work for anyone.

Romans 12:2 says, "Let God transform you into a new person by changing the way you think" (Romans 12:2, NLT). Max, Beth, Serena, and Gayle are all new people because God used their minds to change their thinking. As you read God's Word and install it in your mind, you too will act differently and feel differently.

We are well aware this process can take time. For some it has taken years. Even though we have outlined a few practical and helpful steps, setting your mind free is not about a program but about a Person — Jesus Christ. Trust Him. He wants your mind to be free even more than you do! Ask Him, trust Him, and don't be surprised if He accomplishes something far beyond your wildest dreams.

SERVANT LOVERS: Allow God to set their minds free.

SELFISH LOVERS: Permit wrong images to remain in their minds, hindering their sexual relationships.

SOLOMON TO TIRZAH:
"You are as beautiful as Tirzah, my darling,
As lovely as Jerusalem,
As awesome as an army with banners.
Turn your eyes away from me,
For they have confused me;
Your hair is like a flock of goats
That have descended from Gilead.
Your teeth are like a flock of ewes
Which have come up from their washing,
All of which bear twins,
And not one among them has lost her young.
Your temples are like a slice of a pomegranate
Behind your veil.
There are sixty queens and eighty concubines,
And maidens without number;
But my dove, my perfect one, is unique:
She is her mother's only daughter;
She is the pure child of the one who bore her.
The maidens saw her and called her blessed,
The queens and the concubines also,
and they praised her, saying,
'Who is this that grows like the dawn,
As beautiful as the full moon,
As pure as the sun,
As awesome as an army with banners?'"

SONG OF SOLOMON 6:4-10

chapter thirteen

Be Free to Forgive

Here is a scene played out in bedrooms all across the country:

HUSBAND: "I want sex."

WIFE: "No way, I'm exhausted. Leave me alone."

HUSBAND: "Okay — I will." (rolls over)

Later . . . .

WIFE: "You always think about yourself and *your* needs."

HUSBAND: "And you care more about sleep than loving me."

Here is what we saw happen in Solomon and Tirzah's bedroom in chapter 11:

SOLOMON: "I want sex."

TIRZAH: "It's after midnight! Leave me alone."

SOLOMON: "Okay — I will." (He leaves.)

Later . . .

WIFE (TO HERSELF): You are my lover and my friend.

HUSBAND (TO HER): "You are the most beautiful woman in the world."

Solomon and Tirzah had been hurt. He demanded late-night sex. She rejected him. Yet now Solomon and Tirzah lavish one another with loving words and actions. In this chapter, we see how to respond sacrificially and forgive when our spouse has hurt us.

UNDERSTANDING THE SONG

Solomon to Tirzah: "You are as beautiful as Tirzah, my darling, as lovely as Jerusalem, as awesome as an army with banners." (6:4)

Once again praise flows from Solomon's lips. This is the third *wasf* in the Song. He compares his wife to the city of Tirzah (remember, this reference is what caused us to call the bride Tirzah), the chief city of northern Israel, and to Jerusalem, the capital of southern Israel. Both cities were set on a hill, both were renown for their splendor. First, Solomon says his wife is like Tirzah, a city of natural and rustic beauty with inviting gardens and groves. Then he tells her she is as lovely as Jerusalem, which was called "the perfection of beauty" (Psalm 50:2). Jerusalem was said to stir the soul and evoke awe in those who gazed upon her majesty.[1]

It is possible that these metaphors describe not only her beauty but also her character. *Tirzah* comes from a root meaning "to be pleasant," and the word *Jerusalem* alludes to "a foundation of well-being."[2] Later in the Song, Tirzah describes herself as the one who brings shalom, or peace, well-being, and security (see Song 8:10). The fullness of Solomon's words declares that her inner beauty and outer beauty move him deeply. He exclaims — two times — that she is "as awesome as an army with banners" (see verse 10). It is unclear exactly what this means, but the phrase could possibly be translated as "splendid to look upon."

Solomon to Tirzah: "Turn your eyes away from me, for they have confused me." (verse 5)

So great is the power of his wife's eyes to churn him up inside that Solomon begs her to turn them away from him. He is "overwhelmed, excited, overpowered, unsettled!"[3] A modern-day paraphrase might go something like this:

> Avert your tantalizing eyes,
> Your gaze which threatens danger.
> Your awesome beauty has the power

To churn the depths of deep desire,
To light the fire of yearning strong
That drains me of all strength.
A helpless victim I am left,
A slave at beauty's mercy,
Weak captive of magnificence.[4]

Solomon to Tirzah: "Your hair is like a flock of goats that have descended from Gilead. Your teeth are a flock of ewes which have come up from their washing, all of which bear twins, and not one among them has lost her young." (verses 5-6)

If you are thinking, *I've heard this before,* you are right. Solomon is about to pull out the Top Three Creative Compliments again (we'll explain why in a moment). Remember, while these would not be the compliments we would choose today, they were, nonetheless, compliments (see Song 4:1 on pages 133-134 and Song 4:2 on page 134).

Solomon to Tirzah: "Your temples are like a slice of a pomegranate behind your veil." (verse 7, see also 4:3)

Next, a replay of the pomegranate/cheek compliment. Not once, not twice, but three times Solomon reiterates the same imagery he used on their wedding night. Why? Was it because he'd misplaced his thesaurus and run out of adjectives? No. Solomon understood that the language of love bears repeating. Relationships are oiled and healed with praise. His compliments were well chosen to communicate a vital message to his wife. Instead of withdrawing or lashing out because she had hurt him, he chooses to praise her with the very same words he used to praise her the night they were married.

Tirzah's heart leaps — he loved her just as he loved her *before* she rejected him. Solomon communicates, "Nothing has changed. Regardless of how you respond to me, this does not affect the love I have for you. Yes, you have hurt and rejected me, but I choose to view you through the eyes of love with which I saw you the day we made our vows."

Solomon to Tirzah: "*There are sixty queens and eighty concubines, and maidens without number; but my dove, my perfect one, is unique. She is her mother's only daughter; she is the pure child of the one who bore her.*" *(verses 8-9)*

Some have thought that the eighty concubines and sixty queens mentioned here refer to Solomon's harem, as described in 1 Kings 11:3, but this reference does not mention Solomon by name or in any way indicate that these are *his* queens and concubines. Instead, Solomon looks at all the other women around him and says, "My Tirzah outshines them all." She is unique — her mother's only daughter. She is pure. She is perfect. But Solomon is not the only one overcome by her beauty and worth. All of the women in Jerusalem join their king with effusive praise of the bride.

Solomon to Tirzah: "*The maidens saw her and called her blessed, the queens and concubines also, and they praised her, saying, 'Who is this that grows like the dawn, as beautiful as the full moon, as pure as the sun, as awesome as an army with banners?'*" *(verses 9-10)*

Usually women do not praise other women — there is too much envy among them — but Tirzah's beauty brings forth no such division. A wave of praise rises from the women; like the dawn, Tirzah's beauty becomes brighter as they observe her. She is like the most beautiful of full moons, lighting the atmosphere where she walks. Her purity goes before her like the sun, and just as an army marches with flowing banners that rustle in the breeze, she carries a magnificence about her person.

GROWING AS A SERVANT LOVER

DESIRE: I want to be free to forgive.

OBSTACLE: I withhold forgiveness because I've been hurt.

SOLUTION: I choose to forgive.

OUTCOME: I am now free to praise my mate with my words.

APPLYING THE SONG TO COUPLES

Linda and Lorraine: We like Solomon's response! Even if we hurt Jody and Pete, we want them to heap on the praise.

Jody and Pete: We like Tirzah's response! When we act like jerks, we want Linda and Lorraine to daydream about our bodies.

All four of us *want* to be like Tirzah and Solomon, to respond to our mate as a servant lover rather than as a selfish lover, but unfortunately that doesn't always happen. Our spouse does something that deeply hurts us, so we shut down. What comes out of our lips? Not praise but hurtful words meant to sting and wound.

But Solomon responded to his wife's rejection with praise. How was that possible? Nowhere in the Song does he say, "Tirzah, I forgive you," but it is obvious that he had. In order for Solomon to praise his wife with sincerity and enthusiasm, he had to have forgiven her. Because forgiveness is such a critical component of every marriage, we want to focus on it here.

OFFER A CUP OF FORGIVENESS

Marriage has been called the union of two good forgivers. When you live as one flesh, share the same soap, and constantly rub shoulders, it is impossible not to rub one another the wrong way. As marriage partners, we miscommunicate, misunderstand, and miss the sexual cues given by our partner. When our spouse has been selfish, insensitive, and demanding, what does God want us to do? Forgive.

Tracy and Tom's marriage started out great, but by the time their four kids entered middle school, it was in the pits. Tracy felt that she was doing everything at home and that Tom was happy to let her carry the load. One day, God convicted Tracy's heart that she needed to stop being so critical toward Tom.

She prayed for several days about how to do that. Then the perfect idea came to her. On their wedding day, a friend had given them a "forgiveness cup" and said, "Whenever you do something to offend the other person, fill this cup up with something to drink and say, 'I'm sorry I hurt you. Will you please forgive me?' If the other person accepts your apology, he or she should drink from the cup." Unfortunately, the cup had gotten lost during a move five years earlier. She purchased a new one and then told Tom, "We need to talk." We'll let Tracy tell you what happened.

> Tom was nervous because when I said, "We need to talk," he heard, "I'm going to blast you for something you've done wrong." He sat on the couch. I sat on the floor at his feet. I said, "Before we talk, I have a gift to give you." He looked surprised because a gift was the last thing he expected. He opened it. "Do you know what this is?" I asked. He stammered, "Is it an 'I'm sorry cup'?" "Yes, Tom. That's what I wanted to talk about. I'm sorry that I have been critical and judgmental of you. I was wrong. Will you please forgive me?" He grabbed me and, with tears in his eyes, kissed me.

Six months later, Tracy reports that she and Tom have recaptured the sweetness of love that existed in their early years of marriage. The turning point in their marriage occurred when Tracy humbled herself and said, "Please forgive me."

LEVELS OF FORGIVENESS[5]

Level 1 — *Detached Forgiveness*—There is a reduction in negative feelings toward the offender, but no reconciliation takes place.

Level 2 — *Limited Forgiveness*—There is a reduction in negative feelings toward the offender, and the relationship is partially restored.

Level 3 — *Full Forgiveness*—There is a total cessation of negative feelings toward the offender, and the relationship is fully restored.

FORGIVENESS IS NOT:
- Approval of what they did
- Excusing what they did
- Justifying what they did
- Pardoning what they did
- Reconciliation (something that happens between two people)
- Denying what they did
- Blindness to what happened
- Forgetting
- Refusing to take wrong seriously
- Pretending we are not hurt

FORGIVENESS IS:
- Being aware of what they did and still forgiving them
- Choosing to keep no records of wrongs
- Refusing to punish
- Not telling what they did
- Being merciful
- Graciousness
- An inner condition
- The absence of bitterness

Servant lovers are forgivers. Sometimes it's easier to offer a forgiveness cup than at other times. The Song records Tirzah sexually rejecting Solomon once. But what happens when a husband or wife faces the ultimate rejection — the decision of their mate to have an affair? How do we forgive when the pain thrusts like a knife and cuts to the core of our masculinity and femininity? It seems impossible, but as Jack discovered, it isn't:

> Toni and I sat on the bed, the very bed where we'd made love many times during our eighteen years of marriage, as she confessed that five years ago, she'd had an affair with her former boss. I felt like I'd been stabbed with a knife. Even though our marriage wasn't great, I'd always

trusted her. I couldn't believe she would betray me that way.

For the next two months, anger gripped me. I was mad at myself for being such a blind fool, believing all her lies and deception. And I was angry with Toni. Not only had she let another man touch her sexually, she had pursued him for over a year. Two months later, when I'd come to the place of truly wanting to forgive this woman who was the mother of our three children, she confessed something else that rocked my world. Not only had there been another man, in the last year there had been another woman.

I was devastated and disgusted. I could not fathom what had driven her to do this. Because of her actions, I doubted my own manhood. What was there about me that was so repulsive that she would seek to be intimate with a man *and* a woman, when she was reluctant to have sex with me?

I shut down emotionally. Yes, this was the answer: feel nothing, file for divorce, put this behind me, and move on. But one day as I was reading my Bible, God spoke to me from Malachi: "I hate divorce." He whispered to me, "Fight for your marriage, Jack." *How, God? I have no desire to even be with her!* God assured me, "I will help you. You will learn to forgive her as I have forgiven you."

This began a process that was painfully difficult because I had to dole out more forgiveness than I felt I possessed. God gave me the grace to say, "I forgive you for being unfaithful," but the big decision to forgive was easier to make than the small daily choices to forgive. Memories, images in my mind, accusing thoughts — all were little knives that dug into me.

You lied about having to work late the Friday of Kaley's parent teacher conference. Instead of being with us, you were with him. I forgive you.

You went with him to see the movie I wanted to see with you. I forgive you.

You allowed another woman to satisfy you sexually, but when I wanted to love you, you said, "I'm not in the mood." I forgive you.

On and on and on. The cuts were so deep that the moment one part began to heal, another part began to bleed.

If you think Jack and Toni's story is hopeless, you have grossly underestimated the healing power of the Almighty. Five years later, you would not recognize this couple, very much in love, as they renewed their wedding vows. After five years of tears and counseling — Toni's sexual abuse as a young girl greatly influenced her many wrong choices — she and Jack are truly "new creations" (2 Corinthians 5:17). Formerly the walking wounded, they now serve as living testimonies that "nothing is impossible with God" (Luke 1:37).

> "Lord, how often shall my [mate] sin against me and I forgive [him or her]? Up to seven times?" Jesus said to him, "I do not say to you, up to seven times, but up to seventy times seven." (Matthew 18:21-22, modified)

We believe that God asks us to forgive our spouse because He understands that without forgiveness, the flame of love dies; bitterness and resentment extinguish it.

UPROOT BITTERNESS

Margo understands just how destructive bitterness can be. She says that when she first learned about Butch's affair, she was so angry that if she'd had a gun she would have shot him. "How could you?" she raged. "You promised this would never happen!"

Every day a thousand accusations fed her bitterness:

- ◊ You *promised* on our wedding day to be faithful.
- ◊ When your dad cheated on your mom, you swore you'd never do such a horrible thing to me.
- ◊ Creep. You didn't even have the decency to cheat with a stranger — you chose our friend.
- ◊ Liar. I asked you a few months ago, "Are we okay?" and you said, "Sure, honey, we're fine."

Adding to her sense of injustice was Butch's indifference about the pain he'd caused her. Margo couldn't sleep; she lost weight. Her eyes were puffy from crying. She looked and felt like the walking dead.

She saw no possible way for her and Butch to repair the damage that had been done, so they separated. Three months into the separation, Margo made an appointment to talk to Joyce, her pastor's wife. Margo tells us what transpired:

> Joyce took one look at me and said, "Margo, you look terrible. You are so bitter that it's killing you. You have to forgive Butch — for your sake."
>
> "But he doesn't deserve to be forgiven," I cried.
>
> "No, Margo, he doesn't. None of us deserves forgiveness. But right now, this is not about Butch; this is about you. Your sin of unforgiveness and bitterness is no less than his sin of adultery."
>
> I was stunned. Butch was the one who had sinned. How dare she accuse me of sin. But truth rose above my indignation. *Oh God, she's right! I've been so focused on Butch's sin that I missed my own.*
>
> I sobbed into a wad of tissue and then looked at Joyce. "I can't do this anymore. I want this bitter root gone. I'm ready to forgive Butch. Tell me what to do."
>
> "Close your eyes. Picture in your mind a big fishhook. Now picture Butch hanging from that hook. The reason you feel so much weight is because he is on your hook and you are carrying that with you everywhere you go. You've been carrying this around so long that it has poisoned and weakened you, and the weight has become too much."
>
> I nodded as the tears streamed down my face.
>
> She continued, "Margo, tell the Lord you are going to release Butch from your hook."
>
> "God," I sobbed. "This weight is too much. I release Butch. He is no longer on my hook. I let him go."
>
> Relief was immediate. The weight lifted. Then Joyce said, "Margo, look at your hook. Nothing is there. That is why you feel lighter. But there is another hook — God's hook. Now that you've let Butch off your hook, he is on God's hook, where he belongs, and God will deal with him."

That day, two miracles occurred. The first miracle was that Margo acknowledged her own sin and released Butch to God. This action pulled out the root of bitterness. The second miracle occurred a few hours later when her cell phone rang. It was Butch. They had not spoken in three months. He cried into the phone, "Margo, honey, I've been wrong — so very, very wrong. Can we get together and talk?"

> See to it that no one comes short of the grace of God; that no root of bitterness springing up causes trouble, and by it many be defiled. (Hebrews 12:15)

ANOINT WITH FORGIVENESS

Extending forgiveness is one of the most difficult things we are asked to do as Christians. This is especially true when our mate has betrayed us by being sexually intimate with someone else. Often husbands and wives say to us, "I have tried to forgive. I think I've forgiven, but then when the images come again, I wonder if I really have." This was Connie's problem. Like Margo, Connie's husband had been unfaithful and she wanted out of the roller-coaster ride of questioning if she had forgiven him. To move forward, Connie decided to cement in her mind that she had made the choice to forgive by acting out her forgiveness in a beautiful way:

> I was shaking as I asked my husband to stand in front of me. I took off all of his clothes, and with a bottle of scented oil, I anointed his body.
>
> I touched his forehead: "I forgive your mind for thinking thoughts of her."
>
> I touched his eyes: "I forgive your eyes for looking at her."
>
> I touched his ears: "I forgive your ears for listening to her."
>
> I touched his hands: "I forgive your hands for touching her."
>
> After anointing every part of his body, I came to his feet. "I forgive your feet for walking toward her." As the words came, tears

cascaded down my face. Relief flooded me. The past was truly in the past — for us both.

Every couple knows the agony of making the choice to forgive. It would help if when your mate offended you, he or she would fall on the floor at your feet and, with tears, beg your forgiveness and then, as a sign of deep repentance, run out and buy you a new Ferrari in your favorite color. But God says we are to forgive even if the person has not asked for forgiveness. He says, "Forgive as you have been forgiven":

> Forgive unconditionally
>> Forgive freely
>>> Forgive repeatedly

We encourage you to buy a forgiveness cup and use it often with your mate and kids. You can designate your own cup or buy one at www.intimateissues.com. Apologizing clears the air and offers a new beginning.

> When there is a problem
>> And you are the one to blame
>> Don't demand your rights
>> Be humble in Jesus' name
>> Offer the cup of forgiveness
>> To the one you have offended
>> When you say "I'm sorry,"
>> Relationships are mended.[6]

SERVANT LOVERS: Offer forgiveness when wounded.
SELFISH LOVERS: Hold a grudge and use it as a weapon against their mate.

TIRZAH TO HERSELF:
"I went down to the orchard of nut trees
To see the blossoms of the valley,
To see whether the vine had budded
Or the pomegranates had bloomed.
Before I was aware, my soul set me
Over the chariots of my noble people."

THE CHORUS TO TIRZAH:
"Come back, come back, Shulammite;
Come back, come back, that we may gaze at you!"

TIRZAH TO THE CHORUS AND TO SOLOMON:
"Why should you gaze at the Shulammite,
As at the dance of the two companies?"

SOLOMON TO TIRZAH:
"How beautiful are your feet in sandals,
O prince's daughter!
The curves of your hips are like jewels,
The work of the hands of an artist.
Your navel is like a round goblet
Which never lacks mixed wine;
Your belly is like a heap of wheat
Fenced about with lilies.
Your two breasts are like two fawns,
Twins of a gazelle.
Your neck is like a tower of ivory,

SOLOMON TO TIRZAH (CONTINUED):
Your eyes like the pools in Heshbon
By the gate of Bath-rabbim;
Your nose is like the tower of Lebanon,
Which faces toward Damascus.
Your head crowns you like Carmel,
And the flowing locks of your head
are like purple threads;
The king is captivated by your tresses.
How beautiful and how delightful you are,
My love, with all your charms!
Your statue is like a palm tree,
And your breasts are like its clusters.
I said, 'I will climb the palm tree,
I will take hold of its fruit stalks.'
Oh, may your breasts be like clusters of the vine,
And the fragrance of your breath like apples,
And your mouth like the best wine!"

TIRZAH TO SOLOMON:
"It goes down smoothly for my beloved,
Flowing gently through the lips of those who fall asleep.
I am my beloved's,
And his desire is for me."

SONG OF SOLOMON 6:11–7:10

chapter fourteen

Be Free with Your Body

"When we were discussing sex in marriage during a Bible study,
the teacher said the wife in the Song of Solomon performs a
nude dance as part of their lovemaking. I don't believe it.
Surely this isn't in the Bible! I could *never* do that!"

Is there really such a thing in the Bible? Read on and see for yourself.

UNDERSTANDING THE SONG

*Tirzah: "I went down to the orchard of nut trees to see the blossoms
of the valley, to see whether the vine had budded or the pomegranates
had bloomed." (6:11)*

While there is some disagreement, most commentators believe this is
Tirzah speaking. The imagery suggests she desires a sexual encounter with her
husband. The word translated as "orchard" is the Hebrew word for garden
(*ginnat*), which, as pointed out earlier, refers to the female genitals.[1] This verse
is the only one in the Song where *ginnat* is used to refer to an "orchard of nut
trees," but in extrabiblical literature, references to nuts and nut groves often
had sexual connotations.[2] So when Tirzah speaks of going down to the nut
grove, she is likely expressing her desire for sexual intimacy, as supported by
the fact that she wants to see if the pomegranates had bloomed.

In biblical times, the pomegranate was commonly viewed as an aphrodisiac. The juice of the fruit was often mingled with wine, and its seeds were a
common symbol of fertility.[3] So when Tirzah says she wants to see if the vine
had budded and the pomegranates had bloomed, she is saying she wants to

explore her husband's body. The budding of the vine and the blooming of the pomegranates speak of the blossoming of sexual passion.

Tirzah: "Before I was aware, my soul set me over the chariots of my noble people." (verse 12)

This verse is the most obscure in the Song. It has also been translated, "Before I realized it, I found myself in my princely bed with my beloved one" (NLT) and "Before I was aware, my fancy set me in a chariot beside my prince" (NRSV). Is Tirzah in bed with her beloved, or in a chariot with him? We aren't sure, but in either case, Tirzah's words express strong passion for her husband.

The Chorus to Tirzah: "Come back, come back, O Shulammite; come back, come back, that we may gaze at you!" (verse 13)

By calling her Shulammite, the chorus is referring to Tirzah as Mrs. Solomon. Her thoughts show that her whole being longs to be reunited with her lover. What follows is very erotic. Get ready — this is hot stuff!

Tirzah to Chorus and to Solomon: "Why should you gaze at the Shulammite, as at the dance of the two companies?" (verse 13)

This verse is a tease meant for Solomon's ears. The queen is being coy. As the following verses will show, she is performing an erotic dance before her husband. He can see her entire body, so we assume she is either nude or dressed in very transparent clothing. She toys with him as she sways before him and asks, "Solomon, why are you staring at me?" (Need she ask?)

Her dance is called "The Dance of the Mahanaim" or of the two companies, because Mahanaim was the place where Jacob's company met Esau's army. It was also the place where Jacob wrestled with the angel (see Genesis 32:24-32). Perhaps Tirzah's sensuous swaying dance movements contained beauty as magnificent and transporting as the dance of an angel.[4]

In the five verses that follow, Solomon again employs a *wasf*— the literary device that poetically praises the parts of the body in sequential order. In the first three *wasfs* (see Song 4:1-7,12-14; 5:10-16; 6:4-6), the praise started at the top of the head and progressed downward. But here (7:1-8), Solomon begins with Tirzah's feet and works his way upward:

-   Feet (verse 1)
-   Upper part of thighs, rounding of hips (verse 2)
-   Naval, like a round goblet (verse 2)
-   Belly, like a heap of wheat (verse 2)
-   Breasts, like two fawns (verse 3)
-   Neck, like a tower of ivory (verse 4)
-   Eyes, like pools of Heshbon (verse 4)
-   Nose, like a tower of Lebanon (verse 4)
-   Head, crowns you like Carmel (verse 5)
-   Hair, tresses (verse 5)

Solomon to Tirzah: "How beautiful are your feet in sandals, O prince's daughter! The curves of your hips are like jewels, the work of the hands of an artist. Your navel is like a round goblet which never lacks mixed wine." (verses 1-2)

To speak of the curves of Tirzah's hips is a beautiful way of expressing the exquisite craftsmanship and symmetric beauty of his wife's thighs. The Hebrew word *shor* is translated here as "navel," but it probably does not refer to Tirzah's belly button. While *shor* could mean that, it is generally translated as "vulva."[5] The description that the *shor* "never lacks mixed wine" speaks of it as a source of sexual pleasure and moistness.[6] Furthermore, the belly button is not noted as a place of moisture or sexual pleasure, but this description fits the vulva well.[7] As she dances before him, Solomon views his wife's *shor* and says it looks to him like a "round goblet" or "a bowl in the shape of a half moon."[8] The allusion to her vulva seems obvious and makes sense, given the sequential progression of Solomon's description of his wife's body.

Wine is used throughout the Song (see 1:2; 5:1) and in eastern erotic poems as a symbol of sexual pleasure. Solomon is suggesting that Tirzah's vulva is a never-lacking source of sexual pleasure for him. "Mixed wine" refers to a mixing of his sexual pleasure with hers — of wine and milk (see 5:1). Longman says, "The description of the woman's aperture as containing wine implies the man's desire to drink from the sensual bowl. Thus, this may be a subtle and tasteful allusion to the intimacies of sex."[9]

Solomon to Tirzah: "Your belly is like a heap of wheat fenced about with lilies." (verse 2)

In Syria, perfect skin was compared in color to the yellowish-white of wheat after it had been threshed and winnowed.[10] Here Tirzah's *shor* is described as wine and wheat, food commonly associated with a meal. The combination of these images compose a feast[11] and suggest Solomon's desire to kiss these areas as he later expresses a desire to kiss her breasts.

Solomon to Tirzah: "Your two breasts are like two fawns, twins of a gazelle." (verse 3)

This phrase, also found in Song 4:5, suggests that the softness of her breasts invited his touch.

Solomon to Tirzah: "Your neck is like a tower of ivory. Your eyes like the pools in Heshbon, by the gate of Bath-rabbim. Your nose is like the tower of Lebanon, which faces toward Damascus." (verse 4)

Tirzah's neck is important to Solomon. In Song 4:4 he praised her stately and adorned neck, and he is doing the same here. With her hair swept up, her smooth pale neck looked like a tower of ivory. As he gazes into their depths, her eyes cause him to feel calm and tranquil. Solomon longs to penetrate the mysterious depths of his beloved's body and soul.

Having a neck like ivory is one thing, but the wives writing this book would not like to be told that their noses looked like a tower! One commentator believes that the comparison is linguistic and not visual, for the root of the Hebrew words can mean Lebanon and frankincense. So Solomon could be saying that her nose is straight, like the tower of Lebanon, or he may be saying it's pale and fragrant.[12] (Still, the wives writing this book believe that Solomon, although normally a master of praise, was not up to par with this analogy).

Solomon to Tirzah: "Your head crowns you like Carmel, and the flowing locks of your head are like purple threads; the king is captivated by your tresses." (verse 5)

As majestic Mount Carmel crowned the fertile plains of Palestine, so Tirzah's beautiful face sits exquisitely atop her lovely figure. Purple is a royal color and Solomon sees his wife's hair as queenly. Her magnificent flowing tresses hold him captive.

Solomon to Tirzah: "How beautiful and how delightful you are, my love, with all your charms!" (verse 6)

This verse could be paraphrased, "How beautiful and delightful you are, skilled in giving sexually delightful caresses."[13] The Hebrew word for charm, *tahanug*, is very intensive and refers to "the delights of love"[14] and combines the ideas of luxury and exquisite delight; she was a "daughter for all pleasure."[15] Tirzah is a master at pleasuring her husband.

Solomon to Tirzah: "Your stature is like a palm tree, and your breasts are like its clusters." (verse 7)

Solomon was increasingly aroused as he gazed upon his wife's breasts and swaying body. The palm tree serves as a very exotic description of Solomon's beloved. It sways in the wind with inexpressible gracefulness but seldom breaks.

Solomon to Tirzah: "I said, 'I will climb the palm tree, I will take hold of its fruit stalks.' Oh, may your breasts be like clusters of the vine." (verse 8)

In this verse, Solomon is mixing two images of fruit — the date palm and the grape vine — to say to his wife, "I want you *now!* I will make love to you and caress your breasts."

The phrase *climb the palm tree* has very erotic connotations. Since the earliest times, female flowers on date palms have been artificially fertilized. The male and female flowers grow on separate trees, in clusters among the leaves. In order to fertilize the female tree, one must climb the male tree and get some of its flowers and then ascend the female tree and tie a bunch of the pollen-bearing male flowers among the female flowers.[16] So climbing the palm tree is essentially fertilizing it.

Solomon then changes images from date palms to grape clusters, likely because grapes swell and become increasingly round as they ripen, similar to the female breasts when sexually aroused. This metaphor too is highly erotic. In Palestine, a vine grower had an almost personal relationship with his vines. The farmer had to work lovingly with each one to cause them to ripen and then he would get to taste the yield. In effect, Solomon has aroused Tirzah to the point that her breasts are ripened and engorged and ready to yield the best "wine" possible.

Solomon to Tirzah: "And the fragrance of your breath like apples, and your mouth like the best wine!" (verses 8-9)

Solomon longs to taste not only her breasts but also her breath, which is deliciously scented with apples and like the best-vintage wine. The mingling of the sweet scents enhances the experience of their lovemaking. Also, the use of the word *apple,* which was thought to be an aphrodisiac,[17] indicates Solomon's longing for Tirzah to be excited and eager to reach the heights of pleasure with him.

Solomon is beside himself with desire. His wife has captivated him by dancing seductively before him. God had created him to be aroused through the eyes, and Tirzah was skilled at giving him all any husband could desire in a lover. This grand dance climaxes in exquisite lovemaking. As the two lie together in oneness, Tirzah speaks.

Tirzah to Solomon: "It goes down smoothly for my beloved, flowing gently through the lips of those who fall asleep." (verse 9)

Tirzah says her love is totally and completely satisfying to her husband. "It goes down smoothly" is a reference to the "wine" or high sexual pleasure. As wine causes the body to relax and drift into sleep, so their love has left them sweetly exhausted, and they fall asleep in one another's arms.

Tirzah to Solomon: "I am my beloved's, and his desire is for me."
(verse 10)

As they drift into peaceful oblivion, Tirzah whispers this beautiful benediction before sleep whisks her away: "I belong to him. He desires me. I am blessed among women."

GROWING AS A SERVANT LOVER

DESIRE: I want to be free with my body.

OBSTACLE: I am inhibited and self-conscious.

SOLUTION: I choose to overcome my inhibitions by embracing God's truth about sex and my body.

OUTCOME: I can be free with my body to sexually delight my mate.

APPLYING THE SONG FOR WIVES

Several month's ago, a woman called Linda to ask, "Do you and Lorraine give dance lessons?"

"Excuse me?" Linda replied.

"You know, that wife in the Song of Solomon. Can you and Lorraine give me lessons so I can dance like she did?"

We want to make one thing clear: We do *not* give dance lessons! Nor are we suggesting that you run out and buy a sexy teddy and dance seductively before your husband. Our job is not to approve specific acts such as erotic dances but rather to help you understand the Song so that you can apply God's Word in a way that is unique and personal to your intimacy. So here our focus will *not* be on Tirzah's *actions* but on her *attitude,* which proclaimed, "Because I am sexually free, I can use my body provocatively to delight my mate."

Are you free with your body in the privacy of your intimacy? Or do fears or insecurities inhibit expression? Let's look at some things you can do to overcome your inhibitions, and then talk about the key role your husband plays in helping you become sexually free with your body.

SAY "YES" TO SEXUAL FREEDOM

The word *inhibit* means to restrain, to hinder, to prohibit, to check. Do women suffer from inhibitions? Yes. As we talk to women around the country, we would say 50 percent or more feel that their inhibitions hinder lovemaking with their husbands. They desire to be free, but instead they are tied with ropes of restraint. What are these restraints?

Cultural modesty: Many are brought up to believe that good Christian girls are proper, and proper girls are not wild and crazy in bed.

Guilt or shame: Many wives were sexually free *before* they were married, and now when it is right to be free, they can't get over guilt and shame from their past.

Embarrassment: Some wives think, *I could never provocatively display my body to my husband. I get embarrassed just thinking about it!*

Fear of rejection: What if he laughs or makes a sarcastic comment about my body or ridicules my sexy dance steps?

Sexual abuse: Because of the deep pain of past memories, many wives can hardly make love, let alone be sexually uninhibited.

Inadequacy: Pictures of models and movie stars with voluptuous breasts and flat tummies assault women daily, so at night when they crawl into bed, they cover up because they don't measure up. Most women feel inadequate at some level. Men's magazines are filled with pictures of beautiful women, but so are women's magazines, and it can be intimidating.

Throughout this book, we've said that God wants you to enjoy sex and be uninhibited in bed. We've talked about what God permits and prohibits sexually and about releasing control of your body to your husband. And we've explained how God can set you free from any guilt and shame associated with your past. But we know that the gap between "I can make love only in the dark under the covers" and "I am free and creative in bed" can feel as expansive as the Grand Canyon. Don't give up. It is possible to throw off your fears and be free.

INHIBITION CRUSHERS

Insight from wives who have walked freedom's path:

Get in shape: I think I started to lose my inhibitions when I began regular exercise. It made a big difference in how I felt about myself.

Put on sexy attire: Sexy lingerie helps me overcome my inhibitions. I buy the less expensive stuff at Wal-Mart. If I spent more money on it, I would want to keep it on longer!

See the humor: As I attempted my dance, I turned bright red and felt as clumsy as an elephant in a tutu. We laughed and it blessed us both.

Pray: I'm committed to praying for God to change me. God has shown me that my relationship with Him cannot be right if my relationship is not right with my husband.

Find privacy: Locking the doors of our bedroom helps me be free. I can't be uninhibited when I am worrying if the kids will barge in at an embarrassing time.

For some women, freedom follows quickly on the heels of their commitment to being an uninhibited lover. But for others, freedom is something they grow into — growth comes each time they say "yes" to expression and "no" to the restraints that hold them captive. What is the process to becoming sexually free? How do you know when you have arrived? The key lies in your ability to honestly answer "yes" to the following three questions.

1. Have you embraced God's perspective of sex?

If you don't know whether to say "yes" or "no" to this question, get out a sheet of paper and write five adjectives that describe your attitude about sex. Did you include words such as *fun, adventurous,* or *exciting?* Or did you write words such as *uncomfortable, predictable,* or *duty?* Has your attitude become more aligned with God's attitude since you began reading this book? If your perspective could use more alignment, go back to the beginning and read again all the chapters up to this point. As you read, ask God to speak to your heart.

Getting God's perspective is the most important step you can take to becoming uninhibited with your body. Once you truly understand that God gives *you* permission for pleasure, that He blesses *your* sexual relationship with your husband, you will begin to experience freedom. One woman said, "Knowing that what I am doing in bed is *pure* and *holy* in the eyes of God has set me free. I'm becoming like the uninhibited wife in the Song of Solomon."

The bottom line is this: If you don't have God's perspective of sex, you will continue to feel restraint in the bedroom. But if you answered "yes," you are ready for the second question.

2. Have you given your body to your mate as a gift?

We have a folder filled with stories from women who say that giving the gift of their bodies to their husbands was crucial in their ability to overcome inhibitions in the bedroom. Remember, this is not about giving your body for the purpose of sex but about releasing authority of your body to your husband (see 1 Corinthians 7:4; refer to pages 155-156 about the gift exchange). When you have given your body as a gift to your husband, you will develop an inner desire to please him sexually, as these wives testify:

> "What has helped me to overcome my embarrassment? I see his joy."

> "The thing that has given me the greatest freedom is realizing that letting go in my mind, heart, *and* body is the biggest turn-on for him."

When you have God's perspective concerning intimacy with your husband, it frees your mind before God. When you give the gift of your body to your husband, it frees you before your lover. Most women find that this decision triggers something that enables them to be more expressive with their bodies. Now for the final question. Are you ready? It involves courage and actually doing something to demonstrate your God-given freedom.

3. Will you demonstrate your freedom through new actions?

Being free is part knowledge and part jumping off a cliff and going for it. It involves taking a risk with your body — leaping forward by faith and having no assurance of the outcome. We know — it's scary. *What if he hates what I try? What if I start something and feel like I can't follow through with it? What if I look stupid rather than sexy?*

Every woman has inhibition hurdles over which she must jump. Some have an entire track filled with hurdles every few feet; others have only a few. We can procrastinate and never run the race for sexual freedom, or we can jump — one hurdle at a time. All your jumps won't be perfect. You'll miss a few. At times, you might feel awkward and ungraceful. On occasion, you might fall flat on your face. But next time, it likely will be easier. Here are some comments from a few hurdle jumpers:

> "I love this man. I knew what he wanted, and I never had tried it before. I realized I just needed to go forward and do it. So I shut my eyes and went for it."

> "To get over my inhibitions, first I picture in my mind what I want to do. Then, as the slogan says, I just do it!"

> "When I choose to do something I don't feel comfortable with but that my husband likes, I view my obedience as an act of worship to God that pleases both my husband and my Lord."

> "I made a commitment to grow sexually. I am far less inhibited now than I was five years ago. I hope to be even freer in another five years. By the time I'm fifty, my husband won't even know what hit him."

Wives sometimes look at their inhibition hurdles and think, *I'll wait a while—this will be easier in five years.* Sometimes this might be true, but most often not. Why not decide today to be free? God is a trustworthy God. Trust Him to help you run this race. You won't regret it, nor will your husband. Will you pray?

> *Lord, I want to embrace the beauty and fun that you want me to have. Please give me the courage to become like the wife in the Song of Solomon. I choose today to take a step forward in freedom.*

While you reflect on what you have just read, hand this book over to your husband, because now we have a few things to say to him about how he can help you over the inhibition hurdles.

HUSBANDS: LOVE HER TO FREEDOM

Would you like for your wife to be sexually free, for her to be able to use her body sensuously to arouse you and bring you delight? We thought so. Well, you can help her achieve this noble goal. We surveyed thousands of wives, and they tell us that *you* are key to your wife's overcoming her inhibitions. In chapter 7, you learned that your wife's greatest need is to be loved with a deep, cherishing type of love. This is especially true in the bedroom. Nothing will help her overcome her sexual inhibitions faster than your love, acceptance, praise, and appreciation of her. Let's look at how you can best communicate these concepts.

Solomon encouraged Tirzah to be sexually free by wrapping a cloak of security around her with words of praise. We've talked repeatedly about the power of praise because Scripture repeats this message over and over. Rather than tell you what to say, we will share with you what wives have told us their husbands said that helped them overcome their inhibitions:

> "When I was pregnant with our fifth child. I was very disturbed about my appearance. My husband asked me to undress and relax on the bed, and I automatically pulled a sheet over my body to hide. He gently pulled the sheet off of me and started to tell me the beauty that he saw with each part of my body, beginning at the top of my head and moving down to my toes. We then experienced a deep, intimate time of making love like no other."

"I have one breast and a scar. I can hardly stand to look at myself in the mirror, but my husband kisses my scar and my one breast and tells me that I am beautiful. How can I *not* desire this man when he looks at my flaws and expresses such appreciation?"

"My father looked at pornography and left it around our home. He told dirty jokes and had numerous affairs. I was always ashamed of my femaleness and embarrassed around him. My husband was aware of my body insecurities. For the last fifteen years, he has told me I'm beautiful — every single day. I finally believe him! This has set me free from shame."

Your wife needs to know that the bedroom is a place where you never will judge, criticize, or embarrass her. Instead, let her know your bedroom is a place where you will listen to her, gently love her, and call forth all that is within her as a woman. Caleb's wife describes how he did this for her:

I carried baggage into our intimacy because of my wrong choices, but my husband has made me a new woman by nurturing me. I think of him as a farmer, and I am his garden. He has carefully, patiently, and gently tended this garden. By talking and listening, he's helped me pull the weeds in my mind (wrong images) and then plant flowers (good memories) in their place. He prayerfully seeks God's best for our marriage bed, and I've slowly learned under his care to follow and respond. Even when I was bald from chemotherapy, surgically scarred, and overweight, he still wanted me and gently nurtured me. Now *I'm* the one who not only is responding but also pursuing him. My husband's farming skills are bringing forth much sweet fruit!

Loving acceptance creates within a wife the desire to be free:

My husband helps me overcome my inhibitions by encouraging me to be open to new ideas, but if I'm not ready, he says, "That's okay, princess. I don't ever want you to do anything that doesn't feel right to you." His acceptance of me makes me all the more willing to go for it.

Be patient as your wife grows in her sexual freedom. Let your words tenderly love her. Create an atmosphere where she feels safe and accepted and she will be more likely to step out and try new things. If you are brave (and we are sure that you are), ask your wife:

    ◊ In the bedroom, do you feel loved, or condemned?
    ◊ In the bedroom, do you feel accepted, or judged?
    ◊ In the bedroom, do you feel praised, or ignored?

If she answers negatively to any of these questions, ask her what you can do to help her feel safe, accepted, and loved. Tell her that you want to help her grow sexually and that you know this requires creating an environment where she can be free. We encourage you to grab her hand and pray something like this:

> *Lord, I haven't given my wife the love and acceptance she needs. Please show me how to do this. I want to become an encouraging lover to her. Amen.*

Now that we've talked to you about how you can help your wife be free, we'll discuss the importance of sexual freedom for you.

APPLYING THE SONG FOR HUSBANDS

Do men struggle with sexual inhibition? Yes, but the problem is not as common for them as it is for women, nor does it manifest itself in the same way. Still, certain factors can cause a man to feel restrained or inhibited in the bedroom:

Vulnerability: Part of the "male mystique" is that men are supposed to naturally be super lovers. This is a fallacy. Men don't know everything about pleasing their wives sexually, and sometimes their lack of knowledge causes them to feel vulnerable.

Shame of his body: Men are feeling more pressure these days, as sculpted abs are definitely in.

Guilt from his past: Men who previously treated women with a lack of respect don't know how to move beyond it.

Pornography: Men who have struggled with pornography in the past (or present) are sometimes afraid to be too free for fear of the images that will flood their minds.

Performance: If the ads on television, in newspapers, and in magazines for Viagra, natural performance enhancers, and videos to improve your lovemaking skills are an indicator, performance anxiety is at an all-time high.

A wife's apathy: If his wife is indifferent in the bedroom, it deflates a man's view of himself as a lover.

Contrary to popular perception, husbands are more vulnerable than wives when it comes to sex. The movies characterize men by locker-room bravado. In reality, husbands usually are closed-mouthed about marital sex. Why? Perhaps they don't want it known that their wives aren't panting after their bodies; they want to be viewed as a super lover. A man's masculinity is tied to how he feels about his ability as a lover. Don Meredith says, "Few things in life give a man more a sense of having finished a task well than having satisfied his wife sexually."[18]

Here's what men say when they're being honest:

> "It's about achievement, isn't it? Don't we all walk around afterward and arch our backs and throw out our chests like the roosters we are, our heads bobbing and our steps swaggered and jerked? The next morning, as we survey our surroundings, we think, *I am man, and all that I see is good.*"

> "I hesitate to say the word *conqueror,* but when I look at my wife satiated with pleasure after lovemaking, I feel like running to the highest hill, planting a flag in the ground, and shouting, 'Victory!'"

Every husband wants to feel confident as a lover. If you don't feel this way, what are some practical things you can do?

§ If you have a wrong perspective about your role as a lover, keep reading this book. Ask God to give you His perspective. Also, consider reading *Sex, Men, and God,* by Douglas Weiss.

§ If you have problems related to sexual performance, first talk to your doctor. If he rules out medical problems, then talk with a respected and licensed sex therapist through the American Board of Christian Sex Therapists (ABCST) at www.sexualwholeness.com.

§ If you have a low sex drive, consider using a performance enhancer. Some men have found arginmax (www.arginmax.com) helpful. Check with your doctor or a licensed therapist for other recommendations.

§ If you struggle with guilt over your past, reread chapter 12 and schedule a talk with your pastor. Christ wants you to be free as a lover.

§ If pornography is an issue, bring it out in the open by talking to a pastor or friend. Read *Every Man's Battle.* Go to Focus on the Family's websites www.pureintimacy.org and www.renewingintimacy.com for help. See "Get Rid of Porn," pages 197-198.

We are not telling you things that you have not already heard, but the question is, *Are you doing them?* What can you do right now to enjoy sexual freedom in your intimacy?

Because your wife plays a role in how you feel about yourself as a lover, hand the book over to her, and we'll give her some ways to encourage you.

WIVES: LOVE YOUR HUSBAND TO FREEDOM

Many husbands say that *you* are the key to their overcoming their fears and feeling good about themselves as a lover.

Think for a moment about how God made men and women. Within the body of each female, He intricately wove ways for it to shout, "You are feminine; you are woman!" Every month, a woman is reminded. (Most feel they could do fine without this monthly reminder.) A woman carries a baby and feels her child kick, and with each thrust in her ribs, she is reassured, "You are feminine; you are mother." A mother holds a new baby to her breast and her body whispers, "You are woman. You are mother!" God built *one thing* into a man's body that shouts, "You are masculine; you are man!"

Ladies, we're certain you know what that "one thing" is! This is why a husband's prowess as a lover is directly tied to his masculinity. That is why it is so important that his wife affirm his lovemaking skill. When Tirzah said to Solomon, "I am lovesick; satisfy me," Solomon felt like a superstud. This sometimes surprises women, as the following comment indicates:

> I was shocked to learn (and I've been married over thirty years) that a man's ego is so tied to sex. The idea never occurred to me, and my husband would never tell me that, but he sure confirmed it when I probed him! That is truly a revelation, and it makes me sad that I was so ignorant before.

Certain things you do and say either help or hinder your husband's sexual freedom. You can make him feel like he is Superman and Agent 007 all wrapped into one man, or you can cause him to see himself as an emasculated wimp, as these husbands testify:

> "What's worse than rejection is a begrudged spreading of the legs so she can get it over with and go to sleep. How is a man supposed to feel he is pleasuring his wife after encountering an attitude like that? The most pleasure a man can get from sex is to know he is pleasing his wife."[19]

> "We were making love last night, and right in the middle of it, she asked me, 'How much longer is this going to take?'"

Ouch! Do you feel the pinprick of conviction?

In chapter 7, you learned that your husband's greatest need is for respect. This is especially true in the area of sexual intimacy. One of the key ways you can show him respect is to build him up as a lover. Every husband longs to hear words of affirmation from his wife's lips. When one wife asked her husband how she could encourage him as a lover, she said his simple answer smacked her in the face: "Be available and agreeable and be interested."

Consider this story from our funny friend Darla:

> One evening at our marriage group we were asked to introduce our mate by telling something we appreciated about him or her. The answers were strictly mundane: "He's a great father," "She's a creative cook, " blah, blah, blah. I decided to be more vulnerable and honest, so when it was my turn to introduce Parker, I said, "I am grateful that Parker is such a wonderful lover!" Afterward, every man in the room raced over to Parker and asked, "How did you get her to say that? Tell us what you do!" Parker was very embarrassed, but I know secretly he loved feeling like the "superlover of the century."

Darla told us that six months later, men were still going up to Parker and asking, "How did you get her to say that?"

We are *not* suggesting that you publicly talk about your husband's love-making skills — the privacy of your bedroom is the right place for this. But the response to Darla's statement that her husband was a wonderful lover illustrates a man's deep need to be affirmed about his skill in this area.

Will you talk to God? You might pray something like this:

> *Lord, I see that I have not encouraged my husband in his role as my lover. Please show me what this looks like. I want to build him up.*

Will you talk to your husband this week? Ask him, "What three things can I do to encourage you as a lover?"

GET READY FOR FUN!

God desires that every husband and wife cast off sexual inhibitions and revel in sexual freedom. He wants your intimacy to become a place of fun, excitement, and deep oneness. We pray you have a high level of commitment to grow in this aspect of intimacy. How willing are you to say "yes" to God and "no" to the fears that restrain you? How willing are you to encourage and build one another up? You will ignite your intimacy when you choose to be free!

SERVANT LOVERS: Overcome inhibitions and use their bodies to delight their mate.

SELFISH LOVERS: Allow their fears and insecurities to restrain their ability to give extravagant love.

TIRZAH TO SOLOMON:
"Come, my beloved, let us go out into the country,
Let us spend the night in the villages.
Let us rise early and go to the vineyards;
Let us see whether the vine has budded
And its blossoms have opened,
And whether the pomegranates have bloomed.
There I will give you my love.
The mandrakes have given forth fragrance;
And over our doors are all choice fruits,
Both new and old,
Which I have saved up for you, my beloved.

TIRZAH:
"Oh that you were like a brother to me
Who nursed at my mother's breasts.
If I found you outdoors, I would kiss you;
No one would despise me, either.
I would lead you and bring you
Into the house of my mother, who used to instruct me;
I would give you spiced wine to drink
from the juice of my pomegranates.
Let his left hand be under my head,
And his right hand embrace me.
I want you to swear, O daughters of Jerusalem,
Do not arouse or awaken my love
Until she pleases."

SONG OF SOLOMON 7:11–8:4

❦

chapter fifteen

Be Free to Be Creative

"Everything about our lovemaking is familiar. The bedroom is familiar.
Our bodies are familiar. He touches me; I touch him — always in the same way
and the same place. Ten minutes later, it's over. This is supposed to be thrilling?
How do we get out of this rut?"

Once again, the Song leaps forth with answers to our questions. Once again, solutions are found when we decide to be servant lovers to our mate.

UNDERSTANDING THE SONG

Let's recap Tirzah's choices to be a servant lover. First, she used her mind to shift her body into sexual gear. Next, she performed a dance to the delight of her husband. Surely this was more than enough to let Solomon know she desired to be the lover of his dreams. But she does even more. Here she schedules a weekend away in the country and tells him of her plans to make love with him — not in the predictable environment of a bedroom but outside in the vineyard!

Tirzah to Solomon: "Come, my beloved, let us go out into the country, let us spend the night in the villages." (7:11)

One commentator suggests that Solomon and Tirzah are probably not married at this point, because married couples don't have time to seek out hidden hideaways to make love. We disagree. Married couples desperately need to create new and exciting lovemaking adventures, and Tirzah is superb at planning romantic encounters. She calls to her husband to come away with her — away from the pressure of palace life, away from his daily responsibilities. Together, they will flee to the countryside, where life is lazy and serene. And at the top of Tirzah's agenda for their time together are two key words: *renewal* and *romance*.

Tirzah to Solomon: "*Let us rise early and go to the vineyards; let us see whether the vine has budded and its blossoms have opened, and whether the pomegranates have bloomed. There I will give you my love." (verse 12)*

Notice that Tirzah says, "Let us," four times in verses 11 and 12. This is a time for just the two of them. They will rise early before other people are awake and go to the rows of grapevines, where it is easy to hide among the branches laden with leaves and fruit. They will bask in the fresh air and beauty of the springtime morning — and in one another — for outdoors, in God's glorious creation, Tirzah promises to give Solomon her love.

A striking characteristic of the Song in comparison to the love literature of the Ancient Near East, is its use of metaphors related to fruit to describe the pleasures of love. We read of engorged grapes, ripening, and juicy.[1] The lovers want to be intoxicated with love's sweet fruit (2:3) and its sensuous wine.

When Tirzah asks Solomon to come with her to the country and make love outdoors, she speaks of the opening of grape blossoms and pomegranates in bloom (7:12). She then tells him she will give him the "juice" of her pomegranates (8:2-3). This wife is not a passive partner in their lovemaking. She is eager and active as she dispenses the mixed wine and pomegranate juice.

Tirzah to Solomon: "*The mandrakes have given forth fragrance; and over our doors are all choice fruits, both new and old, which I have saved up for you, my beloved." (verse 13)*

As the couple lies among the grapevines, the walls of their secret hideaway are not carved of wood but fashioned by the Almighty out of His bounty. Mandrakes were a well-known aphrodisiac, but it appears Tirzah doesn't need them. She has taken the initiative, calling her husband to come with her to the vineyards where she will unwrap surprises especially for him. This creative wife entices her husband by telling him, "I have planned new delights for you — things we've never done before. I have old delights — some of your favorites — that are sure to please you." You just *know* this king was beside himself with excitement!

Then, after offering her invitation to a lover's tryst in the outdoors, Tirzah seems to make an abrupt mood shift.

Tirzah: "Oh that you were like a brother to me who nursed at my mother's breasts. If I found you outdoors, I would kiss you; no one would despise me, either." (8:1)

Here we see the young bride's thoughts. Tirzah doesn't wish that they were literally brother and sister; she simply wishes they were as free as siblings are to express their love in public.[2] In that culture, it was acceptable for a brother and sister to hold hands or kiss in public, but not for a husband and wife.[3]

Tirzah: "I would lead you and bring you into the house of my mother, who used to instruct me; I would give you spiced wine to drink from the juice of my pomegranates." (verse 2)

The reason for Tirzah's reference to her mother's home is unclear. But in view of the erotic associations that follow and her request for intimacy in verse 3, it seems likely that Tirzah's mother was the one who first taught her about intimacy.

Tirzah's wish that she and Solomon could demonstrate their love in public quickly turns into a desire for intimacy in private. She again takes the initiative: "I would lead you, I would give you the juice of my pomegranates." Her words express desire for an intimate rendezvous with her lover.

Tirzah: "Let his left hand be under my head and his right hand embrace me." (verse 3)

Tirzah imagines Solomon's left hand under her head as she lies on her back, and his right hand "embracing" or "fondling" her breasts and "garden."[4]

Tirzah: "I want you to swear, O daughters of Jerusalem, do not arouse or awaken my love until she pleases." (verse 4)

This is the third time Tirzah addresses the imaginary chorus with this warning: "Do not arouse or awaken love until she pleases." Here's a quick review of what we believe is the meaning behind these three warnings:[5]

First warning, 2:7: If you want to have the maximum sexual joy and fulfillment in marriage, do not allow sexual arousal to occur with anyone before marriage.

Second warning, 3:5: If you want to objectively evaluate marriage to a particular person, do not allow yourself to become sexually stimulated by this person, or else your objectivity will be lost.

Third warning, 8:4: Here the message seems to be that because there are sexual adjustments to be made after you've said, "I do," do not complicate things further by bringing into the marriage guilt and scars from previous sexual encounters.

When one enters marriage free of guilt, it is easier to become a creative, uninhibited lover like Tirzah.

Did you ever expect to read in God's Word about a husband and wife making love in a vineyard? We think it is wonderful. Our God gives us such freedom. We thank Him, and we thank Tirzah. She shows us that a wife can be assertive and seductive. She takes the initiative and plans this outdoor escapade. This wife is supremely confident of her capacity to delight her husband and articulates all the pleasures she has in store for him.

GROWING AS A SERVANT LOVER

DESIRE: I want to be a creative lover.

OBSTACLE: I feel overworked, overtired, and under-creative.

SOLUTION: I will plan a creative encounter with my mate this month.

OUTCOME: I will grow in my skill as a lover.

APPLYING THE SONG FOR COUPLES

We can become a Rembrandt in the art of loving our mate, or we can stay at the paint-by-numbers stage. We can throw wild colors on the canvas of our lovemaking, or only connect the dots. If we always make love the same way, in the same place, in the same position, it is like an artist who paints using only the color green. Even if green is your favorite color, if all the paintings in your home are shades of emerald, you would eventually shout, "Borrrrring!"

Tirzah was a colorful wife when it came to making love. On the canvas of their sexual intimacy, she splashed vibrant yellows, rich browns, and vivid blues as she invited Solomon to an outdoor escapade under an azure sky. Her example inspires three ideas for how couples can fuel the flame of intimacy in their marriages: consider an outdoor adventure, schedule alone time for loving, and enjoy new and old sexual delights.

The illustrations that follow offer practical ideas for each of these areas. Certain ideas are ones we have tried and found beneficial; others come from creative lovers who have given us permission to share their stories. Some of the ideas may surprise you; others might make you laugh. Our hope is that what you read will inspire you to infuse color and fun into your intimacy and encourage you to grow as a Rembrandt in your sexual art!

CONSIDER AN OUTDOOR ADVENTURE

Perhaps when you read of Tirzah and Solomon making love in the vineyards, you thought, *No big deal, we've made love outside before.* Or maybe for you it is a big deal and Tirzah's outdoor adventure left you gulping, "I could never do that." One wife said this is how she felt:

> I was definitely out of my comfort zone. Whatever possessed me to tell Garrett I was up for finding a secluded area and spending a night of wild lovemaking in the back of his new truck? As we drove around looking for the perfect spot, visions of police with flashlights filled my mind. *God,* I silently prayed, *help me here. I'm trying to be creative, but I need someplace that feels safe and private.*
>
> A few minutes later, we spotted a sign for a Christian retreat

center. We drove in and the caretaker, with a knowing smile, said we could park our truck anywhere on the grounds for the day and the night! My husband said it was the perfect christening for his truck.

If you are fearful of being discovered, consider something closer to home:

Our outdoor adventure was not in the light of day but under a canopy of stars — on our son's trampoline. We snuggled under the blanket, and with each shooting star, things began to heat up. We discovered that the spring of the trampoline offered a fun bounce to a most memorable night.

You might want to plan a picnic by moonlight. It's easy and fun. Here's what you'll need:

Props: lantern, two blankets, cheese, crackers, grapes, sparkling cider, snack-size candy bars, portable CD player with batteries, romantic CD, sleeping children, and one backyard free of yipping pets and biting mosquitoes. (If you are concerned about being in the backyard while your children are alone in the house, take a baby monitor with you.)

Directions: In your backyard, spread out a blanket, food, cider, and a CD player. Lay aside the second blanket for later. After the kids are asleep, venture to your picnic spot by lantern light. Sit on the blanket and enjoy quiet conversation and words of affirmation as you share tasty delicacies. When you have finished the main meal, pull the second blanket over you and enjoy dessert — chocolate and each other.

We've given you three outdoor lovemaking possibilities. Perhaps one is right for you, perhaps not. A couple does not have to make love in the wild to be creative in their sexual intimacy. Ask your mate, "Honey, would you feel comfortable making love outdoors?" If the answer is "no," consider other things you can do to add adventure to your sexual relationship. If the answer is "yes," discuss where you could go and when you could enjoy this creative encounter.

Each couple must seek how creativity is spelled for them. One way to develop creativity is to plan time for just you and your mate.

SCHEDULE TIME ALONE FOR LOVING

How many times have you said to each other, "We desperately need a weekend away together"? How many times have you read in a marriage book or heard your pastor say, "It's critical that husbands and wives carve out time for one another so that they can stay connected in their marriage"? We've made similar suggestions in this book. All the while you nod your head in agreement, *Yes, we need time alone.* The question is, When was the last time you scheduled time for just the two of you for intimate loving?

We know that scheduling alone time is difficult. We know it can be expensive. We know you worry about whom you can trust to care for the children. We know all this and yet we also know that it is imperative that you occasionally get away from the pressures and demands of ordinary life so that you can reconnect and refresh one another.

Consider making every anniversary your primary escape time. Lorraine and Peter do this. Each year, they get away and do something together they have never done before. Sometimes the new thing is sexual; other times it is going to a new place. One year they hiked a mountain trail rated "most beautiful in all of Colorado." Another year they danced on the beach to the music of crashing ocean waves. Over the years, they have built twenty-four memories that only the two of them share.

Half the fun of an anniversary getaway is preparing for it. So visit a travel agency and grab some brochures, or hop online and print out vacation destinations not far from where you live. Here are some tips for planning that special time:

- Dream about the possibilities and brainstorm about where you would like to go.
- Set the date (and an alternate date as a backup). Cross out the days on your calendar, hopefully on or near your anniversary.
- Discuss resources you will need for the weekend (budget, babysitting, someone to take your place teaching Sunday school, pet or plant care, and so on).
- Write down several expectations each of you have for your time away.

As the date draws near:

- Build anticipation by writing each other e-mails or notes of your excitement to be away together.
- Purchase items you may need (lingerie, foods, gifts for each other).
- Make a packing list. Include items that will contribute to romance, such as music and candles. You may want to take this book and set aside time to read out loud to one another. The chapters will put you in the mood for loving, and the Couple Time questions in the Bible study will serve as fodder for the fire of many intimate moments together!

If you are on a tight budget, commit to putting one dollar each day in a special getaway fund; 365 dollars is enough for a fun weekend. And the anticipation you feel each time you deposit a dollar in the box is worth more than a dollar. But if a dollar a day is beyond your budget, take heart and learn from this wife who planned a million-dollar anniversary night for under a hundred dollars:

> First, I told Jeff not to schedule anything for the night of our anniversary. Then, I booked a hotel (I found a special forty-five-dollar weekend offer). After I left the children at their grandma's, I put our motel key in an anniversary card and wrote, "Meet me at _____ motel, Room _____." Jeff found this on the kitchen table when he came home from work. Meanwhile, I purchased a takeout meal from his favorite Italian restaurant (twenty dollars), bought some roses for half price, and placed rose petals all over the bed and floor of our hotel room. I set up a CD player with romantic music, and seven dollars' worth of candles all around our hideaway. He unlocked the door with a huge grin on his face to find a candlelit room, the aroma of rose petals, romantic music, lasagna, and me in a skimpy nightie.

Another husband, Gregg, surprised his wife on their tenth anniversary with a weekend at a ski resort:

Our romantic condominium, complete with cozy fireplace and a view of snowcapped mountains, would have been enough to delight Karen, but further surprises awaited her one evening as she walked into the bedroom and found a box filled with twelve different items. Some of the items were coupons; others were fun gifts. Each had a message attached to it and was labeled with a month of the year. I told her, "Start with January and go progressively through each month. Everything in this box is my way of showing you that I intend to love you not only today, which is our anniversary, but all year long." Here are the items I included:

January: Anniversary card. "After a day of slipping down the slopes, I want to make love to you by the fire."

February: Five-dollar certificate for Barnes & Noble. "Let's sip coffee and look at books and dream about where we want to go for next year's anniversary."

March: Blockbuster video pass and popcorn. "Good for a night of munching, watching the movie of your choice, and holding hands."

April: Bath gel and massage lotion. "For us to enjoy April showers."

May: Thirty-five-dollar certificate to a local nursery. "For you and me to enjoy planting May flowers."

June: Bag of marshmallows. "Meet me at the fire pit in our backyard after the kids are asleep."

July: Lemon. "Meet me on the patio for lemonade on a warm Saturday afternoon when the kids are not at home."

August: Handmade coupon: "Good for one ice cream cone and ten compliments about why I love you."

September: Handmade coupon (with a leaf taped to it). "Good for a walk to remember among the falling leaves."

October: Bag of Hershey's Kisses. "Each chocolate good for one kiss placed exactly where you request."

November: Blank coupon. "Good for _____ (fill in the blank)."

December: An angel Christmas ornament. "Because you are my angel, I will do three chores of your choice (wrap presents, put up the lights, assemble toys for the kids, and so on)."

Getting away requires planning and creativity. The key is to leave your own environment and go someplace where you can enjoy each other and temporarily leave the worries of life. Do you know someone who lives in another state you'd like to visit? Ask if he or she would like to house-swap for a few days. Or plan a road trip to one of the national forests and camp at the grounds. An anniversary is *not* going to visit relatives, but it *is* finding alone time for the two of you.

Most of our life is not made up of vacation getaways but of routine days in which the responsibilities of life demand our attention. So what can you do when you're not on vacation? How can you add adventure and the vibrant color of creativity to your ordinary days? This next section contains plenty of ideas.

ENJOY NEW AND OLD DELIGHTS

After a few years of marriage, most husbands and wives have a storehouse of old delights. You know what has pleased each other in the past and trust that those ways of loving will please in the future — you know each other's favorite time to make love; you know each other's favorite position; and you know the touches that arouse, the scents that excite.

Spend an evening together sharing your most memorable times of lovemaking. Reminisce about the where, when, and why that made it one of your favorites. It feels good to speak of the things only the two of you share, doesn't it? This is the joy of old delights.

We admit there's an element of danger in trying something new. What if your spouse doesn't like your new creative position, or says, "But I like what we always do"? What if your plans turn out less pleasurable than what you've done in the past? This is likely. "When you try the floor instead of the bed, you may end up with carpet burns on your knees and a sore back the next morning. If you sneak out in the dead of night to enjoy your lover by the light of the silvery moon, you may both end up with the worst case of chiggers in three counties."[6]

But you took a risk, and that's the point. You tried something new. You created a memory together. You ventured out into the realm of the unknown. If you aren't sure where to begin, we suggest you ask each other the following question: What is your idea of a dream lovemaking encounter? One wife who asked her husband this question related the following story:

He replied with little hesitation, "After a foot massage, in front of a fire — on a bearskin rug." Well, I had massage creams and a fireplace, but the bearskin rug presented a challenge. After a series of phone calls, I located a trapper in British Columbia. I told him what I wanted and why, and luckily he said he had a bearskin to help me fulfill my husband's dream. A month later, the rug arrived. I called my husband at work and told him to come home promptly at 6:00 PM because I had a surprise for him. The look on his face when he saw me, the blazing fire, and the bear's eyes was worth all the effort and expense. The bearskin rug now hangs on our bedroom wall as a fun memory for us.

Some husbands and wives don't ask what new adventure their spouse would like; they just prepare, plan, and then involve their mate in the outcome. Jennifer's husband was in the hospital for minor surgery. She donned her nurse's uniform — without undergarments — and snuck into his room while he was sleeping. Then she took his wrist in her hand and said, with her blouse wide open, "Let me take your pulse, sir." He awoke with a smile.

Another creative wife blindfolded her husband and gave him some simple ground rules:

I told him, "No talking and no using hands; just lie back and enjoy. This is an evening to arouse all your senses using love potions, until we're standing on the edge of ecstasy and we dive together into the Lake of Love." Then I did various things to please him using the five senses. I appealed to his sense of taste with love potions of chocolate sauce, blueberry sauce, cheesecake, and so on; his sense of smell with scented candles and perfumed lotions; his sense of hearing with the sounds of ocean waves crashing from our CD player; and his sense of sight by removing his blindfold and dancing nude over him. Afterward, we did indeed dive into the Lake of Love!

Creative lovers plan new delights custom-made for their mate. If your husband or wife likes sports or working on your home or cars, the following creative ideas may inspire your thinking:

"My husband loves cars, and he often suggested we wash our car together. So one night when our teenagers were out for the evening, I closed the blinds in our garage (it had a drain and hot and cold running water) and brought out new bright flip-flops, a bucket of suds for the car, a new ladder for me to use, and sponges for the car and for us. When I appeared in flip-flips and nothing else, my car-loving man was beside himself with joy. I think he even liked washing me more than he did the car!"

"I am a big baseball fan and get caught up every year in the World Series. My husband always says I major in baseball during the series and not in loving him. He had been out of town for a few days and was coming back the night of the seventh game. I wanted to please him but also wanted to watch the game, so I set the stage for love and a ball game. In front of the television, I placed two stadium chairs, pom-poms, a big stadium blanket, and two baseball caps (which were the only clothing allowed in our stadium). I made something to drink and also some hot dogs and popcorn — things we could feed each other. Dessert was, well . . . you can guess. I had everything set up (myself included) when he walked in the door. It brought my husband much joy, and I got to watch most of the game! From that night on, he said that fall is his favorite season because the World Series is on."

"When we need some home improvements, my wife and I have found painting walls in the nude to be fun as well as efficient. The job is shared, it's fun, and your clothes don't get paint on them!"

You have probably laughed at some of the delights described here, but what do you do if ordering a bearskin rug or blindfolding your mate and saying, "No hands, no talking; just lie back and enjoy" is outside your comfort zone? What do you do if you feel God missed you when He passed out creative genes?

Our best advice would be this: Be persistent, and don't expect perfection. We wish we could promise you that every creative encounter will turn out exactly as you have planned. But after being married for many years and enduring broken-down cars, sick children, and arguments the morning of the getaway, we know that reality can overtake the ideal of what we plan. Linda tells what happened when she planned a new delight for Jody:

> We were long overdue for a romantic adventure, so I called a friend and scheduled her mountain condominium for a romantic weekend getaway. I was determined to plan something new sexually, but I had no ideas. I walked around our house and prayed, *God, show me something fun that will build a memory for us*. In the hallway closet, I spied an Easter basket filled with brightly colored plastic eggs that I'd gotten for the grandchildren. Instantly, I knew what to do.
>
> I went to the grocery store and purchased a large box of Milk Duds, Jody's favorite candy, which would be his "sweet treat." Then I wrote out on tiny pieces of paper a "sexual treat." In each plastic egg, I put both some sweets and sexual treat. *Perfect!*
>
> Each morning, I tossed Jody a plastic egg from the basket. One morning I tossed him a hot pink egg. He opened the egg, popped the Milk Duds in his mouth, and smiled in expectation as he read the sexual treat. All at once, he yelled, "Oh, no!" He pulled the Milk Duds out of his mouth, and with the candy came a bridge with four crowns. We quickly dialed the number of a local dentist. As Jody stood at the door with his teeth in his hands, I said, "Grandpa, I'll be here waiting for you when you get your teeth glued back in."

That particular creative sexual encounter cost six thousand dollars. Most likely, your teeth will not fall out, nor will it cost you a fortune when you plan a creative sexual encounter, but something discouraging may happen. Don't give up! The memories you create together will be worth the effort. Be persistent. Also, keep in mind the privacy factor. If you plan an outdoor adventure in a national forest, consider the possibility of bird-watchers with binoculars who might also be in the area. If you arrange for an afternoon of loving in front of a fire, make sure that UPS is not scheduled for a delivery. And if you are at a family reunion in a house filled with people, be careful that — well, we'll let Gavin tell you in his own words about certain precautions you may need to take.

We were in a living room full of relatives attending a family reunion. It was 2:00 PM, time for the baby's feeding, so Erika bounded up the stairs to breastfeed our three-month-old daughter. Bored with family gossip, I joined Erika in the bedroom. Together, we put the baby down for her nap and then proceeded to have a quick, passionate romp on the carpet. Afterward, we ventured back down the stairs to utter silence. Many sat with heads hung. Others squirmed uncomfortably in their seats, avoiding eye contact. We wondered if someone had died! What had happened here? Then we saw on the table the reason for their silence: the baby monitor, turned to high volume!

So our caution is: Ensure privacy! But our encouragement is: Have fun! Be free:

Free to use your mind in creative and sensuous ways
Free to forgive and use your words to delight your mate
Free to use your body to intoxicate your lover
Free to be creative

We hope this chapter has spurred your creativity. A servant lover is a creative lover who enjoys sexual freedom, schedules alone time, and discovers new ways to delight his or her mate sexually. Will you tell God that you are willing to grow in creativity and adventurous lovemaking?

Gracious Lord, thank You for giving us such joy and freedom in our intimacy. Take us deeper in all it means for us to be free to be creative.

SERVANT LOVERS: Are free to be creative in their lovemaking.
SELFISH LOVERS: Are unwilling to try creative new ways to please their mate.

THE CHORUS:
> *"Who is this coming up from the wilderness*
> *Leaning on her beloved?"*

SOLOMON:
> *"Beneath the apple tree I awakened you;*
> *There your mother was in labor with you,*
> *There she was in labor and gave you birth."*

TIRZAH TO SOLOMON:
> *"Put me like a seal over your heart,*
> *Like a seal on your arm.*
> *For love is as strong as death,*
> *Jealousy is as severe as Sheol;*
> *Its flashes are flashes of fire,*
> *The very flame of the LORD.*
> *Many waters cannot quench love,*
> *Nor will rivers overflow it;*
> *If a man were to give all the riches of his house for love,*
> *It would be utterly despised."*

TIRZAH'S BROTHERS:
> *"We have a little sister,*
> *And she has no breasts;*
> *What shall we do for our sister*
> *On the day when she is spoken for?*
> *If she is a wall,*
> *We will build on her a battlement of silver;*
> *But if she is a door,*
> *We will barricade her with planks of cedar."*

TIRZAH:
"I was a wall, and my breasts were like towers;
Then I became in his eyes as one who finds peace.
Solomon had a vineyard at Baal-hamon;
He entrusted the vineyard to caretakers.
Each one was to bring a thousand shekels of silver for its fruit.
My very own vineyard is at my disposal;
The thousand shekels are for you, Solomon,
And two hundred are for those who take care of its fruit."

SOLOMON TO TIRZAH:
"O you who sit in the gardens,
My companions are listening for your voice—
Let me hear it!"

TIRZAH TO SOLOMON:
"Hurry, my beloved,
And be like a gazelle or a young stag
On the mountains of spices."

SONG OF SOLOMON 8:5-14

chapter sixteen

Fan the Fire of Lifelong Love

"Today in the newspaper there was a picture of a couple who have been married fifty years. They look like they are still so much in love. How can anyone keep passion alive for fifty years? It seems impossible."

Is lifelong passion possible? Yes. We began this book by asking, "Where did all the passion go?" Each succeeding chapter has demonstrated creative ways to ignite and fuel the flame of intimacy in marriage by becoming a servant lover. Now we come to the culmination of the teaching of the Song. It ends as it began — with the declaration, "Enjoy your sexual love!"

Because 8:5-14 is the longest scene in the Song, we've organized the commentary under four subjects so that you can better understand the poet's intent in explaining lifelong love: love awakened, love defined, love developed, and love enjoyed.

UNDERSTANDING THE SONG

LOVE AWAKENED

The Chorus: "Who is this coming up from the wilderness leaning on her beloved?" (8:5)

Apparently, Solomon and Tirzah have just come from their outdoor hideaway, where they shared their love. This description of Tirzah as leaning on her lover denotes intimacy and mutual dependence and alludes to their recent lovemaking.

Solomon: "Beneath the apple tree I awakened you; there your mother was in labor with you, there she was in labor and gave you birth." *(verse 5)*

Here Solomon reflects on Tirzah's home and birthplace. The reference to the apple tree could be literal, suggesting an actual tree next to her childhood home, or it could be symbolic. The apple tree, which is a fruit tree with a sensuous scent, produces an appropriate atmosphere for awakening love. We have seen the apple connected with the place of sexual excitement and arousal before (see 2:3,5; 7:8).

The two verses that follow present the theme of the Song. Let's look at them first in their entirety and then phrase by phrase. What will unfold is one of the most beautiful definitions of love ever penned.

LOVE DEFINED

Tirzah to Solomon: "Put me like a seal over your heart, like a seal on your arm. For love is as strong as death, jealousy is as severe as Sheol; its flashes are flashes of fire, the very flame of the LORD. Many waters cannot quench love, nor will rivers overflow it; if a man were to give all the riches of his house for love, it would be utterly despised." *(verses 6-7)*

How can you describe love? It is so wide, so high, so deep. In an attempt to capture the depth and expanse of her emotion, Tirzah uses a series of images to communicate that her love for Solomon is intimate, intense, indestructible, and invaluable.

Tirzah: "Put me like a seal over your heart, like a seal on your arm." *(verse 6)*

Love is intimate.

The seal spoken of here is the seal of ownership and personal identification;[1] it's an allusion to the seals of that day — engraved tablets, worn openly over the breast, or a signet, worn on the arm or hand.[2] (Today the seal for married couples is a wedding ring.) To possess someone's seal is to have access to all that the person represents or owns. Tirzah wants to deeply and openly imprint her claim on her lover.³ She pleads with Solomon to display that ownership over his heart, the symbol of affection, or on his arm, the source of strength, so that it is immediately apparent to anyone he meets that he belongs to her, and she to him.

Tirzah: "For love is as strong as death, jealousy is as severe as Sheol."
(verse 6)

Love is intense.

Tirzah says that love is as strong as death. Upon first glance, this imagery may not seem romantic. But think with us. Death is final, permanent, and irreversible. Like death, Solomon and Tirzah's love is permanent; it will endure because it is irresistible, resolute, and unshakable.

Next she says that love is jealous. We often think of jealousy as a green-eyed monster, but here jealously denotes single-minded devotion. Scripture describes two relationships in which jealousy is positive and appropriate: God's jealousy for His people, and the jealousy between a husband and wife. God insists upon exclusive devotion, which is also essential in the marriage. If this love is compromised, jealousy is a proper response because so much hangs on the integrity of the relationship. It is so basic, so deep that it stirs up strong emotions and passions.

Tirzah: "Its flashes are flashes of fire, the very flame of the LORD."
(verse 6)

The picture here is holy and beautiful. The hotly burning flame illustrates the great power and energy of *ahabah* (covenant) love between a husband and wife. The flashes of *ahabah* are the very flame of the Lord. The Hebrew word *Shalhebetyah,* translated as "flame of the Lord," may mean "extremely intense, a mighty flame or a vehement flame." However, the suffix *yah* refers to Yahweh and therefore specifically identifies this flame as the flame of Yahweh.

Ahabah was fueled by erotic passion, *dod.* The flame grew brighter when the fuel of companionship, *rayah*, was poured on. Solomon and Tirzah show us that couples fuel *ahabah* love by responding to each other with a blessing when hurt, by putting the needs of the other first, and by committing to persevere through the hard times so that love is characterized by lifelong commitment. The Song has been building to this point. Then an even more astonishing claim is made.

This love, this *ahabah*, is given the highest appellation possible: Its "flashes" are the very "flame of the Lord." What are these "flashes"? The flashes of *ahabah* include the sparks of sexual passion, but the intensity of the passion comes from the companionship, service, sacrifice, loyalty, and commitment the couple bestow on each other. This is not the "passion" of one-night stands. This kind of sexual explosion flashes forth only from a certain kind of love, *ahabah*.

The Hebrew word for "flashes," *resheph*, is often translated as "lightning bolts."[4] These "fire bolts" burst forth from the *ahabah* of a couple who has devoted themselves to building lifelong love that is the "flame of the Lord." God Himself is in the midst of these wonderful fire bolts![5]

This stirring declaration seems like a perfect climax to the vivid and erotic pictures of Solomon and Tirzah's sexual love. But there is more: Tirzah proclaims that *ahabah* love, love fueled by God, is indestructible.

Tirzah: "Many waters cannot quench love, nor will rivers overflow it." (verse 7)

Love is indestructible.

Normally, the way to extinguish a flame would be to douse it with water, but Tirzah says that not even a raging river can extinguish the flame of *ahabah*. The images of fire and water, together with the verb *quench,* powerfully illustrate the indestructibility of love. Water can put out flames, but their deep love, which is fueled by the energy of God Himself, will triumph and overcome all adversities.

Then she makes a final statement about love:

Tirzah: "If a man were to give all the riches of his house for love, it would be utterly despised." (verse 7)

Love is invaluable.

Though all the gems of the world, all the wealth of the universe, be gathered in one place, it would not be enough to purchase this powerful flame of love whose flashes are the lightning bolts of God Himself.

In the culmination of these images, Tirzah sets out the ideal of love. Obviously, love is not always ideal. We can make wrong choices and stray from God as the source of our love, but the Song lifts up *ahabah* and declares that this powerful love is possible for all couples who choose to become servant lovers.

As we read these words, our hearts soar on the winds of *ahabah*, carried away by the reality of a love that is intimate, intense, indestructible, and invaluable. We want to pause and consider the possibilities. But the poet moves us on in the next verse and abruptly shifts our thinking to a discussion of Tirzah's breasts by her brothers. This seems out of place, but we must trust that God has something to say through the poet in what seems out of order to us. The previous verses defined love. Here the Song mentions two final ingredients that contribute to committed love: growing up in a caring family and making responsible choices about your own sexuality.

LOVE DEVELOPED

Tirzah's Brothers: "We have a little sister, and she has no breasts; what shall we do for our sister on the day when she is spoken for?" (verse 8)

In this flashback, the Song takes us back to Tirzah's childhood. Apparently, we are to see in the conversation between her brothers something central to the development of a deep love. Tirzah's father is not mentioned, but her brothers are concerned for her future marriage and happiness. In the absence of their father's influence and in light of the fact that she is the only daughter, the brothers assume certain responsibilities in preparing her for the "day she is spoken for" — the day of her marriage. At this point, Tirzah's breasts are not yet developed, but soon she will become a mature woman, and young men will come calling. The brothers' strategy is simple and wise, offering sound instruction that holds true for parents today.

Tirzah's Brothers: "If she is a wall, we will build on her a battlement of silver. But if she is a door, we will barricade her with planks of cedar." (verse 9)

The brothers' strategy depends on Tirzah's character. If she is a wall—impervious to sexual advances from young men—her brothers will adorn her with praise just as a "battlement of silver" adorns a wall and adds an element of beauty. But if she chooses to be a door—easily entered, easily seduced—the brothers will take a different approach. They will be strict with her, barricading her with planks of cedar in order to protect her virtue.

These verses tell us that Tirzah grew up in a caring home characterized by encouragement and discipline. The poet singles out this kind of environment as one factor in Tirzah's ability to develop an intense and committed love for her husband.

No matter what kind of home environment we are provided with (some of the writers of this book did not come from safe, caring homes, but God filled in the gaps of childhood), we must make responsible choices regarding our sexuality that represent our own values and not simply those of our parents. In the following verses, Tirzah informs us she made such choices.

Tirzah: "I was a wall, and my breasts were like towers; then I became in his eyes as one who finds peace." (verse 10)

Tirzah chose to be a wall. When she matured, her breasts were "like towers." Before you imagine Tirzah with breast implants, let us explain. Although the reference to her breasts as towers is somewhat ambiguous, it appears that they, "like the silver battlements, are decorative and attractive. She is not flat-chested, but full, mature and ripe for love. She will give her 'consoling breasts' only to the one to whom she is committed."[6]

The next phrase is emphatic in the Hebrew. "*Then* I became in his eyes as one who finds peace." When? *After* deciding to be a wall. As a result of assuming personal responsibility for her virtue, Tirzah found favor in Solomon's eyes. The phrase seems to be a play on words. Tirzah's name in the Hebrew sounds like the word *Shulamith*. Solomon's name in the original Hebrew sounds like *Shulomoh*. The Hebrew word for peace is *shalom*. Tirzah says, "Shulamith has found shalom with Shulomoh." She found love and romance when she found Solomon. Her responsible behavior concerning her own sexuality attracted the king's love.

Tirzah: "Solomon had a vineyard at Baal-hamon; he entrusted the vineyard to caretakers. Each one was to bring a thousand shekels of silver for its fruit. My very own vineyard is at my disposal; the thousand shekels are for you, Solomon, and two hundred are for those who take care of its fruit." (verses 11-12)

Tirzah often refers to herself as a vineyard (see 1:6; 2:15) and earlier complains that the workload imposed on her by her brothers kept her from tending her own vineyard — her feminine charms (see 1:5). When she says that "my very own vineyard is at my disposal," Tirzah is asserting that her brothers' work is completed. Her vineyard is now under her own authority and control, and she freely gives of herself to her lover, the king.

Tirzah's brothers protected her and prepared her to make wise personal choices. When she came of age, she chose wisely. This flashback tells us three important things about the development of an intense and vibrant love:

- ◊ It is rooted in a home where love is coupled with discipline.
- ◊ It is the result of responsible behavior.
- ◊ It is freely given.

We have seen love awakened, love defined, and love developed. In the last verses of the Song, we see love enjoyed.

LOVE ENJOYED

Solomon to Tirzah: "O you who sit in the gardens, my companions are listening for your voice—let me hear it!" (verse 13)

As the lovers prepare to leave Tirzah's country home, Solomon tenderly turns to his beloved and whispers these words to her. In the Hebrew text, the word *my* does not appear, so the companions referred to here are likely Tirzah's childhood friends who desire to tell her goodbye. But while her friends desire to say their farewells, Solomon says there are words he longs to hear her whisper. Tirzah privately responds with very erotic imagery.

Tirzah to Solomon: "*Hurry, my beloved, and be like a gazelle or a young stag on the mountain of spices!*" *(verse 14)*

The Hebrew here would be better translated as "sneak away, my beloved," as the original text denotes the idea of escape or flight.[7] The references to a young stag and gazelle communicate playfulness and sexual potency. The mountain of spices refers to the "mountain of myrrh and . . . hill of frankincense" (see 4:6) — her perfumed breasts and "garden."[8] Her private message to her beloved is, "Sneak away quickly, my lover! I long for your body as you long for mine. The time for passionate love is here!"

Solomon and Tirzah experienced the joy of committed, lifelong *ahabah,* a love whose flashes are the very "flame of the LORD." Lightning bolts burst forth from the flame of this intense, intimate love. This love can be yours too!

APPLYING THE SONG FOR COUPLES

> *Lorraine:* Dressed in white from head to toe, Peter and I stood before several hundred people who had come to witness the exchange of our marriage vows. For a moment, they faded into the background.
>
> There was only Peter, me, and the light from two candles. Peter held a taper in his left hand, and I held a matching one in my right. Together, we lowered our individual candles toward the wick of a much larger unity candle on the altar before us. The fire of my candle joined his, igniting a new flame that was brighter and more vibrant than the ones we'd each brought to it. We withdrew our individual candles and blew them out. The flame before us was a public symbol of what God would accomplish privately tonight. No longer would we be two but one.
>
> The flame on the altar glowed brightly. This flame was our love, the very flame of the Lord. And God Himself was in the midst of the flame.

Your love is a flame. For a moment, picture this flame and all it represents. Your flame is precious and holy to the Lord. He ignited it. He wants you to fuel the flame by becoming a servant lover to your mate. He desires that you keep the flame burning forever because it is a reflection of Him.

How can a couple keep the flame burning bright? By providing the right fuel.

- *Ahabah love:* service, sacrifice, loyalty, and commitment
- *Dod love:* passion rooted in sexual desire
- *Rayah love:* companionship and friendship

It takes all three types of love to keep the flame burning for a lifetime. The fire of sexual love (*dod*) will eventually burn out if not fueled by committed, servant love (*ahabah*). A marriage based on friendship love (*rayah*) — with no sexual love (*dod*) — will seem cool and passionless. But when all three fuel the flame, love builds and grows until it becomes an unquenchable bonfire.

MARRIAGE

A bond of love	*The joining of two lives*
Between two people	*Becoming one*
That holds them together	*Through love and adoration*
Forever	*Forever*
A shared commitment	*A holy union*
To live united	*Created by God*
Through harmony or discord	*Honored by you*
Forever	*Forever*

BY ROBIN HAPPONEN, WRITTEN FOR HER PARENTS, JODY AND LINDA, FOR THEIR THIRTY-SEVENTH WEDDING ANNIVERSARY

PURSUE LIFELONG LOVE

We were created for so much — to experience deep, blazing love — but we often settle for so little. God calls from heaven through all generations, "Revel in the gift of love I have given you. Pursue passionate, lifelong love." To pursue something means to run after it, to chase it with intent and purpose. No passive ho-hum spirit here but a tenacious pursuit of a faithful, forever love.

What does this kind of love look like?

We see lifelong love on the faces of Billy and Ruth Graham. In a recent interview, one author described the couple: "Billy will be 85 in November. He and his wife just celebrated their 60th wedding anniversary. Neither of them is doing well at all, but Billy said, 'We've discovered we can continue our love affair at this age with our eyes.'"[9]

We see lifelong love demonstrated in the lives of Bill and Vonette Bright. At the funeral of Bill Bright, the founder of Campus Crusade for Christ, Vonette, his wife and co-laborer of fifty-four years, shared how in the last hours of her husband's life, she had crawled in bed beside him and held his hand and prayed, thanking God for their years of love together.

During the service, Bill's assistant shared, "After a long day in the office, Bill would bound up the steps to their home, open the door, and call out, 'Love! Love! Where are you, my love?' By watching Bill Bright, I learned how to love my God. I also learned how to love my wife."[10]

Do you want what Solomon and Tirzah had — what the Grahams and the Brights forged over a lifetime — a love that is intimate, intense, indestructible, and invaluable? We do! We desire to strike a match and ignite a white-hot burning intimacy. We want this not just during the first year of our marriages but *every year*. This was Cheri and Scott's desire also.

Cheri and Scott had been married for sixteen years. In general, their relationship was enjoyable; they were good friends and deeply committed to each other. But Cheri knew something vital was missing. While their marriage wasn't completely sexless, it may as well have been. All their married life, Cheri had struggled with sexual intimacy and rarely initiated sex. She didn't even enjoy deep kissing with her husband.

But that began to change when she read the manuscript of *Intimacy Ignited* and decided to ask God to free her in this area. God graciously answered Cheri's prayers. Cheri tells the rest of her story:

> God has given me an incredible freedom and desire to love and respect
> my husband. It is as if we are brand-new lovers. After I finished reading
> the book, Scott and I cuddled on the couch and talked. Then I was able,

as never before, to bless him from head to toe with a holy kind of intimacy. It meant so much to him that he wept. For ten days in a row, we enjoyed intimacy in an incredible way, but it was more than just sexual intimacy we enjoyed. We are more deeply in love and passionate about one another. Scott has a greater desire to serve me in romantic ways. He has said, "You have my heart." He has even written me poetry! I think of him often and can hardly wait to be intimate and enjoy his company. His mouth is pure sweetness to me, and I love kissing him.

Perhaps you are wondering, *How did these changes come about? Were they overnight, as it sounds?* No. Cheri made some responsible choices that God used to personally transform her and the intimacy in their marriage. Again, Cheri shares,

> God gently used a number of things to make the difference in my heart. This included confessing sexual sin with my husband before we were married and forgiving him for pushing me to be intimate. It involved committing Scripture on intimacy to memory, giving my body as a gift to my husband and receiving his body as a gift to me, confessing my negative and selfish attitudes on sex, and choosing to think about my husband in a sexual way.

Cheri is becoming a servant lover. Every time she says, "Yes, God," she takes another step toward igniting intimacy in her marriage. She has embraced God's perspective and vows to live it out in her marriage on a daily basis.

How about you? As you read each chapter and saw the characteristics of a servant lover, did you step toward your mate and say "yes" to God, or did you take a step back and say, "No, this just seems like too much work"?

As you read each chapter of the book, you discovered the traits of a servant lover. According to the Song, servant lovers:

1. Are teachable
2. Give themselves permission to extend — and receive — passion
3. Express admiration through encouraging words and actions
4. Seek to make sexual love a place of refreshment

5. Develop a sexual language so they can communicate lovingly to one another
6. Catch the little foxes that threaten their love
7. Make their marriage a safe place by communicating love and respect
8. Daily honor their wedding vows
9. Are romantic, in and out of bed
10. Give the gift of their body to their mate
11. Admit their selfishness and learn from it
12. Allow God to set their minds free
13. Offer forgiveness when wounded
14. Overcome inhibitions and use their bodies to delight their mate
15. Are free to be creative in their lovemaking
16. Actively pursue lifelong intimacy

Are you wondering, *How can I ever begin to live this out?* Each of us changes and becomes a servant lover in the same way that Cheri did, one step at a time. We encourage you to prayerfully consider the following plan. You can follow this plan by yourself, but we strongly encourage you to do it with your mate, if possible.

◊ Each week take one trait and ask God to make it your own. Write a paragraph about what the quality described means to you, vow to incorporate the quality into your life, and consider various ways you can do that.
◊ Read the chapter that corresponds with that vow.
◊ If possible, do the Bible study for that chapter during the week.
◊ Do any personal application suggested in the chapter and Bible study.
◊ Talk to God every day about how you can personally live out this vow in your marriage.
◊ Be accountable to your mate or to a friend about your progress.

This is a sixteen-week program. Does this seem too hard? We admit, following this plan will require effort, but isn't the potential benefit to your marriage worth the time you'll invest? Look ahead and visualize how you will change. Four months out of a lifetime is not a long time. Four months from now you can be different — you can become a servant lover! As you continue on the path of becoming a servant lover, you will find the joy and beauty of lifelong love in your marriage.

The Beauty of Old Love[11]

Is there anything more beautiful in life than a
boy and a girl clasping clean hands
and pure hearts in the path of marriage?

Can there be anything more beautiful than young love?

Yes, there is a more beautiful thing.

The sight of an old man and an old woman
who have walked the path of marriage for a lifetime.

Their hands are gnarled but still clasped;
their faces are seamed but still radiant;
their hearts are physically bowed and tired
but still strong with love and devotion for one another.

Yes, there is a more beautiful thing than young love.

Old love!

SERVANT LOVERS: Actively pursue lifelong intimacy.
SELFISH LOVERS: Give up when marriage gets tough.

The Flame

[Love's] flashes are flashes of fire, the very flame of the LORD.
(Song 8:6)

God says that a couple's love is a flame and that He is in the midst of that flame. As you read the following fictional story based on Scripture, ask the Lord to open your eyes to why sexual intimacy is important to God and why it matters so much to the Enemy.

~

In the beginning, before all things, there existed only A Holy Consuming Fire,[1] the Holy God. He created the heavens and filled them with angelic beings. The most beautiful was Lucifer, the Bright Shining One.[2] Lucifer served the Holy Fire faithfully until the day came that he exalted himself because of his great beauty. In defiance, he said:

> *I will ascend to heaven.*
> *I will raise my throne above the stars of God.*
> *I will sit enthroned on the mount.*
> *I will ascend above the tops of the clouds.*
> *I will make myself like the most high God.*[3]

Selfishness was born, a monstrous evil emerging from a pool of pride. In his self-exaltation, Lucifer became Satan, God's adversary.[4] The Holy Fire could have addressed such blasphemy with raw power, destroying Satan immediately. Instead, He brought into existence a plan that would forever answer the idol called "I" — a plan that would involve the Holy One Himself in a moral demonstration of the superiority of servanthood over selfishness.

God banished Satan and his followers to earth.⁵ Then He announced to all of creation,

> "We shall set up a drama on earth and allow the universe to watch it unfold. We shall give this rebellion a thorough trial. We shall permit it to run its full course. The universe shall see what a creature—even the greatest—can do apart from Me. The wrack and ruin that will result will demonstrate forever the superiority of my plan, servanthood, over Satan's plan, selfishness."⁶

Creation held its breath in anticipation as the Holy Fire formed a creature similar to Himself, not a blazing furnace, but a spark, a tiny reflection of His light. He breathed into the creature and it glowed with life. "You shall be called man," the Holy Fire announced. Then God caused the man to sleep. Reaching deep inside him, He removed a part of the man and fashioned another being whom He named woman because she was taken from the man.⁷

The Holy Fire blessed the creatures. Then He gave them a divine mandate that, if followed, would defeat Satan and prove the superiority of God's ways:

> "Reflect my image.
> Be fruitful and increase in number.
> Fill the earth and subdue it."⁸

The creatures frowned. "How will we accomplish such great tasks?"

"I will give you a gift called sexual desire. As you live in dependence upon me and in service to one another, this gift will help you fulfill the mandate."⁹

Satan observed this exchange and threw back his head in laughter. "What kind of plan is this?" he mocked. "These sputtering sparks pale in comparison with me, the Bright Shining One. They will not rule my world. They will never subdue me."

The angels, who looked on as well, were perplexed. Indeed, the creatures were inferior to Satan. Why had God placed them in Satan's world and told them to rule the earth?¹⁰ How could such insignificant creatures, much lower than the angels,¹¹ possibly defeat Satan?

Several days passed. Satan and his demons watched as the two small lights went about their work, serving God and one another without incident. But then the creatures paused to unwrap the Holy One's gift to them. At first glance it appeared small and insignificant, but as the wrappings fell away, they realized that the gift possessed great power. The universe watched in utter disbelief; this gift was unlike any they'd ever seen.

The two individual lights pressed together, making it difficult to tell where one began and the other ended. The glowing sparks rubbed together, creating an intense heat that grew hotter, brighter. Then — a miracle! They were no longer two but one.[12] The separate sparks of their love had joined together to ignite a single vibrant flame.

The angels recognized the flame immediately. In some mysterious way the couple's love — their oneness — had produced a flame that was an image of the Holy Fire, the very "flame of the Lord."

Satan seethed as he glimpsed for the first time the larger plan of God. This gift enabled the creatures to multiply the image of the Holy Fire. One such image is no threat, but many flames, each living in dependence upon God and in service to one another, would mean his defeat.[13]

Satan looked at the gift of sex and despised its power:

- The gift enabled two to become one.
- The gift, rooted in God, enabled the creatures to reflect the Holy Fire.
- The gift enabled the flame to multiply.

I know what I must do, Satan reasoned. *I must separate the gift from its Source. I must pervert its purposes. I will convince the creatures to use the gift apart from its Creator and render the gift ineffective.*

Satan announced to all,

> *I will create a counterfeit gift and convince the creatures that it is better.*
> *God made the gift exclusive; I will let it be used indiscriminately.*
> *God created sex for oneness; I will use it to bring division.*

*God made sex pure; **I** will pervert it.*
*God designed sex to produce life; **I** will use it to bring death.*
The counterfeit will deceive God's creatures. Sex apart from its
Source will cause them to serve self, not God. And I will win.

At Satan's words, the demons cheered. The angels wept. The war began.

Marriage is about something much bigger than the drama of our daily disagreements and disappointments. Every Christian couple, whether they acknowledge it or not, is caught up in a greater drama—a heavenly battle involving the armies of God and the armies of Satan. The focus of the battle is our oneness. Satan's goal is to destroy marital oneness because it reflects God. God seeks to fortify oneness, to fuel the flame of love so that we might create a vibrant light that reflects Him.

What is our role in the grand drama today? You have a choice every day to give in to selfishness and follow the ways of God's enemy, or to be a servant lover and follow the ways of Christ. Which will you choose?

Sexual Acts That God Prohibits

This material is taken from Linda and Lorraine's book *Intimate Issues*[1] and is used with permission.

GOD'S TEN SEX PROHIBITIONS:

1. Fornication: Fornication is immoral sex. It comes from the Greek word *porneia,* which means "unclean." This broad term includes sexual intercourse outside of marriage (see 1 Corinthians 7:2; 1 Thessalonians 4:3), sleeping with your stepmother (see 1 Corinthians 5:1), and sex with a prostitute (see 1 Corinthians 6:13).

2. Adultery: Adultery, or sex with someone who is not your spouse, is a sin and was punishable in the Old Testament by death (see Leviticus 20:10). In the New Testament, Jesus expanded adultery to mean not just physical acts but also emotional acts in the mind and heart (see Matthew 5:28).

3. Homosexuality: The Bible is very clear that for a man to have sex with a man or a woman to have sex with a woman is detestable to God (see Leviticus 18:22; 20:13; Romans 1:27; 1 Corinthians 6:9).

4. Impurity: There are several Greek words that are translated as "impurity." To become "impure" (in Greek, *molyno*) can mean to lose one's virginity,[2] or to become defiled due to living out a secular and essentially pagan lifestyle (see 2 Corinthians 7:1; 1 Corinthians 6:9). The Greek word *rupos* often refers to moral uncleanness in general (see Revelation 22:11).

5. Orgies: For a married couple to become involved in sex orgies with other couples is an obvious violation of (1), (2), and (4) and therefore doesn't need to be discussed.

6. Prostitution: Prostitution, which means paying for sex, is morally wrong and condemned throughout Scripture (see Leviticus 19:29; Deuteronomy 23:17; Proverbs 7:4-27).

7. Lustful passions: First, let us tell you what this does not mean. Lustful passion does not refer to the powerful, God-given sexual desire a husband and wife have for one another. Instead, it refers to an unrestrained, indiscriminate sexual desire for men or women other than the person's marriage partner (see Ephesians 4:19; Mark 7:22).

8. Sodomy: In the Old Testament, *sodomy* refers to men lying with men.[3] The English word means "unnatural sexual intercourse, especially of one man with another or of a human being with an animal."[4] Unfortunately, some Christian teachers have erroneously equated sodomy with oral sex. This is not the way the term is used in the Bible. In the Bible, *sodomites* refers to male homosexuals[5] or temple prostitutes (both male and female).[6] In contemporary usage, the term *sodomy* is sometimes used of anal intercourse between a man and woman. This is not the meaning of the biblical word.

9. Obscenity and coarse jokes: In Ephesians 4:29, Paul says, "Let no unwholesome word proceed from your mouth." The Greek word is very descriptive and literally means "rotten" or "decaying." In Ephesians 5:4, the Bible warns us to avoid "silly talk" or "coarse jesting." We have all been around people who can see a sexual connotation in some innocent phrase and then begin to snicker or laugh. This is wrong. However, this does not rule out appropriate sexual humor in the privacy of marriage but rather inappropriate sexual comments in a public setting.

10. Incest: Incest, which means sex with family members or relatives, is specifically forbidden in Scripture (see Leviticus 18:7-18; 20:11-21).

A Journey to
Igniting Intimacy

Dear Couple,

Do you want to ignite the flame of passion in your marriage? If so, this study is for you. It can be life-changing, as demonstrated by the following comments from couples who field-tested this study for us:

> "We had the best talk about sex we've ever had in our thirty years of marriage." — John and Valorie

> "Homework is something we look forward to!" — Ron and D.J.

> "For the first time in our lives, we are truly understanding and applying God's perspective of intimacy." — Brian and Pam

Before we begin the first lesson, we wanted to answer a few questions you may be asking.

HOW IS THIS STUDY SET UP?

We've designed the study to fit an eight-week format. Each Bible-study session covers two chapters in *Intimacy Ignited* and has corresponding study questions and exercises. However, you can easily adjust the material for a shorter or longer time period to better suit your needs. The reading and application will take from one and a half to two hours a week. The more time, prayer, and discussion you put into the study, the more you will benefit.

IS THE STUDY DESIGNED FOR A COUPLE OR A GROUP?

Both. The Bible-study questions are designed for group use. The sections called "Private: For Couples Only" contain discussion questions designed just for the two of you and should not be part of what you share with the group.

WHAT DO I NEED FOR THE STUDY?

A teachable heart, a Bible, a copy of *Intimacy Ignited*, a pen, and a notebook in which to write your responses to the questions.

HOW DOES A GROUP TALK ABOUT SEX TOGETHER?

Very sensitively and with discretion. The facilitators of your study will help your group establish ground rules that all participants will agree on. When sexual intimacy is presented and discussed within the context of God's Word and under the guidance of the Holy Spirit, it becomes holy and sanctified.

Here are a few guidelines for a group doing this study:

- All discussions are to be kept confidential.
- No negative or embarrassing comments about spouses are allowed.
- Keep your focus on what changes you need to make, not on those your spouse needs to make.
- No one will be asked to talk about anything that makes him or her feel uncomfortable.
- Each couple will commit to the eight-week period.
- Expect to have fun, grow, and be amazed at God and His beautiful plan for intimacy. We are convinced the Song of Solomon can change you and your marriage forever. So get ready for adventure!

May God richly bless you and transform your marriage.

Jody and Linda Dillow
Peter and Lorraine Pintus

LESSON ONE

This week read:

> Introduction: Sex At Its Best
>
> Chapter 1: Where Did All the Passion Go?
>
> Chapter 2: Give Permission for Passion

INTRODUCTION: SEX AT ITS BEST

1. Write a paragraph describing God's perspective of sex. Save this — you'll compare it with a paragraph you'll write near the end of this study, after you have spent much time in God's Word learning things that may impact your current viewpoint.

2. Read the Song of Solomon prayerfully and thoughtfully.

   a. List any questions or observations you have about the Song and what it says about sex in marriage.

   b. Does what you read in the Song differ from what you were taught growing up? If so, how?

CHAPTER 1: WHERE DID ALL THE PASSION GO?

3. Are you willing to say to God, "I want to be teachable; I desire to ignite intimacy in my marriage"? If so, write a prayer expressing this.

CHAPTER 2: GIVE PERMISSION FOR PASSION

4. Read Ephesians 5:31. Write answers to the following questions:

   a. How would you describe the meanings of *leave, cleave,* and *one flesh*?

   b. In Ephesians 5:31, we learn a great mystery: Sexual intimacy with our mate is a picture of our spiritual intimacy with Christ. How does this insight influence your perspective of intimacy?

   c. How does this help you give yourself permission for passion?

5. Read Proverbs 5:15-19. Also read the paraphrase of verse 19 on page 29. Write a paragraph expressing how this passage encourages you to give yourself permission for passion.

6. Write out Philippians 2:3-4 on a card and look at it every day. (Philippians 2:3-4 is one of the theme verses for *Intimacy Ignited*.)

   a. On pages 32-33, read about being a servant lover.

   b. List three ways you are being a servant lover to your mate now.

   c. List three ways you want to grow in becoming a servant lover to your mate.

7. Do husbands and wives view intimacy differently? If yes, how? What gets in the way of couples fully enjoying intimacy?

Private: For Couples Only

Servant lovers are teachable.

- Each of you name two positive things about your sexual relationship.
- Each of you identify two ways you hope your sexual relationship will grow during this study.
- List two ways you hope to grow personally as a lover during this study, and share them with your mate.

Servant lovers give permission to extend and receive passion.

- Discuss how you can, as a couple, give yourselves permission for passion.
- Has kissing changed since you got married? How?
- Talk about one thing you like about the way you kiss and one new thing you would like to try.

LESSON TWO

This week read:

Chapter 3: Soothe Insecurities

Chapter 4: Offer Sexual Refreshment

CHAPTER 3: SOOTHE INSECURITIES

Some of the principles in this chapter apply to wives, and others apply to husbands. In this study, we want to apply all principles to both husbands and wives.

1. Read 1 Corinthians 6:19-20. Write a paragraph about how you are to view your body according to this verse. How should this perspective influence the way you look at yourself and your mate?

2. Review "View Your Body as God's Temple," pages 41-42. Write practical steps you can implement to take better care of your body in these three areas:

   a. For your mate

   b. For yourself

   c. For God (Ask the Lord, "Is there anything you would have me do about my appearance that would bless my mate?")

3. List two physical attributes that you find attractive about your mate. Show your mate what you wrote, and ask if you can share it with the Bible-study group.

4. On pages 48-50, read "Implement a Thirty-Day Praise Plan." This week, begin to praise your mate daily in one of the following areas: acts of service, physical attributes, or character attributes. To help you get started praising your mate, try one of the following ideas or come up with your own idea:

   a. Write a poem or song and share it with your mate.

   b. Make a list of positive adjectives that describe your mate and post them where your kids can see them.

   c. On poster board, create a montage of pictures that describes your mate.

   d. Write a letter to your children, describing why Mom or Dad is so wonderful.

   e. Place an ad in the paper expressing why your mate is so wonderful.

f. Write a short paragraph expressing three things you appreciate about your mate. Earn Brownie points by reading it to the Bible-study group.

CHAPTER 4: OFFER SEXUAL REFRESHMENT

5. First Samuel 24:1 talks about Engedi as a stronghold, a place of safety and an oasis of beauty. The Song expands the idea to include a hideaway for lovers. List three words or phrases that describe the current stressors in your life that keep you from creating your personal Engedi.

6. Read Proverbs 11:25. What does this verse mean as it might relate to your sexual relationship?

7. Read 2 Samuel 12:24 and Genesis 24:66-67.
   a. According to these verses, what is one reason God gave the gift of sex to married couples?
   b. Sexual union can be a source of comfort in stressful times, such as the death of a loved one. Name some other circumstances in which intimacy might give comfort to your mate when he or she is in pain or under extreme stress.

8. Take a bedroom inventory. List anything you'd like to do in the next month that would improve your bedroom ambiance.

PRIVATE: FOR COUPLES ONLY

SERVANT LOVERS EXPRESS ADMIRATION THROUGH ENCOURAGING WORDS AND ACTIONS.

- Identify two things about your mate's body that create sexual desire in you. Then look your mate in the eye and tell him or her.

SERVANT LOVERS SEEK TO MAKE SEXUAL LOVE A PLACE OF REFRESHMENT.

- Each of you identify one or two current emotional or sexual needs. Discuss how your sexual intimacy might help meet these needs.
- Plan together one night of "refreshment" this week.

LESSON THREE

This week read:

Chapter 5: Trade Sexual Compliments

Chapter 6: Catch the Little Foxes

CHAPTER 5: TRADE SEXUAL COMPLIMENTS

1. *Wives:* Write what you learned from Tirzah about being a creative lover.

2. *Husbands:* Write what you learned from Solomon about being a creative lover.

3. Read Proverbs 16:24, Ephesians 4:29, and 1 Thessalonians 5:11. List three things you learned from these verses that you can apply directly to how you speak to your mate.

4. Read Ephesians 5:4. Write a paraphrase of this verse. What does this say about how you should speak in public and in private about your sexual intimacy?

5. Read "Establish Sexual Boundaries" on pages 77-80 and "Get Rid of Porn" in chapter 12 on pages 197-198.

    a. What does this say about a husband or wife looking at pornography?

    b. List five reasons why God would say "no" regarding pornography.

    c. What would you say to a friend involved in viewing pornography?

CHAPTER 6: CATCH THE LITTLE FOXES

6. Identify two "little foxes" that were problems earlier in your relationship that are no longer an issue. What did you do or what circumstances caused these foxes to go away?

7. Identify two or more "little foxes" that currently gnaw at your love relationship. How can you trust God with these? How can you work together to keep these foxes from causing permanent damage?

8. Take the Marriage Minutes (MM) test on page 93. If you scored less than 180 minutes, identify two ways you can increase your Marriage Minutes together this week, and then implement them.

9. Review the "Top Ten Time Grabbers" on pages 94-96. Which ideas do you think would help you find time as a couple? Think of another time grabber, and write it here. Come prepared to share it with the group.

PRIVATE: FOR COUPLES ONLY

SERVANT LOVERS DEVELOP A SEXUAL LANGUAGE SO THEY CAN COMMUNICATE LOVINGLY TO EACH OTHER.

- Reread the exercise on pages 72-75 about developing a sexual language. Discuss how you can create your own sexual vocabulary of words and phrases that will enable you to talk freely about intimate body parts and to communicate, "Let's make love."
- Reread "Establish Sexual Boundaries" on pages 77-80 and "God's Ten Sex Prohibitions" in the appendix on pages 273-274. Discuss these questions: Are you permitting something in your sexual relationship that God prohibits? Are you prohibiting something in your sexual relationship that God permits?

SERVANT LOVERS CATCH LITTLE FOXES THAT THREATEN THEIR LOVE.

- Go on a date with your mate and talk about the "little foxes" in your marriage. Discuss specific ways to deal with the little foxes you have identified so that they do not hinder your marriage.

LESSON FOUR

This week read:

Chapter 7: Create a Safe Place for Loving

Chapter 8: Remember Your Vows

CHAPTER 7: CREATE A SAFE PLACE FOR LOVING

1. In your notebook, draw a vertical line, forming two columns. In one column, write any words or phrases you have communicated in the past that might have caused your spouse to feel emotionally or sexually abandoned. In the second column, write words or actions that communicate a sense of security and well-being. Prayerfully ask God for opportunities to communicate these to your mate this week.

2. Fifty years ago, the word *divorce* was whispered with trepidation. Today, Christian couples casually throw around the "D" word. What contributes to the casual use of the "D" word?

    a. Read Malachi 2:13-17 and Matthew 19:3-9. List three reasons why you think God uses such strong language and emotion in connection with divorce.

    b. If you have spoken or communicated the "D" word to each other in any way, express your regret and then talk about ways you can keep this from happening in the future. If the "D" word is not part of your vocabulary, write down two things you can do to reinforce your positive attitude.

3. *Husbands:* Review "Love Your Wife" on pages 106-107. In your notebook, list one way that you can love your spouse in each of these areas:

    a. Help

    b. Affection

    c. Listening

4. *Wives:* Review "Respect Your Husband" on pages 110-112. In your notebook, list one way that you can show respect to your spouse in each of the following areas:

a. Honor
b. Support
c. Response to sexual needs

CHAPTER 8: REMEMBER YOUR VOWS

5. Reflect on the vows you made to each other on your wedding day.
   a. Record two vows you made, and describe how you are actively fulfilling them.
   b. Identify any vows you are not fulfilling.
   c. Write a prayer asking God to show you ways you can practically demonstrate these vows to your mate this week.
6. *Husbands:* Review the information on pages 127-130 about how to protect your bride.
   a. Write three ways that you feel you protect your wife. Then write several more ways that you can protect her. Share this with her.
   b. Look up Psalms 7:1, 11:1, and 18:2. What do these verses tell you about where you should ultimately turn for protection?

PRIVATE: FOR COUPLES ONLY

SERVANT LOVERS MAKE THEIR MARRIAGE A SAFE PLACE BY COMMUNICATING LOVE AND RESPECT.

For Husbands:

- Make a list of your actions and attitudes that communicate love to your wife. Don't rush this exercise. Look at 1 Corinthians 13 to spur your thinking.
- Ask your wife to list the actions and attitudes that communicate love to her. Instruct her to include attitudes as well as actions. Did her comments match items on your list?

- What difference would it make in your marriage if you loved your wife in this way?

For Wives:
- Review Ephesians 5:33 from the *Amplified Bible* (page 111). Write a sentence following each descriptive word to illustrate how you could demonstrate this to your husband.
- Ask your husband to write a list of what communicates respect to him.
- What difference would it make in your marriage if you respected your husband in this way?

SERVANT LOVERS HONOR THEIR WEDDING VOWS DAILY.

- Take some time to relive your wedding day. Look through pictures, share memories, and call up others who were involved and reminisce.
- If you remember your wedding vows, recite them to one another. If not, consider writing some new ones that reflect what you want in your marriage today.
- Revelation 2:5 says that to return to the passion of first love, you should "do the deeds you did at first." What did you do at first for one another? Make a list together.
- Discuss how you have grown as lovers since your wedding day. Consider what it would look like for you to commit to a year of sexual delight (pages 126-127). How would this look? What might you do?

LESSON FIVE

This week read:

Chapter 9: Be Romantic In and Out of Bed

Chapter 10: Give Your Body as a Gift

CHAPTER 9: BE ROMANTIC IN AND OUT OF BED

1. Write a definition of romance based on what you have learned in this study.

2. Romance includes the unexpected.

    a. Describe a time you romanced your mate with the unexpected.

    b. List three ways you can include unexpected romantic encounters in the future.

3. Romance includes the impractical.

    a. Describe a time you included the impractical in a romantic encounter.

    b. List any barriers you have to being impractical and how they can be overcome.

4. Romance includes being intentional.

    a. Intentional spontaneity often creates anticipation. What role does anticipation play in lovemaking, and what can you do to increase anticipation?

    b. Describe a time you were intentionally romantic toward your mate. What was the response?

CHAPTER 10: GIVE YOUR BODY AS A GIFT

5. Memorize Song of Solomon 5:1: "Eat, friends; drink and imbibe deeply, O lovers."

    a. Paraphrase this verse in today's language.

    b. Review pages 154-155. Have you received God's blessing on your intimacy? If not, why not?

6. Write out 1 Corinthians 7:4 on a notecard and put it in a place where you will see it every day (taped on your bathroom mirror, car steering wheel, or fridge). Read this verse and pray it back to God every day this week.

7. Review "Give Your Body as a Gift" on pages 155-156.

   a. Write three things that keep a wife from giving authority of her body to her husband.

   b. Write three reasons why a husband might not give authority of his body to his wife.

8. Write a paraphrase of Proverbs 5:15-19 to share at the Bible study.

PRIVATE: FOR COUPLES ONLY

SERVANT LOVERS ARE ROMANTIC, IN AND OUT OF BED.

- Discuss how you can intentionally include romance in your marriage and sexual intimacy.
- Make a list of intentional actions you can take (a date night every month, buying *Simply Romantic Nights*, a creative sexual encounter next week, and so on).
- List two romantic things you would like to do in the next month.

SERVANT LOVERS GIVE THEIR BODY AS A GIFT.

- How could you give yourself as a gift to your mate?
- *Wives:* Describe how your intimacy would grow if you gave authority of your body to your spouse.
- *Husbands:* Read "Keep Your Eyes on Your Wife," pages 162-164. If you made a covenant with your eyes, how would your intimacy grow with your wife?
- On a card, in a letter, or in your mate's notebook, write, "I, _____ (fill in your name), choose with my free will to give my body to you as a gift. I hand over authority to you because I love and trust you." Sign your commitment and date it.

LESSON SIX

This week read:

Chapter 11: Stamp Out Selfishness

Chapter 12: Be Free in your Mind

CHAPTER 11: STAMP OUT SELFISHNESS

1. Memorize this important verse: "Marriage is a decision to serve the other, whether in bed or out" (1 Corinthians 7:4, MSG).

2. Read 1 Corinthians 7:5. What reason does Paul give for not having sexual intimacy? Name five other reasons (excuses) husbands and wives give to one another for not wanting to make love.

3. Review Philippians 2:4. Write a short paragraph about how this verse applies to demanding that your spouse have sex.

CHAPTER 12: BE FREE IN YOUR MIND

4. *Take inventory of your mind.* Review Max and Beth's story on pages 191-197. Be still before God for at least fifteen minutes. Ask Him to show you what is in your mind as it relates to sex. Record this on paper, using Max and Beth's charts on pages 193-194 as guidelines.

5. *Remove the corrupted files.* "If we confess our sins, He is faithful and righteous to forgive us our sins and to cleanse us from all unrighteousness" (1 John 1:9). Ask God to remove anything in your mind that is displeasing to Him and harmful to you. This includes any thinking that has resulted from wrong actions or attitudes on your part, or painful images from wrong that was done to you by others. Take your time — this could be one of the most important exercises you will do in this study.

6. *Install a new program.* Review the Scriptures on page 201. Choose a verse or passage and commit it to memory this week. Write it on a three-by-five

card and tape it to your bathroom mirror, reviewing it each morning and evening as you brush your teeth. Challenge your mate to do the same.

7. Use your mind creatively to shift into sexual gear.

   a. In your notebook, write two reasons why you think God gives us the example of Tirzah using mental imagery to shift her mind into sexual gear.

   b. What is one way that you can apply sexual imagery in a godly and positive way?

PRIVATE: FOR COUPLES ONLY

SERVANT LOVERS ADMIT THEIR SELFISHNESS AND LEARN FROM IT.

- If God has revealed selfishness to you, admit it and ask your mate for forgiveness.
- Ask your spouse what you can do to demonstrate selflessness in your sexual intimacy — and then do it!

SERVANT LOVERS ALLOW GOD TO SET THEIR MINDS FREE.

- Make a commitment to maintaining truth in your sexual relationship. Because pornography is one of the greatest dangers to intimacy in marriage, ask each other, "Have you ever looked at pornography or been tempted to do so?" Then discuss what you can do to safeguard each other and your children from porn.
- Share what you have done this week to transform your mind.
- Tell your spouse how he or she can encourage you to be free in your mind.

LESSON SEVEN

This week read:

Chapter 13: Be Free to Forgive

Chapter 14: Be Free with Your Body

CHAPTER 13: BE FREE TO FORGIVE

1. Review the stories about the pain of sexual betrayal on pages 211-216.

    a. Write five adjectives that describe the emotions someone might feel upon learning of sexual betrayal by his or her mate.

    b. Why do you think sexual betrayal is one of the most difficult sins to forgive?

2. Read Matthew 6:14-15. Paraphrase these verses in your own words, and explain how they apply to your marriage.

3. Read Matthew 18:21-35.

    a. According to Jesus, how many times must we forgive someone for the same offense?

    b. Do you think Jesus was referring to an actual number of times, an attitude, or both?

    c. Is unforgiveness a sin? Is it a lesser or worse sin than someone committing adultery?

4. Words can be used to create pain and they can be used to heal. One way that words are used for healing is when they seek or offer forgiveness.

    a. What does Nehemiah 9:17-21 tell us about God's perspective of forgiveness?

    b. Read Luke 17:4 and identify what it says about your role in the forgiveness process.

5. Review the sidebar on pages 210-211 about forgiveness. What do you think Jesus means when He says we are to forgive as we have been forgiven?

6. Review the story about the forgiveness cup on page 210. This week, buy a forgiveness cup. Be prepared to use it!

CHAPTER 14: BE FREE WITH YOUR BODY

7. What causes inhibitions in wives? In husbands? Write your thoughts down in your notebook. Are the causes the same or different?

8. *Wives:* Review "Say 'Yes' to Sexual Freedom" on pages 226-230.

   a. Write a paragraph describing God's perspective of sex. Compare this to the paragraph you wrote for lesson 1.

   b. How has your view of sex changed since lesson 1? How has the Song and this study shaped your thinking?

   c. Are you growing and embracing God's perspective? If so, how? If not, why not?

9. *Husbands:* Review "Love Her to Freedom" on pages 230-232. Describe two ways you can offer loving acceptance to your wife.

10. *Wives:* Review "Love your Husband to Freedom" on pages 234-236. Describe two ways you can encourage your husband as a lover.

Private: For Couples Only

Servant lovers offer forgiveness when wounded.

- As a couple, pray and ask God to reveal areas within your intimate relationship where you need to forgive your mate. Also ask Him to show you wise words that will bring healing (see Proverbs 12:18).
- Then write a note of forgiveness in each other's notebook or offer the forgiveness cup.

Servant lovers overcome inhibitions and use their body to delight their mates.

- Discuss what inhibits your freedom of sexual expression.
- Share with your mate what he or she can do to encourage you in becoming free.
- Commit to "loving one another to freedom."

LESSON EIGHT

This week read:

Chapter 15: Be Free to Be Creative

Chapter 16: Fan the Fire of Lifelong Love

CHAPTER 15: BE FREE TO BE CREATIVE

1. Describe three things that characterize adventure for you.
2. What is your favorite creative idea in chapter 15? Why is it your favorite?
3. List three things that will help you grow in becoming a more creative lover.
4. Reread "Schedule Time Alone for Loving" on pages 245-248.
   a. Describe your dream anniversary getaway.
   b. What can you do to make your dream a reality — even if you have to plan and save for five years?
   c. List two things you can do to find time for just you two for intimate loving this month. Refer to "Top Ten Time Grabbers" on pages 94-96.

CHAPTER 16: FAN THE FIRE OF LIFELONG LOVE

5. Read Jeremiah 31:3. God says He will love us for how long? If He is the source of our love, how long should we love one another?
6. Paraphrase the beautiful definition of love in Song of Solomon 8:6-7. Be prepared to share your paraphrase with the Bible-study group.
   a. What does it mean that God is in the midst of the flame of your love? (Refer to pages 257-258 under "Love Is Intense.")
   b. Consider love in light of these four words: *intimate, intense, indestructible,* and *invaluable.* In what ways do you demonstrate these words to your mate?

7. List four ways you are pursuing lifelong love. What can you add to what you are already doing?

8. Reread the sixteen qualities of servant lovers on pages 265-266. Consider doing the sixteen-week project together to reinforce your desire to fan the flame of lifelong love.

PRIVATE: FOR COUPLES ONLY

SERVANT LOVERS ARE FREE TO BE CREATIVE.

- Discuss how you both feel about an outdoor lovemaking adventure.
- Share your favorite "old" lovemaking delight, and tell each other why it is your favorite.
- Name one "new" lovemaking delight you would like to try.
- Ask your mate, "What is your idea of a dream lovemaking encounter?"

SERVANT LOVERS ACTIVELY PURSUE LIFELONG INTIMACY.

- Plan a special time this week to celebrate your intimacy. Enjoy one another. Delight in your sexual love!

Bible Study Facilitator's Guide

When we field-tested this Bible study, we were amazed by the significant impact our few weeks together had on the husbands and wives in the group. One couple told us, "We were going through a really tough time; I'm not sure our marriage would have survived without this group and what we learned about loving one another."

Following is a guide to assist you in facilitating the Bible study. Please feel free to customize these Bible-study sessions as you see fit. Groups differ in their pace, time commitment, and needs. While we've formatted the information for eight weeks (an average of two chapters per week), some groups may prefer a longer program in order to cover the material in more depth.

GETTING STARTED

OVERVIEW

Ideally, a husband-and-wife team should lead the study together. As leaders, your role is not so much to teach as it is to foster and create an environment for authentic conversation that will help participants learn from each other.

Our goal is to help couples immerse themselves in the truth of God's Word as it relates to marital intimacy and to encourage accountability among couples. Each session is designed to maximize learning and to help participants get to know each other. You may wish to conclude your time together with a celebration ceremony so that couples can rededicate themselves to one another by expressing the vows of a servant lover.

A TRUST-BASED ENVIRONMENT

It's critical that the participants of the study feel comfortable and safe, so judgmental comments and interruptions should be discouraged. Maintaining confidentiality is key to the success of a study on intimacy. Everyone in the group needs to agree not to relay information shared during the study to anyone outside of the group unless they have permission to do so.

Encourage the participants to listen closely, respond thoughtfully, and exercise unconditional regard for one another. Because sensitive and perhaps controversial issues will be discussed, insist on an atmosphere of trust and respect among all members of the group. As facilitators, your role is to create a trust-based environment by modeling this way of being and by encouraging participants to do the same. Regularly remind everyone of these two things: (1) feel free not to answer any question that makes you feel uncomfortable; and (2) never divulge information that will embarrass or offend your spouse.

Promoting the Study

Here are some ideas for publicizing the study:

- Have it announced on Sunday morning during church or in Sunday school.
- Write about it in your church bulletin, newsletters, and e-mails.
- Encourage interested couples to promote the study through word of mouth.
- Approach a current couples' study group about their interest in studying *Intimacy Ignited*.

Size of Group

Discussion is a cornerstone in this study, so the optimum size is between six and ten couples.

Building Relationships

Encourage couples to connect with each other between sessions by phone, by e-mail, or in person. You might suggest that all of the couples meet together once or twice for a social event, such as a potluck, group hike, or barbecue.

Materials Needed

Each couple will need a Bible, notebook, pen, and copy of *Intimacy Ignited*. As facilitators, you might find it helpful to use an overhead, flip chart, or projector that allows you to run a PowerPoint presentation. Consider using a CD player to play relaxing music at the beginning and end of the study. It sets a nice mood as people enter and exit the meeting.

ENCOURAGE HOMEWORK

The participants repeatedly told us, "We loved the homework." Encourage everyone to do the practical exercises in the study and to keep up with the reading. Also reiterate that the questions that appear in the "Private: For Couples Only" sections are *not* for group discussion.

GROUND RULES

Take a few minutes at the beginning of the first session to brainstorm and come up with ground rules that all can agree upon. If necessary, periodically revisit these rules and modify them as needed. Here are some ground rules your group might want to adopt:

- Start and end on time.
- Turn off cell phones.
- Maintain confidentiality.
- Don't force anyone to talk about anything that makes him or her feel uncomfortable.
- Focus on what *you* can do, not what *your mate* should do.
- Don't dominate the discussion time.
- Use "I" statements — don't speak for others.
- Follow the lead of the facilitator.
- Come prepared.
- Have fun!

LESSON FORMAT

Plan approximately two hours for each session. Include time for socializing, reflecting, and participating. Here is a suggested format:

- Socializing
- Opening prayer
- Brief review of previously covered material, if necessary

    ◊ Eighty minutes for discussion of the material

    ◊ Review of next week's assignments

    ◊ Closing prayer

    ◊ Socializing

GO FOR IT

Because your first meeting will establish the framework for future sessions, lesson 1 contains more suggestions than the lessons that follow. While much of your time will be focused on processing the questions in the Bible study, we have added some tips that will help you as you lead the group.

LESSON ONE

Introduction: Sex At Its Best

Discuss the framework of the Song of Solomon, the primary characters, and the purpose of the book. Be prepared to answer the question *Why is Solomon, a man who had many wives by the end of his life, qualified to write this book?* Many people cannot receive the rich information in the Song unless this basic question is answered.

Chapter 1: Where Did All the Passion Go?

Some natural discussion questions that emerge from this chapter are: *What attitudes about sex were communicated to you while you were growing up? Did you talk with your parents about sex? If you have kids, how do you intend to communicate sexual information to them?* These questions can help the group open up and begin to share.

Chapter 2: Give Permission for Passion

Focusing on Philippians 2:3-4, this chapter introduces what it means to be a servant lover and shows that in Scripture, God gives permission for passion. Because these themes will surface again later, be sure to discuss what constitutes a servant lover and what sorts of things keep a person from experiencing passion as God desires.

Facilitator Tips:

- ẟ Building relationships is critical. Because this is the first study, you might begin the meeting by asking each couple to tell how long they've been married and a special anniversary memory, or ask them to identify a goal for the study.

- ẟ Establish ground rules as a group and write them on a whiteboard or overhead. Make sure everyone agrees to the ground rules. During the week, prepare handouts summarizing these rules, and pass them out to each couple at the next session.

- ẟ Let couples know that at the next study, they will be asked to share a creative way they praised their mate that week.

LESSON TWO

Chapter 3: Soothe Insecurities

Body image is a huge issue for most women. Empathize with the women, but encourage them not to buy in to the world's message that shouts, "Be dissatisfied with your body." Urge them instead to embrace God's message, "Rejoice in the body I gave you" (see Psalm 139:14). Try to help the men understand what it would be like if they were bombarded day in and day out with messages designed to make them feel inadequate or dissatisfied with their bodies. Emphasize the key role a husband plays in helping his wife accept her body so that she can use it creatively during sex.

Chapter 4: Offer Sexual Refreshment

The key point of this chapter is that a married couple's sexual relationship can be a place of refreshment, renewal, and refuge.

Facilitator Tips:

- ẟ Focus on the Family has a video that contains amazing images of Engedi that can help couples visualize this point. It is part of a series called *That the World May Know.* Call (800) 232-6459 or go to www.family.org to purchase set 3, which includes *Faith Lesson 18: Living Water* (about Engedi).

❧ Tell the couples that next week's study includes taking a Marriage Minutes test. Encourage them to start on the test right away, and let them know that in the next study, you will ask them to talk about what they learned.

LESSON THREE

Chapter 5: Trade Sexual Compliments

Due to the sensitive nature of this chapter, reiterate the ground rules at the start of this session. Explain that it's important for couples to develop a private sexual language. Talk generally about the merits of doing this, but avoid specific references.

Chapter 6: Catch the Little Foxes

What happens if we fail to catch the "little foxes" in our marriage? Stress the importance of being willing to work on small problems so that they do not become large ones. Ask couples to share what they learned from taking the Marriage Minutes (MM) test.

Facilitator Tips:

❧ Pornography is a huge problem in many marriages. Be prepared to address this problem and encourage couples to pray not only for themselves and their kids but also for our nation. If the statistics prove true, half of the men in your group will be into porn on some level. Have the couples share what advice they would give to a friend who is into pornography.

❧ Ask each couple to bring a wedding photo or their wedding album next week. Let them know that you will spend some time at the start of the class looking at each other's pictures.

LESSON FOUR

Chapter 7: Create a Safe Place for Loving

Talk about what situations can cause someone in the marriage to feel unsafe, and then discuss the three ideas presented for making your marriage a safe place: (1) Eliminate the "D" word—discuss how divorce has impacted our country and the families who have suffered from divorce; (2) Husband, *love* your wife — have the men share what they learned about what speaks love to their wives; and (3) Wife, *respect* your husband — have the women share what they learned about what speaks respect to their husbands. Talk about practical ways a husband communicates love to his wife, and a wife communicates love to her husband.

Chapter 8: Remember Your Vows

Talk about the importance of a covenant and why God values it so much. You might want to look up verses in the Bible relating to *covenant* and *vow*. Talk about the practical aspects of *protection*.

Facilitator Tips:

- Open by having everyone swap wedding photos and sharing fun wedding memories. (You will need to set a time limit.)
- End by praying for one another — that each couple will make their marriage a safe place and that they will commit to keeping their marriage covenant before God.

LESSON FIVE

Chapter 9: Be Romantic In and Out of Bed

As a group, define "romance for a man" and "romance for a woman." Then ask the couples to talk among themselves and modify the definition so that it is tailored to their mate. Sometimes it helps to determine what romance is not (for example, eating garlic bread). This too will include individual preferences.

Chapter 10: Give Your Body as a Gift

The concept of giving authority of your body is one that many people do not understand. Stick to Scripture. Try to help couples understand that it's possible to give your body to your mate in sex but still have the attitude that "my body is my own, and I'll give it when I want." The goal is to help couples understand God's ideal and how it can be lived out in marriage.

Facilitator Tips:

- ◊ Have each couple share a romantic memory.
- ◊ Because this lesson is about offering our bodies as gifts, consider bringing a wrapped gift and presenting it to the couple who offers the greatest insight on this important concept.
- ◊ Explain that next week you will talk about how to "clean up our minds" and that it is important that they do the exercises in chapter 12 in order to get the most out of the study.

LESSON SIX

Chapter 11: Stamp Out Selfishness

Satan is the external enemy of intimacy; selfishness is the internal enemy of intimacy. Both are defeated when we live in dependence upon God and as servant lovers to one another.

Chapter 12: Be Free in Your Mind

Strongly encourage every group member to work through the exercises for this lesson. Stress the importance of Scripture memorization and meditation. If applicable, share examples of how memorizing Scripture has helped you. Review this chapter thoroughly, and ask couples to share how the exercise of "renewing your mind" impacted them.

Facilitator Tips:

- ◊ To introduce the chapter on selfishness, arrange some toy blocks or Scrabble letters in the form of the idol altar (I, ME, MINE, MYSELF) on page 180. Point out that if you remove the "self" at the bottom, it causes the altar to collapse.
- ◊ Introduce chapter 12 with this visual exercise. Fill a glass pitcher with water. Tell the group this represents our minds early in life. As you're explaining that what we see, hear, and experience pollutes our minds, add the following things to the water: blue food coloring (represents movies or pictures we see that color our perspective of sex) and a handful of dirt (represents dirty images or filthy words

we hear). Then ask the group how we should renew a mind filled with junk. Respond with:

> "Pour out your sins before God." (Pour polluted water into a bucket.) "Receive God's forgiveness." (Rinse glass pitcher with clear water.) "Memorize God's Word." (Fill glass pitcher with clear water.) "*Voila!* A renewed mind! But this process can take time and will need to be repeated throughout the course of your life to keep your mind new."

LESSON SEVEN

Chapter 13: Be Free to Forgive

Review and discuss the sidebar about forgiveness on pages 210-211. Focus on what forgiveness is, what it is not, and the role it plays in marriage.

Chapter 14: Be Free with Your Body

Be careful that the conversation for this chapter does not turn too personal. Talk in general about what creates inhibitions among women and what causes men to be inhibited.

Facilitator Tips:

- ◊ If you have stories to share about how you have used a forgiveness cup, tell the group. Spend a lot of time on the topic of forgiveness, as it is not only crucial to a healthy marriage but also in your relationship with your children.
- ◊ Tell everyone that next week you will be talking about creative lovemaking encounters. Ask them to think of creative ideas they've heard or read about that are appropriate and in keeping with the ground rules you established as a group.

LESSON EIGHT

Chapter 15: Be Free to Be Creative

Discuss how creativity contributes to maintaining lifelong love.

Chapter 16: Fan the Fire of Lifelong Love

Focus on how the flame is central to understanding how our love can be lifelong.

Epilogue: The Flame

Talk about why it is important to understand the small drama of our marriage within the context of the large drama of what God is doing in our world.

Facilitator Tips:

- After the couples express their vows to one another, consider giving a small unity candle to each couple. This will serve as a flame of love to remind them of their oneness and their vows to become servant lovers to one another.
- Discuss how their perspective of sex has changed during the eight weeks.
- Consider planning a "Commemoration Dinner" to celebrate all the group has learned. Spend time in worship and thanksgiving. Pray and ask God to keep the couples growing in lifelong love.

Notes

INTRODUCTION

1. Rabbi Benjamin Blech, *Understanding Judaism: The Complete Idiot's Guide* (Indianapolis: Alpha Books, 1999), p. 92.
2. Richard G. Moulton, "Lyric Idyl: Solomon's Song," *The Literary Study of the Bible: An Account of the Leading Forms of Literature Represented in the Sacred Writings Intended for English Readers* (London: Isbiter, 1903), pp. 207-224.

CHAPTER 1

1. Philip Yancey, "Holy Sex," *Christianity Today* (October 2003), pp. 48-49.
2. Yancey, p. 49.
3. Ruth Smythers, "Instruction and Advice for the Young Bride," *The Madison Institute Newsletter* (New York: Spiritual Guidance Press, Fall 1894).
4. Adapted from Sylvanus Stall, D. D., *What a Young Husband Ought to Know* (Philadelphia: The Vir Publishing Company, 1907), pp. 79, 91, 95.
5. Tom Gledhill, *The Message of the Song of Songs* (Downers Grove, Ill.: InterVarsity, 1994), p. 171.

CHAPTER 2

1. Tom Gledhill, *The Message of the Song of Songs* (Downers Grove, Ill.: InterVarsity, 1994), p. 95.
2. Attributed to French singer Mistinguett.
3. The scholarly protocols for transliteration of Hebrew words have no meaning to those who do not know Hebrew. Therefore, throughout this book we will use the transliteration system employed in *The New American Standard Exhaustive Concordance to the Bible* (Nashville: Holman, 1981), p. 1481. The Hebrew word *dod* has a wide range of meanings and in some contexts means "Uncle!" However, when applied to one's lover in a marriage relationship, it takes on more erotic connotations. See J. Swanson, *Dictionary of Biblical Languages with Semantic Domains: Hebrew Old Testament*, electronic ed. (Oak Harbor, Wash.: Logos Research Systems, Inc., 1997), s.v. "*dod*"; Franz Delitzsch, "Song of Songs," *Commentary on the Old Testament* (Grand Rapids: Eerdmans, n.d.), p. 20. *Dod* as "love" itself is extolled or described by "thy love is better than wine" (Song 1:2), "we will remember thy love more than wine" (1:4), "how fair is thy love" and "how much better is thy love than wine" (4:10), and "there will I give thee my love" (7:12). Ezekiel speaks of the Lord's kindness toward Israel when "thy time was the time of love" (16:8). But the Babylonians "came to her into the bed of love" and defiled her (23:17). In Proverbs 7:18, the harlot says to the foolish young man, "Come, let us take our fill of love until the morning."
4. J. D. Douglas, ed., *The New Bible Dictionary* (Grand Rapids, Mich.: Eerdmans, 1962), p. 906.
5. Tremper Longman III, *Song of Songs*, The New International Commentary on the Old Testament (Grand Rapids, Mich.: Eerdmans, 2001), p. 94.

6. Adapted from *How to Romance the Man You Love*, by the editors of *Prevention* magazine health books (Emmaus, Penn.: Rodale Press, 1997), p. 27.

7. Adapted from Dr. Clifford and Joyce Penner, *52 Ways to Have Fun, Fantastic Sex: A Guidebook for Married Couples* (Nashville: Nelson, 1994), p. 73.

8. Adapted from *How to Romance the Man You Love*, pp. 27-28.

9. "Kiss Me, Please," *Health* (October 2002), p. 196.

CHAPTER 3

1. Franz Delitzsch, "Song of Songs," *Commentary on the Old Testament* (Grand Rapids, Mich.: Eerdmans, n.d.), p. 32.

2. Tremper Longman III, *Song of Songs*, The New International Commentary on the Old Testament (Grand Rapids, Mich.: Eerdmans, 2001), p. 100.

3. Longman, p. 100.

4. Longman, p. 102.

5. Dr. Don Dunlap, *The Power of Praise* (Family Life Association for Ministry and Education, 2004), www.christianity.com.

6. Adapted from *The Marriage Masterpiece: A Bold New Vision for Your Marriage*, by Al Janssen (Wheaton, Ill.: Tyndale, 2001), pp. 66-67. "Johnny Lingo's Eight-Cow Wife," by Patricia McGerr, was originally published in *Woman's Day* in November 1965.

7. Used with permission.

8. C. J. Mahoney, "The Fine Art of Romantic Communication," in *Simply Romantic Nights*, by Dennis Rainey and others (Little Rock: FamilyLife, 2003), p. 36.

9. Gary Thomas, *Sacred Marriage: What If God Designed Marriage to Make Us Holy More Than to Make Us Happy?* (Grand Rapids, Mich.: Zondervan, 2002), p. 216.

CHAPTER 4

1. J. Swanson, *Dictionary of Biblical Languages with Semantic Domains: Hebrew Old Testament*, electronic ed. (Oak Harbor, Wash.: Logos Research Systems, Inc., 1997), s. v. "*rayah*."

2. J. D. Douglas, ed., *The New Bible Dictionary* (Grand Rapids, Mich.: Eerdmans, 1962), p. 906.

3. Tremper Longman III, *Song of Songs*, The New International Commentary on the Old Testament (Grand Rapids, Mich.: Eerdmans, 2001), p. 106.

4. Alan R. Hirsch, M.D., in *How to Romance the Man You Love*, by the editors of *Prevention* magazine health books (Emmaus, Penn.: Rodale Press, Inc., 1997), p. 34.

5. Hirsch, p. 35.

CHAPTER 5

1. R. B. Laurin, "The Song of Songs and Its Modern Usage," *Christianity Today*, XI, no. 22 (August 3, 1962), p. 10.

2. Craig Glickman, *A Song for Lovers: Including a New Paraphrase and a New Translation of the Song of Solomon* (Downers Grove, Ill.: InterVarsity, 1976), p. 40.

3. Franz Delitzsch, "Song of Songs," *Commentary on the Old Testament* (Grand Rapids, Mich.: Eerdmans, n. d.), p. 42.

4. Otto Zockler, "The Song of Songs," in *Commentary on the Holy Scriptures: Critical, Doctrinal, and Homiletical*, ed. John Peter Lange, trans. Philip Schaff (Grand Rapids, Mich.: Zondervan, 1960), 6:62.

5. Stewart Pernowne, *Roman Mythology* (London: Hamlyn, 1965), p. 78.

6. Samuel Noah Kramer, *The Sacred Marriage Rite: Aspects of Faith, Myth, and Ritual in Ancient Sumer* (Bloomington, Ind.: Indiana University Press, 1969), pp. 96, 105.

7. Joseph C. Dillow, *Solomon on Sex* (Nashville: Nelson, 1977), p. 31; Carey Ellen Walsh, *Exquisite Desire: Religion, the Erotic, and the Song of Songs* (Minneapolis: Fortress, 2000), pp. 128-129.

8. G. W. Bromiley, ed., *The International Standard Bible Encyclopedia*, rev. ed. (Grand Rapids, Mich.: Eerdmans, 2002), 1:384.

9. Literally "the love of mercy."

10. See Genesis 29:20.

11. See 1 Kings 10:9; Isaiah 63:9; Hosea 11:4; Zephaniah 3:17.

12. J. Swanson, *Dictionary of Biblical Languages with Semantic Domains: Hebrew Old Testament*, electronic ed. (Oak Harbor, Wash.: Logos Research Systems, Inc., 1997), s.v. *"ahabah."* See Deuteronomy 31:8.

13. See Proverbs 5:19.

14. See Proverbs 10:12.

15. See Genesis 25:28.

16. See Genesis 22:2.

17. See Ruth 4:15.

18. G. Kittel, G. W. Bromiley, and G. Friedrich, eds., *Theological Dictionary of the New Testament* (Grand Rapids, Mich.: Eerdmans, 1976), 1:21.

19. Later, Solomon says that *ahabah* is a fire that cannot be quenched, no matter how much water you pour on it (see Song 8:7).

20. Tom Gledhill, *The Message of the Song of Songs* (Downers Grove, Ill.: InterVarsity, 1994), p. 126.

21. D. N. Freedman, ed., *The Anchor Bible Dictionary* (New York: Doubleday, 1996), 3:295.

22. L. Koehler, W. Baumgartner, M. Richardson, and J. J. Stamm, *The Hebrew and Aramaic Lexicon of the Old Testament*, electronic ed. (New York: Brill, 1999), s.v. "chabaq."

23. Swanson, s.v. "chabaq."

24. Delitzsch, p. 45. See Proverbs 5:20; Song of Solomon 8:3.

25. Toben and Joanne Heim, *Happily Ever After: A Real-Life Look at Your First Year of Marriage* (Colorado Springs, Colo.: NavPress, 2004), p. 127.

26. W. Arndt, F. W. Gingrich, F. W. Danker, and W. A. Bauer, *A Greek-English Lexicon of the New Testament and Other Early Christian Literature:* A translation and adaption of the fourth revised and augmented edition of Walter Bauer's Griechisch-deutsches Worterbuch zu den Schrift en des Neuen Testaments und der ubrigen urchristlichen Literatur. (Chicago: University of Chicago Press, 1996), p. 913.

27. Adapted from Linda Dillow and Lorraine Pintus, *Intimate Issues: 21 Questions Christian Women Ask About Sex* (Colorado Springs, Colo.: WaterBrook, 1999), pp. 203-204.

CHAPTER 6

1. Tremper Longman III, *Song of Songs*, The New International Commentary on the Old Testament (Grand Rapids, Mich.: Eerdmans, 2001), p. 121.

2. See Nehemiah 4:3; Ezekiel 13:4.

3. Roland E. Murphy, *The Song of Songs: A Commentary on the Book of Canticles or the Song of Songs* (Minneapolis: Fortress, 1990), p. 139.

4. Tommy Nelson, *The Book of Romance: What Solomon Says About Love, Sex, and Intimacy* (Nashville: Nelson, 1998), p. 68.

5. L. Koehler, W. Baumgartner, M. Richardson, and J. J. Stamm, *The Hebrew and Aramaic Lexicon of the Old Testament*, electronic ed. (New York: Brill, 1999), s.v. "batar."

6. R. L. Harris, G. L. Archer, and B. K. Waltke, *Theological Wordbook of the Old Testament*, electronic ed. (Chicago: Moody, 1999), p. 138.

7. Longman, p. 126.

8. Marvin H. Pope, *Song of Songs*, The Anchor Bible (Garden City, New York: Doubleday, 1977), p. 410.

9. Kathleen Deveny, "We're Not in the Mood," *Newsweek*, June 30, 2003, p. 42.

10. Steven Greenhouse, "Report Shows Americans Have More 'Labor Days,'" *New York Times* (Sept. 2001), www.contemporaryfamilies.org/public/articles/change50.htm.

11. Dan Rutz, "Marriage Research: Working Outside of Home Does Not Affect Sex Life," *CNN Interactive*, December 12, 1998, www.cnn.com/HEALTH/9812/12/work.sex.

12. Adapted from "Sexual Healing," by Alice Park, in *Time*, January 19, 2004.

13. Adapted from Deveny, p. 43.

14. Deveny, pp. 153-154.

15. Dennis and Barbara Rainey, "Controlling Busyness in Your Family Life," adapted from *Parenting Today's Adolescents: Helping Your Child Avoid the Traps of the Preteen and Teen Years* (Nashville: Nelson, 1998).

16. Adapted from Dr. Paul Pearsall, *Super Marital Sex: Loving for Life* (New York: Ivy Books, 1987), pp. 16-18.

CHAPTER 7

1. "All night long" expresses the full force of the Hebrew. G. Lloyd Carr, *The Song of Solomon: An Introduction and Commentary*, Tyndale Old Testament Commentaries (Downers Grove, Ill.: InterVarsity, 1984), p. 105.

2. The perfect verb "qal" is often translated "grasp, take hold, take possession." F. Brown, S. R. Driver, and C. A. Briggs, *Enhanced Brown-Driver-Briggs Hebrew and English Lexicon*, electronic ed. (Oak Harbor, Wash.: Logos Research Systems, 2000), s.v. "qal."

3. Tremper Longman III, *Song of Songs*, The New International Commentary on the Old Testament (Grand Rapids, Mich.: Eerdmans, 2001), pp. 130-131.

4. Dennis Rainey, *Lonely Husbands, Lonely Wives: Rekindling Intimacy in Every Marriage* (Colorado Springs, Colo.: Focus on the Family, 1989), p. 17.

5. Adapted from Rainey, p. 15.

6. Harville Hendrix, "Ten Ways to Get What You Want," *Family Circle*, April 1, 1992, p. 31.

7. Mike Mason, *The Mystery of Marriage* (Portland: Multnomah, 1985), p. 95.

8. W. E. Vine, M. F. Unger, and W. White, *Vine's Complete Expository Dictionary of Old and New Testament Words* (Nashville: Nelson, 1996), p. 184.

9. W. E. Vine, *Vine's Expository Dictionary of Old and New Testament Words* (Grand Rapids, Mich.: Revell, 1981), s.v. "thalpo." See Deuteronomy 22:6.

10. Hebrew word *sakan* (see I Kings 1:2).

11. Gary Thomas, *Sacred Marriage: What If God Designed Marriage to Make Us Holy More Than to Make Us Happy?* (Grand Rapids, Mich.: Zondervan, 2000), p. 185.

12. Dr. Emerson and Sarah Eggerichs, *Motivating Your Man God's Way* (Love and Respect Ministries, Inc., 2003), p. 45.

13. Robert Lewis and William Hendricks, *Rocking the Roles: Building a Win-Win Marriage* (Colorado Springs, Colo.: NavPress, 1991), pp. 120-121.

14. W. Arndt, F. W. Gingrich, F. W. Danker, and W. Bauer, *A Greek-English Lexicon of the New Testament and Other Early Christian Literature:* A translation and adaptation of the fourth revised and augmented edition of Walter Bauer's Griechisch-deutsches Worterbuch zu den Schrift en des Neuen Testaments und der ubrigen urchristlichen Literatur. (Chicago: University of Chicago Press, 1996), p. 1062.

15. Robert Lewis and David Boehi, *Building Teamwork in Your Marriage,* The HomeBuilders Series (Loveland, Colo.: Group, 2001), pp. 46-47.

16. Dr. Laura Schlessinger, *The Proper Care and Feeding of Husbands* (New York: HarperCollins, 2004), pp. 145-146.

17. Tommy Nelson in *Simply Romantic Nights,* by Dennis Rainey and others (Little Rock: FamilyLife, 2000), p. 14.

CHAPTER 8

1. Rabbi Dr. S. M. Lehrman, "The Song of Songs," *The Five Megilloth,* ed. Dr. A. Cohen (New York: The Soncino Press, 1946), p. 12.

2. Lehrman, p. 12.

3. Tim Alan Gardner, *Sacred Sex: A Spiritual Celebration of Oneness in Marriage* (Colorado Springs, Colo.: WaterBrook, 2002), pp. 193-195.

4. Gardner, p. 196.

5. L. Koehler, W. Baumgartner, M. Richardson, and J. J. Stamm, *The Hebrew and Aramaic Lexicon of the Old Testament,* electronic ed. (New York: Brill, 1999), s.v. "samach."

6. Dr. Howard Hendricks, e-mail message to author, April 2, 2004.

7. Adapted from C. W. Neal, *Your 30-Day Journey to Being a Great Husband* (Nashville: Nelson, 1992), pp. 40-41.

8. Adapted from Neal, pp. 40-41.

9. Ron Allen, *Worship: The Missing Jewel of the Christian Church* (Portland: Multnomah, 1982), p. 120.

CHAPTER 9

1. Tremper Longman III, *Song of Songs,* The New International Commentary on the Old Testament (Grand Rapids, Mich.: Eerdmans, 2001), p. 141.

2. Leland Ryken, Jim Wilhoit, Tremper Longman, and others, *Dictionary of Biblical Imagery* (Downers Grove, Ill.: InterVarsity, 1998), p. 881.

3. Tom Gledhill, *The Message of the Song of Songs* (Downers Grove, Ill.: InterVarsity, 1994), p. 157.

4. Gledhill, p. 157.

5. Otto Zockler, "The Song of Songs," in *Commentary on the Holy Scriptures: Critical, Doctrinal, and Homiletical,* ed. John Peter Lange, trans. Philip Schaff (Grand Rapids, Mich.: Zondervan, 1960), 5:63.

6. Longman, p. 156.

7. Tommy Nelson, *The Book of Romance: What Solomon Says About Love, Sex, and Intimacy* (Nashville: Nelson, 1998), p. 99.

8. Dennis and Barbara Rainey, "Why Romance Is Important," in *Simply Romantic Nights,* (Little Rock: FamilyLife, 2000), p. 16.

9. Adapted from Joseph C. Dillow, *Solomon on Sex* (Nashville: Nelson, 1977), pp. 108-109.

10. Adapted from Rainey, pp. 21-22.

CHAPTER 10

1. Gary Thomas, *Sacred Marriage: What If God Designed Marriage to Make Us Holy More Than to Make Us Happy?* (Grand Rapids, Mich.: Zondervan, 2000), p. 226.

2. Westenholz, "Love Lyrics from the Ancient Near East," p. 2474.

3. L. Koehler, W. Baumgartner, M. Richardson, and J. J. Stamm, *The Hebrew and Aramaic Lexicon of the Old Testament,* electronic ed. (New York: Brill, 1999), s.v. "dod."

4. Tremper Longman III, *Song of Songs,* The New International Commentary on the Old Testament (Grand Rapids, Mich.: Eerdmans, 2001), p. 155.

5. R. L. Harris, G. L. Archer, and B. K. Waltke, *Theological Wordbook of the Old Testament,* electronic ed. (Chicago: Moody, 1999), p. 168.

6. G. W. Bromiley, *The International Standard Bible Encyclopedia,* rev. ed. (Grand Rapids, Mich.: Eerdmans, 2002), 2:400.

7. Bromiley, p. 156.

8. Otto Zockler, "The Song of Songs," in *Commentary on the Holy Scriptures: Critical, Doctrinal, and Homiletical,* ed. John Peter Lange, trans. Philip Schaff (Grand Rapids, Mich.: Zondervan, 1960), 5:90.

9. Gledhill, p. 166.

10. Longman, p. 58. It is certainly possible that the metaphors refer to oral sex.

11. Certain commentators' notes attribute these words to the choir. We agree with Charles Caldwell Ryrie's view that God is speaking these words to the couple; *Ryrie's Study Bible* (Chicago: Moody, 1995).

12. This concept is mentioned in Linda and Lorraine's book for single women called *Gift-Wrapped by God: Secret Answers to the Question "Why Wait?"* (Colorado Springs, Colo.: WaterBrook, 2002), but we've expanded it further here and developed the concept of giving authority of your body to your mate.

13. Stephen Arterburn and Fred Stoeker, *Every Man's Battle: Winning the War on Sexual Temptation One Victory at a Time* (Colorado Springs, Colo.: WaterBrook, 2000), pp. 125, 133.

CHAPTER 11

1. This assumption can't be proven. However, we and many commentators believe that this is the probable intent of the poet.

2. Tremper Longman III, *Song of Songs,* The New International Commentary on the Old Testament (Grand Rapids, Mich.: Eerdmans, 2001), p. 162.

3. The Hebrew word *dapaq* is used elsewhere for driving a herd of cattle or for demanding knocking (see Judges 19:22). See R. L. Harris, G. L. Archer, and B. K. Waltke, *Theological Wordbook of the Old Testament,* electronic ed. (Chicago: Moody, 1999), p. 194.

4. Longman, p. 166.

5. Otto Zockler, "The Song of Songs," in *Commentary on the Holy Scriptures: Critical,*

Doctrinal, and Homiletical, ed. John Peter Lange, trans. Philip Schaff (Grand Rapids, Mich.: Zondervan, 1960), v. 103.

6. Zockler, v. 103.

7. Duane A. Garrett, *Proverbs, Eccelsiastes, Song of Songs*, The New American Commentary, vol. 14 (Nashville: Broadman, Holman, 2001), s.v. "Song 5:5."

8. G. Lloyd Carr, *The Song of Solomon: An Introduction and Commentary*, Tyndale Old Testament Commentaries (Downers Grove, Ill.: InterVarsity, 1984), p. 136.

9. Longman, p. 169.

10. Adapted from Joseph C. Dillow, *Solomon on Sex* (Nashville, Tenn.: Nelson, 1977), pp. 108-109.

11. Gary Thomas, *Sacred Marriage: What If God Designed Marriage to Make Us Holy More Than to Make Us Happy?* (Grand Rapids, Mich.: Zondervan, 2002), p. 226.

12. This story was related to us by a professional counselor who said it happened to a woman she knew. We have heard similar stories on three separate occasions. The message is: Satan's followers are praying that Christian marriages will fail; are *we* praying that Christian marriages will *succeed?*

13. Thomas, p. 195.

14. Thomas, p. 195.

CHAPTER 12

1. Tom Gledhill, *The Message of the Song of Songs* (Downers Grove, Ill.: InterVarsity, 1994), p. 184.

2. G. Lloyd Carr, *The Song of Solomon: An Introduction and Commentary*, Tyndale Old Testament Commentaries (Downers Grove, Ill.: InterVarsity, 1984), p. 140.

3. Tremper Longman III, *Song of Songs*, The New International Commentary on the Old Testament (Grand Rapids, Mich.: Eerdmans, 2001), p. 172.

4. Gledhill, p. 185.

5. J. Swanson, *Dictionary of Biblical Languages with Semantic Domain : Hebrew Old Testament,* electronic ed. (Oak Harbor, Wash.: Logos Research Systems, Inc, 1977), s.v. "me eh." Or as Koehler and Baumgartner say it, "That part of the body through which people come into existence." See L. Koehler, W. Baumgartner, M. Richardson, and J. J. Stamm, *The Hebrew and Aramaic Lexicon of the Old Testament,* electronic ed. (New York: Brill, 1999), s.v. "me eh."

6. Longman, p. 173.

7. Longman, pp. 175-176.

8. Jimmy Evans and Ann Billington, *Freedom from Your Past: A Christian Guide to Personal Healing and Restoration* (Amarillo: Majestic Media, 1994), p. 22.

9. From "I Stand Amazed," by Dennis Jernigan. Used with permission.

10. Kelly Hollowell, "America's Sexual Holocaust," WorldNetDaily (2004) www.worldnetdaily.com/news/article.asp?ARTICLE_ID=37868.

11. Pamela Paul, "The Porn Factor," *Time*, January 19, 2004.

12. Paul.

13. Pornographic Statistics 2003, Internet Filter Review at www.internetfilterreview.com/internet-pornography-statistics.

14. Pornographic Statistics 2003.

15. Pornographic Statistics 2003.

16. Pornographic Statistics 2003.

17. Paul.

18. Elmer L. Towns, *Biblical Meditation for Spiritual Breakthrough: 10 Biblical Ways to Meditate and Draw Closer to the Lord* (Ventura, Calif.: Regal, 1998), p. 22.

CHAPTER 13

1. Tremper Longman III, *Song of Songs*, The New International Commentary on the Old Testament (Grand Rapids, Mich.: Eerdmans, 2001), p. 180.

2. Tom Gledhill, *The Message of the Song of Songs* (Downers Grove, Ill.: InterVarsity, 1994), p. 191.

3. Longman, p. 80.

4. Gledhill, p. 192.

5. Adapted from R. T. Kendall, *Total Forgiveness* (Lake Mary, Fla.: Charisma House, 2002), pp. 11-34.

6. Written by Lorraine Pintus.

CHAPTER 14

1. Tremper Longman, *Song of Songs*, The New International Commentary on the Old Testament (Grand Rapids, Mich.: Eerdmans, 2001), p. 184.

2. See Marvin H. Pope, *Song of Songs*, The Anchor Bible (Garden City, New York: Doubleday, 1977), pp. 574-579, for extensive comment. Pope goes so far as to associate the "nut" with the male and female genitalia—the "nut" referring to the testicles and an open nut to the female vulva. He cites an Italian rabbi and physician, Isaac Ben Samuel Lampronti (1679-1756), in the Talmudic encyclopedia, suggesting that the nut represents Eve's vulva. Tremper Longman III, pp. 184-185, accepts this as well, but it seems a stretch. The extrabiblical parallels cited come from a different era and cultural milieu.

3. Irene and Walter Jacob, "Flora," in *The Anchor Bible Dictionary*, ed. D. N. Freedman (Garden City, New York: Doubleday, 1992), 2:808. "The fruit, which is ripe about September, is apple-shaped, yellow-brown with a blush of red, and is surmounted by a crown-like hard calyx; on breaking the hard rind, the white or pinkish translucent fruits are seen tightly packed together inside. The juicy seeds are sometimes sweet and other times somewhat acidic and need sugar for eating. The juice expressed from the seeds is made into a syrup for flavoring drinks and in ancient days was made into wine: 'I would cause thee to drink of spiced wine, of the juice of my pomegranate' (Song of Songs 8:2)"; E. W. G. Masterman, "Pomegranate," in *The International Standard Bible Encyclopedia*, ed. J. Orr (Albany, Ore.: Ages Software, 1915).

4. Franz Delitzsch, "Song of Songs," *Commentary on the Old Testament* (Grand Rapids, Mich.: Eerdmans, n. d.), p. 122.

5. William Gesenius, *A Hebrew and English Lexicon of the Old Testament*, eds. Brown, Driver, and Briggs (London: Oxford University Press, 1966), p. 1057.

6. See Longman, pp. 194-195, for further discussion. Roland E. Murphy translates *shor* as "valley" and understands it as "a euphemism for the pudenda." See *The Song of Songs* (Minneapolis: Fortress, 1990), p. 185.

7. Longman, p. 195.

8. Robert Gordis, The Song of Songs (New York: The Jewish Theological Seminary of America, 1954), p. 26.
9. Longman, p. 195.
10. Rabbi Dr. S. M. Lehrman, "The Song of Songs," *The Five Megilloth*, ed. Dr. A. Cohn (New York: The Soncino Press, 1946), p. 26.
11. Craig Glickman, *A Song for Lovers* (Downers Grove, Ill.: InterVarsity, 1977), p. 83.
12. Tom Gledhill, *The Message of the Song of Songs* (Downers Grove, Ill.: InterVarsity, 1994), p. 207.
13. Otto Zockler, "Ecclesiastes," in *Commentary on the Holy Scriptures: Critical, Doctrinal, and Homiletical*, ed. John Peter Lange, trans. Philip Schaff (Grand Rapids, Mich.: Zondervan, 1960), p. 56.
14. F. Brown, S. R. Driver, and C. A. Briggs, *Enhanced Brown-Driver-Briggs Hebrew and English Lexicon*, electronic ed. (Oak Harbor, Wash.: Logos Research Systems, 2000), 772:2.
15. L., Koehler, W. Baumgartner, M. Richardson, and J. J. Stamm, *The Hebrew and Aramaic Lexicon of the Old Testament*, electronic ed. (New York: Brill, 1999), s.v. "tahanug." See Ecclesiastes 2:8, where the concept is associated with the sexual pleasures offered by concubines.
16. J. Orr, *The International Standard Bible Encyclopedia* (Albany, Ore.: Ages Software, 1915), 4:2235.
17. Longman, p. 198.
18. Don and Sally Meredith, *Two Becoming One: Experiencing the Power of Oneness in Your Marriage* (Chicago: Moody, 1999), p. 187.
19. Dr. Laura Schlessinger, *The Proper Care and Feeding of Husbands* (New York: HarperCollins, 2004), p. 135.

CHAPTER 15
1. Carey Ellen Walsh, *Exquisite Desire: Religion, the Erotic, and the Song of Songs* (Minneapolis: Fortress, 2000), p. 85.
2. G. Lloyd Carr, *The Song of Solomon: An Introduction and Commentary*, Tyndale Old Testament Commentaries (Downers Grove, Ill.: InterVarsity, 1984), p. 166.
3. Tremper Longman III, *Song of Songs*, The New International Commentary on the Old Testament (Grand Rapids, Mich.: Eerdmans, 2001), p. 204.
4. Joseph C. Dillow, *Solomon on Sex* (Nashville: Nelson, 1977), p. 139.
5. Adapted from Dillow, pp. 139-140.
6. Stephen and Judith Schwambach, *For Lovers Only* (Eugene, Ore.: Harvest House, 1991), p. 198.

CHAPTER 16
1. Tremper Longman III, *Song of Songs*, The New International Commentary on the Old Testament (Grand Rapids, Mich.: Eerdmans, 2001), p. 209.
2. John Wesley, "Commentary on Song of Solomon 8," *John Wesley's Explanatory Notes on the Whole Bible*, http://bible.crosswalk.com/Commentaries/ WesleysExplanatoryNotes/ wes.cgi?book=so&chapter=008%201754.
3. G. Lloyd Carr, *The Song of Solomon: An Introduction and Commentary*, Tyndale Old Testament Commentaries (Downers Grove, Ill.: InterVarsity, 1984), p. 169.

4. J. Swanson, *Dictionary of Biblical Languages with Semantic Domains: Hebrew Old Testament*, electronic ed. (Oak Harbor, Wash.: Logos Research Systems, Inc., 1977), s.v. "resheph." See Psalm 78:48.

5. Swanson, s.v. "resheph."

6. Tom Gledhill, *The Message of the Song of Songs* (Downers Grove, Ill.: InterVarsity, 1994), p. 237.

7. Longman, pp. 221-221.

8. Joseph C. Dillow, *Solomon on Sex* (Nashville: Nelson, 1977), p. 155.

9. Berta Delgado, "Author's Latest Novel Imagines a World That Outlaws Religion," *The Dallas Morning News*, October 15, 2003.

10. Jody and Linda Dillow attended the memorial service for Dr. Bill Bright in Fort Collins, Colorado, and heard this said.

11. We have searched for the author of this poem and are unable to find it, but we applaud whoever wrote it!

EPILOGUE

1. God appeared to Abraham in the form of a flaming torch (see Genesis 15:17), to Moses as a burning bush (see Exodus 3:2), and to the children of Israel as a pillar of fire (see Exodus 13:21). He was the Consuming Fire on Mt. Sinai and the eternal flame on the altar of sacrifice (see Judges 12:20). Given these manifestations, it is understandable that God would associate Himself with the flame of love between a man and his wife in Song of Songs 8:6 (NASB).

2. Adapted from Joseph Dillow, *The Reign of the Servant Kings* (Miami Springs, Fla.: Schoettle, 1992), p. 2.

3. See Isaiah 14:13-14.

4. Satan means "adversary"; see William F. Arndt and F. Wilbur Gingrich, *A Greek-English Lexicon of the New Testament and Other Early Christian Literature* (Chicago: University of Chicago Press, 1952), p. 152.

5. See Isaiah 14:12.

6. See Ezekiel 28:17.

7. See Genesis 1:27.

8. Summary of Genesis 1:27-28.

9. God gave the gift of sex to the first couple. While sex is one factor that helps man accomplish God's mandate (to reflect Him, to multiply and fill the earth, and to subdue it), it is important to acknowledge that single men and women also accomplish aspects of the mandate apart from sex. Each man and woman is made in God's image, all have the ability to multiply in ways other than through childbearing, and all can participate in subduing the earth as they submit to the headship of Christ.

10. It is noteworthy that it was a combination of "them" both, what the man and woman in their uniqueness brought to the totality.

11. See Psalm 8:5; Hebrews 2:7.

12. This image is based on Genesis 2:24, where, through sexual intercourse, two become one in the eyes of God. The authors do not intend to imply that Satan is defeated through a couple engaging in the pleasures of sex but rather that Satan is threatened when a husband and wife live out their oneness in dependence upon God and in service to one another.

13. Paul described the sexual union between a husband and wife as a picture of Christ and the church (see Ephesians 5:31). It is this picture, not the act of sex, that poses a threat to Satan.

APPENDIX

1. Linda Dillow and Lorraine Pintus, *Intimate Issues: 21 Questions Christian Women Ask About Sex* (Colorado Springs, Colo.: WaterBrook, 1999), pp. 199-202.
2. William F. Arndt and F. Wilbur Gingrich, *A Greek-English Lexicon of the New Testament* (Grand Rapids, Mich.: Zondervan, 1957), p. 440.
3. Arndt and Gingrich, s.v. "crime."
4. Dana F. Kellerman, ed., *The Lexicon Webster Dictionary* (The English Language Institute of America, 1976), 2:922.
5. G. W. Bromiley, ed., *The International Standard Bible Encyclopedia*, rev. ed. (Grand Rapids, Mich.: Eerdmans, 1988), s.v. "sodomite." See Leviticus 18:22; 20:13.
6. R. L. Harris, G. L. Archer, and B. K. Waltke, *Theological Wordbook of the Old Testament*, electronic ed. (Chicago: Moody, 1980), 2:788.